GROWING UP WITH
America

GROWING UP WITH

America

YOUTH, MYTH, AND
NATIONAL IDENTITY
1945 TO PRESENT

Emily A. Murphy

THE UNIVERSITY OF GEORGIA PRESS
ATHENS

Designed by Kaelin Chappell Broaddus
Set in 9.5/13.5 New Century Schoolbook LT Std Roman
by Kaelin Chappell Broaddus

Most University of Georgia Press titles are
available from popular e-book vendors.

Printed digitally

Library of Congress Cataloging-in-Publication Data

Names: Murphy, Emily A., 1987– author.
Title: Growing up with America : youth, myth, and national identity,
    1945 to present / Emily A. Murphy.
Description: Athens : The University of Georgia Press, 2020. |
    Includes bibliographical references and index.
Identifiers: LCCN 2019057951 | ISBN 9780820357805 (hardback) |
    ISBN 9780820357812 (paperback) | ISBN 9780820357799 (ebook)
Subjects: LCSH: Children's literature, American—History and criticism. |
    Young adult literature, American—History and criticism. | National
    characteristics, American, in literature. | Children in literature. |
    Young adults in literature. | Child authors.
Classification: LCC PS374.C454 M87 2020 | DDC 810.9/9282—dc23
LC record available at https://lccn.loc.gov/2019057951

FOR

Zoey Sofia

MAY YOU NEVER

LET HISTORY DEFINE

YOUR PLACE IN THE WORLD.

CONTENTS

ACKNOWLEDGMENTS

Writing a book is never easy, and there were certainly times when I thought this one would never see completion. I'd like to thank my husband, Roberto Acevedo, for his patience over the years while I have worked on this project. His unending support and confidence in me is a large reason why I was able to persist in the intense work involved in the research, writing, and revision of *Growing Up with America*. I'd also like to thank my family and friends for their emotional support—without it I would surely have failed to reach my goals.

This project developed out of my own interest in answering a question at the heart of *Growing Up with America*: what does it mean to be an American? I was born in 1987, toward the "official" end of the Cold War, and while I didn't share in the experiences of those who lived during this historical period, I often wished I knew what my generation was all about: who we were, where we were headed, and how we fit in with the national ideals taught to us from a young age. As with most projects, I changed faster than my book could, and while I'm mostly satisfied with what I've written here, the answer to my question still eludes me. Having left the United States in 2015—first to China and then to the United Kingdom—I can no longer base an answer to this question on what the IRS describes as "physical presence" (those who know the joys of doing U.S. taxes from abroad will understand).

A special thanks goes to the scholars who helped support me in my career and who provided invaluable feedback on the manuscript version of this book. To Anastasia Ulanowicz, I have no words. You have always been a mentor and a friend, and your empathy and kindness for others, as well as your political activism and concern for world events, continue to inspire me. I also appreciate the feedback of Carol Singley, Julia Mickenberg, Sara Schwebel, and Kenneth Kidd. I appreciate being challenged to push my ideas further and to think more critically about how I position myself within the fields of children's literature and American studies. Most of all, I'm grateful for the models of scholarship they have provided that blend the best of these two fields of study. If I failed to meet the challenges they posed to me, it is through my own fault.

To others who did not directly comment on this book but who supported me nonetheless, I also want to thank you. Having your work acknowledged as an early career scholar is incredibly meaningful and helps give you the hope and resilience you need to get through the challenges of graduate school and the academic job market. My first memory of such an instance goes back to my first year as a master's student, when the curator of the de Grummond Children's Literature Collection, Ellen Ruffin, enthusiastically responded to my ideas about the archive. Lissa Paul, Andrea Mei-Ying Wu, and Vanessa Joosen have also given me encouragement and advice at different points during my PhD studies and in my first years after graduation. For this I am truly grateful.

I also owe thanks to my new colleagues at Newcastle University. Both Lucy Pearson and Kim Reynolds provided feedback on different chapters of this book and have been extremely kind and generous with their time, supporting me in my different roles as a lecturer and helping guide me in my transition to life in the UK. Our amazing graduate students and postdoctoral fellows who attend our weekly CLUGG sessions also listened to a version of my introduction and gave insightful feedback, providing a friendly community for me when I needed it most.

To my past colleagues, in particular Joshua Paíz, I also owe a great debt. We had many good times in Shanghai, including our joint Thanksgiving dinner, and his friendship during the early days of securing a contract for this book and during the difficult personal times I had were invaluable. Even after our work took us to different parts of the world, he's continued to provide support and a good laugh when I need it most.

In looking over my acknowledgments, I think what I feel grateful for most of all is to have so many strong role models from diverse backgrounds. A big part of this project is recovering lost voices, and making the history of those who have been marginalized by myth visible. We need these voices in the academy and as support for those who may not be able to speak so easily. I'm lucky to be in a position where I can write freely and receive so much mentorship from brilliant scholars all over the world, and I hope that I can be as generous with my time and knowledge as those whom I have looked up to—and continue to look up to—have been to me.

GROWING UP WITH

America

The Specter of Youth in the Cold War

[I]t is difficult to read the literature of young America without being struck by how antithetical it is to our modern rendition of the American Dream. How pronounced in it is the absence of that term's elusive mixture of hope, realism, materialism, and promise. For a people who made much of their "newness"—their potential, freedom, and innocence—it is striking how dour, how troubled, how frightened and haunted our early and founding literature truly is.

—Toni Morrison, *Playing in the Dark*

O n the cover of two 1950s special issues from the popular magazine *Life*, the future of the United States is envisioned in starkly different ways: in the first, the familiar image of the mushroom cloud threatens its readers with the potential of nuclear annihilation, while the second provides these same readers with the delightful promise of world peace in its depiction of a U.S. ambassador, dressed in a casual plaid shirt, sitting on the floor laughing and chatting with a group of Buddhist monks from Laos. The correlation between these two images—namely, that the United States has achieved this false sense of peace due to its own participation in nuclear warfare—is left unsaid, and instead there is a celebration of what *Life* magazine's founder, Henry Luce, famously described as the "American Century." In his 1941 editorial for *Life*, Luce earnestly urged Americans to adopt an internationalist view that positioned the United States as a leader of the free world; the special issue from 1957, in comparison, confidently demonstrates the ease with which American citizens engage in the world beyond U.S. borders. The ambassador depicted on the cover page has a wide grin as he leans in, at ease in his environment despite standing out as a foreigner. His youthful appearance—sparkling white teeth, dark brown hair, and smooth tan skin—are contrasted with signs of maturity: a wristwatch, a wedding ring, and a carefully folded envelope (perhaps notes or a plane ticket) in his shirt pocket.

A closer look at *Life*'s special issue on "America's World Abroad" provides a useful framework for analyzing the image of the youthful ambassador. In an editorial by Robert Coughlan entitled "How We Appear to Others," Americans are described as "immature, with the heedlessness and rough manners of the adolescent," and also as having "the adolescent's optimism, exuberance, simplicity, desire to please and other charming qualities" (152). To support this claim about Americans, Coughlan provides a series of testimonials from people around the world: "They are delightfully *adolescent*," an English librarian suggests (emphasis mine). Praising the energy of visitors from across the pond, she adds, "They have that zest for life and love of fun and just ache to be told how wonderful they are" (qtd. in Coughlan 152). A Lebanese artist, an Italian policeman, and Irish lawyer provide equally colorful descriptions that emphasize Americans' youthfulness. They are nothing more than "bighearted boys" or "noisy but goodhearted children," who have "a freshness and enthusiasm about them bordering on naïveté" (152). The data gathered for the editorial signals the ubiquity of the perception of the United States as an adolescent. Through images such as the one featuring the ambassador, who functions as a symbol of America's global presence, the adolescent becomes more than a set of characteristics attributed to American travelers; it serves as a metaphor for the nation itself. Embodying characteristics of adolescence developed over the course of the twentieth century, the nation, previously viewed as an innocent child, began to put its youth behind it following the close of World War II and embarked on a new stage of development that required it to grow up and mature to fulfill its new role as world leader.

This cultural shift away from innocence can be attributed to a growing discomfort with the immaturity associated with childhood, which no longer seemed to have a place in mid-twentieth-century America following the mass death and destruction of World War II. The child was cast aside in favor of the adolescent, whose promise of future maturity was compelling to a 1950s generation still struggling to determine how its war experiences had changed it.

Neither child nor adult, the adolescent is caught between these two stages of growth, and it is from this status of being in between that this figure gained its power. Child psychologist G. Stanley Hall described this "awkward age" of physical development as a period in which the adolescent is "very rarely understood, and understands himself still less" ("Awkward Age" 149). Adolescence is viewed here as a reflective period and time of identity construction, and medical professionals like Hall wanted to help young people through this process by documenting the mental and physical developments they could expect to encounter during puberty. Youth were encouraged to follow guidelines that would lead them slowly toward the experience of adulthood rather than crashing into it at full speed. Those in the health industry emphasized the "immaturity, innocence, and dependent status of youth" while encouraging these same youth to "achieve new standards set for the mature self marked by autonomy, rationality, and moral responsibility" (DeLuzio 49).

The problem with these guidelines for American youth was that they did not transfer so easily when applied to the nation. The slow and steady approach to adulthood recommended for adolescents was impractical at a time when the United States was racing to increase its global power. Indeed, insecurity about national progress in the twentieth century led to a splitting of youth and "adult" culture. In her comprehensive 2003 study of children's literature in the academy, Beverly Lyon Clark, an expert in the field of children's literature, identifies how efforts to secure a national identity associated with the maturity of adulthood marked a growing trend to distinguish between literature for adults and children, in contrast to the more fluid border that existed during the nineteenth century—that is, long before the "crossover" novel became a staple of marketing in children's literature, adults and children were reading the same books without issue. Following World War II, young people began to be viewed in terms of what Marah Gubar, another scholar of children's literature, describes as a "deficit model of childhood" (451), according to which they were defined by the qualities and traits that they lacked compared with adults. This view of the insufficiency of children in such areas of development as maturity, Clark suggests, is apparent in several common phrases used to describe youthful behavior, including "immature response," "childish reaction," "adolescent quarreling," "juvenile behavior," and "puerile thinking" (4). Applied to children and youth, these phrases may seem normal and appropriate; yet when an adult is their object, their negative connotations come into focus and reveal "our cultural anxiety of immaturity, our unwillingness to take children seriously" (Clark 49–50).

The marginalization of childhood, Clark argues, extended into the academy, where scholars in the burgeoning field of American literature rejected children's literature in an effort to build cultural capital for the set of works they felt best represented the national character and voice. With the development of major publications such as *American Literature* (established in 1929) and the *Cambridge History of American Literature* (1917–21), a new canon started to form that did not include children's books (Clark 58, 62). The object of study for these academics included canonical and popular works of American literature—*The Last of the Mohicans* (1826), *The Scarlet Letter* (1850), *Moby Dick* (1851)—that had previously been associated with the "shameful" position of children's books (Lawrence 11). The equation of highbrow American literature, in particular, with "kiddie lit" explained in part these scholars' eagerness to keep the child and children's things in the shadows by turning to the more mature figure of the adolescent. Clark suggests that American literature academics sought to establish the field as a respectable profession "by shedding femininity and appropriating the language of science, a change fueled by two world wars" (Clark 58). Her overview of the diminished status of children's literature in the academy—a situation I will address in further depth in chapter 1—still rings true in an environment where the position of the child in American culture remains hotly debated.[1] However, Clark does not take full account of the emerging associations of the adolescent with the United States, a gap I address through my argument about the relationship between youth and national identity in *Growing Up with America*. The adolescent, while originally a means for marginalizing certain groups of Americans based on gender, race, class, sexuality, and age, became a powerful metaphor for imagining new social structures and relations both domestically and abroad.

Prior to the early twentieth century, when attention began to shift to adolescence, it was the child that dominated in conversations about national identity. Beginning with the Puritan "errand into the wilderness" that emerged sometime in the sixteenth century, the United States formulated an identity closely tied to youth, especially young children, and the land that was believed to reinvigorate those who had emigrated from Europe. In the work of several childhood studies scholars, including Kenneth Kidd, Carol Singley, Anna Mae Duane, Caroline Levander, Sara Schwebel, and Courtney Weikle-Mills, the figure of the child serves as an important means for testing and authorizing new ideas about what it means to be an American. In her 2010 study of colonial America, for example, Anna Mae Duane argues that it was the suffering body of the child that enabled a critical rethinking of the "often violent process of nation-making" (*Suffering Childhood* 3). The child's body, while often white and middle class, was an emotionally powerful figure that came to symbolize the domestic conflicts within the nation that arose from U.S. imperialism, including but not limited to the colonization of Native peoples and the forced subjugation of Africans as part of the slave trade. Duane acknowledges that much of the time the child figure became a way to excuse these colonial exploits, but the violence that the child's body alluded to still aided in drawing attention to the atrocities of empire building. In this manner, the child became an essential "bridge that linked familiar ways of thinking about power and discipline with the novel problems raised by the New World" (5).

The child, as Duane describes here, is a figure for thinking through complex ideas related to nation building and has the potential to both support or refute the national narrative of the dominant powers. Duane describes this child, at alternating moments, as an "image," "symbol," or "figure," then spends an extensive amount of time explaining how the child functions as a metaphor in early America. In her words, metaphor is about acts of transfer, which create the opportunity for creative, "conceptual thinking" (9). Drawing on the work of recent cognitive scientists, Duane explains that metaphor enables a person to take a word and apply it in a new context which disrupts the existing meaning of that word, thereby creating a new meaning in the process. In the context of the suffering child, the dialectic that emerges through the use of this figure enables a radical restructuring of historical events and their meaning. Importantly, although historically this aided the white colonists in power, Duane underscores how the "specters of dependence and fragility that surround the suffering child" can also work to uncover the histories of those who were disempowered by this enduring metaphor, a point that begins to trouble Clark's reading of metaphors of children and youth as merely serving to support the status quo.

The figure of a damaged, suffering child who "haunts" the history of a nation is by no means new. As British cultural historian Carolyn Steedman eloquently argues in her 1995 study of modern concepts of human interiority, childhood in the early nineteenth century was understood as a "category of dependence, a term that defined certain relationships of powerlessness, submission and bodily inferiority or weakness, before it became descriptive of chronological age" (7). It wasn't until the late nineteenth century, she suggests, that this term became inextricably linked to a specific age in the process of growing up. That for Steedman the child figure who would most represent the "dependence," "powerlessness," and "bodily inferiority" that she defines as integral to the original definition of childhood was the deformed and abused child acrobat Mignon is not insignificant. Mignon would go on to gain a host of meanings as she became more than a character in Johann Wolfgang von Goethe's bildungsroman, *Wilhelm Meister's Apprenticeship* (1795–1796). A cultural figure for thinking through the rapid shift in understanding about the inner self gained through advances in biological, medical, and psychological sciences, Mignon helped establish the child as a figure for a "lost past." As the century progressed, the child began to signify different forms of symbolic development that included the individual and the nation (10–12).

As Steedman's and Duane's work demonstrates, the figure of the child has served to give a metaphorical body to human fears and anxieties about societal change and to make sense of historical events and their repercussions. But, as Karen Sánchez-Eppler argues in *Dependent States: The Child's Part in Nineteenth-Century American Culture* (2005), metaphor and other forms of figurative language, including the act of figuring, frequently lead to a "slippage between what is and what is not a person" (xxiii). "The relation between childhood as a discourse and children as persons," she continues, "has proven so entangled because American society has so frequently employed children to give personal, emotional expression to social and institutional structures" (xxiii). Courtney Weikle-Mills makes a similar claim in her 2013 study of childhood and describes how metaphors of childhood were often used by adults at the expense of children (3–4). Children became the means for thinking through ideas of citizenship or nationality, but these rights were rarely extended to them and were even a means for excluding other disempowered groups such as women, slaves, and American Indians (Weikle-Mills 4; Schwebel, *Child-Sized History* 35–36). While I believe this message is important and worth acknowledging, real children are not the subject of this book. However, it is worth remembering that the ideas associated with these imaginary children did in fact have an impact on real ones. Indeed, many of the novels I use as case studies were directed at young readers and would inevitably shape these children's understanding of what it meant to be a member of the American nation.

Although metaphors and figures of childhood risk turning our attention away from the very children who shape and are shaped by them, they remain one of the most significant markers of an emerging American national identity. Indeed, as Caroline Levander and Carol Singley remark in their introduction to *The American Child: A Cultural Studies Reader* (2003), "the American nation, since its inception, has been identified with and imagined as a child, yet the full significance of this alliance and its relevance to critical inquiries into the figure of the child have yet to be fully understood" (4). Childhood studies scholars, as I have started to show already, have provided persuasive evidence to support the claim that Americans have continually turned to the figure of the child as a way to articulate their experiences and understand how these experiences are part of a uniquely American national identity. Carol Singley locates the child in adoption narratives that dominated the writing of prominent figures in early America, including Benjamin Franklin, and would reach its peak in the works of nineteenth-century writers like Louisa May Alcott. For Singley, the adoption narrative, and the children that populated these narratives, helped define an "evolving American character and nationhood" (*Adopting America* 4). Similarly, Sara Schwebel's 2011 study of twentieth-century American historical children's fiction demonstrates how the child often serves as a means for exploring popular American ideals, such as democracy and self-reliance, and how

these works of historical fiction also aim to mold their young readers into good citizens based on these ideals. Each of the authors
of these nineteenth- and twentieth-century narratives establishes
a pattern of turning to national mythology, in this case the "fresh
starts afforded by the genealogical break with the birth country"
(*Adopting America* 7), and using these narratives to answer the
question first posed by J. Hector St. John de Crèvecoeur in 1782:
What does it mean to be an American?[2] It is through the repeated
joining of myth and childhood that answers to this question began
to take shape.

The shift in metaphoric possibilities of the figure of the child
that emerged in early America is relevant to an understanding
of the massive reinterpretation of national myths in the mid-
twentieth century, a time when authorized national narratives of
the United States began to come under fire as these narratives
threatened to push the nation closer to nuclear annihilation in the
race for world domination between the United States and the Soviet Union. As the nation began to gain power as a world leader
in the aftermath of World War II, the child figure that was previously employed to articulate ideas about national identity shifted
as well. It became increasingly common to turn to images of older
children, or adolescents, for inspiration and to discard the images
of innocent children that populated previous narratives about
American national identity. Though there were indeed exceptions,
the adolescent predominated in large part because he (and it typically *was* a he) was poised between innocence and experience, reflecting the Cold War sentiment that Americans were caught between one developmental stage and another. Throughout this
book, I refer to these images of children and adolescents as both
"metaphors" and "figures" as a way of describing how ideas associated with childhood and adolescence began to inform the ongoing
conversation about American national identity in the Cold War.
Carolyn Steedman describes this process as the act of figuring,
where the child is "used for the purposes of personification, to give
a name and a face (and a body . . .) to abstract ideas and bodies of
theory" (19). Figures, Steedman notes, differ from symbols because
they do not simply stand in for something else (e.g., a dove that
symbolizes peace); rather, the figure is a way for a culture to give

body to ideas that would otherwise be difficult to process. To figure, then, is to put together an idea until it quite literally takes shape.

The brief overview I have provided of how metaphors of childhood in the United States have been employed historically demonstrates the potential of the figure of the adolescent in revealing the dark underside of American history and the difficulty, if not impossibility, of securing a unified national identity. It also begins to reveal the problem with Clark's assertions about the place of the adolescent within the academy in the mid-twentieth century, which focuses on the negative reception of adolescence during this period. In contrast to Clark's views, I believe that something more was at work in the rise of this figure within cultural debates about national identity during the Cold War—that in fact the adolescent became the means for renegotiating the master narrative about American exceptionalism by revealing the previously silenced voices within this narrative. Clark begins to attend to this connection when she addresses key works of literary criticism, including R. W. B. Lewis's *The American Adam* (1955) and Richard Chase's *The American Novel and Its Tradition* (1957), and notes how the authors of these works aimed to construct a literary canon by touting the novels of Henry James, Herman Melville, Nathaniel Hawthorne, and Ralph Waldo Emerson, among others, as exemplars of a distinguished tradition in American literature. These authors were celebrated both for being quintessentially American and for the literary merit of their writing (67). Clark suggests that if children's literature was included at all in the master narrative of an American literary tradition constructed by Cold War scholars, it was only in the form of "an adolescent male rebelling against the status quo—becoming a melodrama of beset adolescence, if you will—but then the work would no longer be considered children's literature" (67).

In American studies, a field that contributed to the master narrative that Clark identifies, it is true that the contribution of the adolescent in the shaping of national identity has, for the most part, been downplayed due to cultural anxieties about innocence. One striking example is in American studies scholar Amy Kaplan's frequently cited essay, "'Left Alone with America': The Absence of Empire in the Study of American Culture" (1993), in which Kaplan unpacks one of the central "paradigm dramas" within the field: Perry Miller's "jungle epiphany" (Wise 174). In the opening of her essay, Kaplan recounts how Miller, who codeveloped Harvard University's American Civilization program, journeyed abroad as a young man and "discovered" America during his youthful exploits. Miller's identification of the distinguishing features of American national identity while working along the coast of the Belgian Congo, Kaplan notes, is made possible in part by his contrasting of the "blankness of Africa" with the "fullness of America." From this absence, Miller begins to construct a "coherent [American] national identity" ("Left Alone" 4), one that is only made possible through a break with the national imperialism that is deeply embedded in the history of the United States. Kaplan suggests that in Miller's reflection on his youth, Africa serves as the "repository—and thus uneasy reminder—of those repressed alternatives [in American history]," including the massacre of American Indians and the enslavement of Africans (4). However, in her efforts to distance herself from the master myths that upheld the "state fantasy" of American exceptionalism (Pease, *New American* 1), Kaplan overlooks the cultural significance of Miller's turn to youth in his account of his journey to discover "my America" (qtd. in Kaplan 3).

The postwar investment in proving the United States' maturity, a turn that coincided with the rise of American studies, created a cultural climate where adolescence, and the middle state between innocence and experience that it represented, became deeply embedded in the long-term effort to identify the new voice of American literature. A project that at its heart intended to help unravel the very meaning of what it meant to be American, it was in many ways detrimental to the value attributed to the child and children's literature. As my reading of Kaplan's essay indicates, the centrality of the figure of the adolescent in American studies continues to be little acknowledged, in part due to the marginalization of childhood studies in the humanities. Anna Mae Duane points out in her introduction to *The Children's Table* (2013) that fields of study representing marginalized groups, such as the area studies that arose in the 1950s, have all criticized the deployment of child metaphors to disempower certain social groups. She insists that

childhood studies offers a new way to view these power relationships by examining how and why childhood is a position of mar-
ginality, and that "without rethinking the structures of thought
that render childhood an implicitly shameful position in the first
place, we are at an intellectual impasse" (6). Duane's call to recon-
sider the position of childhood in the humanities echoes Clark's
earlier claim in *Kiddie Lit*, where she asks her readers to "revalue
the status of childhood" (4). Following on these scholars' previous
claims, we might ask what it would mean to rethink the position of
the child, *at all stages of growth*, within the field of American studies? How might the process of negotiating and revising national
myths appear differently if the child is not merely a means for disempowering groups of marginalized people? What if instead this
figure helped cast off the developmental rhetoric tied to narratives
of national progress in order to gain new historical perspectives on
the myths central to the founding of the United States?

The resistance to this revaluation of childhood and children's
literature in American studies is evident in the different responses
from experts in the field to landmark essays published over the
years in *American Quarterly*. As Sharon O'Brien writes in her
commentary on R. Gordon Kelly's "Literature and the Historian"
(1974)—an essay, incidentally, that was published at a time when
children's literature was securing its place within the academy—
Kelly's essay "never attained the almost totemic stature of an article like Barbara Welter's 'The Cult of True Womanhood.' Perhaps
this is because the genre Kelly chose to explore—children's literature—is of less interest to American studies scholars than wom-
en's writing" (113). It is no wonder that earlier stages of growth, including childhood and adolescence, were viewed as suspect in light
of such scathing remarks as literary critic James F. Scott's declaration: "I fear . . . [that there are] powerful social forces now active
beneath the surface of American life, forces which glorify immaturity and thus obscure an essential distinction between adolescent
spontaneity and adult creativity" (151). Scott's comment, from his
1962 essay "Beat Literature and the American Teen Cult," attests
to the assumption that adolescence is a stage of life associated
with immaturity, one that should not be returned to once passed
through.

It is only with the increase of childhood studies in the early 2000s that Americanists more generally have begun to take seriously the importance of the child. This turn is evidenced in several recent book reviews in *American Quarterly*. American literary scholar Maude Hines notes, "Critical interest in childhood has grown in American studies in the last few years." New studies of childhood, Hines continues, "[follow] a trend in recent scholarship that looks at the child, along with its treatment and figuration, as a barometer of cultural pressures. . . . [T]hese books help us to see the breadth of possibility for playing with the role of the child in American studies" (152). Julia Mickenberg, an American studies scholar who has written extensively on radical politics in children's literature, adds that "only relatively recently have works with children as their focus begun to gain the sustained attention of American studies scholars"; yet Mickenberg insists that childhood studies should matter to those in American studies due to the child's ability to "[provide] crucial insights into [the] core values and practices of our society, revealing how American culture reproduces itself in the younger generation" (1217). More recently, Kristen Proehl, a scholar of children's literature and queer theory, asserts: "Recent scholarship in childhood and adolescent studies . . . offers new insights into how the politicization of youth is, in fact, part of a broader American historical and cultural legacy" (172). The growing trend to focus on youth in American scholarship on national identity marks a break from previous attempts to avoid associations with childhood and innocence in first-generation scholarship in the field and opens up possibilities for understanding how youth contributed to cultural debates in the twentieth century that both redefined the nation and its national literature.

In order to examine the role that the figure of the adolescent plays in the making and remaking of U.S. national identity, I employ what can be identified as a childhood studies approach. While the scientific study of childhood emerged as early as the 1800s with the increase in attention to the young in the fields of biology, physiology, and medicine,[3] and reached its full fruition at the turn of the twentieth century through the work of such notable figures as psychologists G. Stanley Hall and Havelock Ellis, I refer here to the institutionalized study of children and children's literature within the academy. Particularly in the twenty-first century with the launch of interdisciplinary programs of childhood studies in higher education, which are separate and distinct from the children's literature programs that originally developed out of library science and gradually found a home in English departments in the 1970s and 1980s, a bridge began to close the divide between the sciences and the humanities. The emerging field of childhood studies employs an interdisciplinary approach to thinking about power and how it impacts children, and it takes issue with the use of metaphors of childhood to oppress others. It seeks to consider why childhood is a place of dependence, of shame, and of vulnerability and viewed as a stage of life that must be passed through as quickly as possible. This line of inquiry goes beyond simply thinking about how fictions of childhood impact real children; it reconsiders the very fictions themselves. In sum, childhood studies seeks "to include the child in any field of study . . . [by] realign[ing] the very structure of that field, changing the terms of inquiry and forcing a different set of questions" (Duane, *The Children's Table* 1).

A childhood studies approach can help us better understand the cultural shifts that began taking place following World War II, as innocence was cast aside for experience. Within academic and intellectual circles that included the consensus historians, myth and symbol critics, and New York Intellectuals, the 1950s narrative of national progress created a welcome departure from the New Criticism popular in the previous decade, which failed to account for cultural and political influences on literature, and opened up a new method of defining the unique qualities of the American experience that suited the national mood. But like the childhood they wanted to leave behind, it was a narrative that only described the experiences of an elite few: highly educated white men with considerable influence due to their academic positions and social connections. In publications that included Richard Hofstadter's *The American Political Tradition* (1948), Lionel Trilling's *The Liberal Imagination* (1950), R. W. B. Lewis's *The American Adam* (1955), Leslie Fiedler's *An End to Innocence* (1955), Louis Hartz's *The Liberal Tradition in America* (1955), Perry Miller's *Errand into the Wilderness* (1956), Henry May's *The End of American Innocence* (1959), and Leo Marx's *The Machine in the Garden* (1964), this disillusioned generation decried the flaws of those who came before them and sought new ways of moving forward into what they recognized as a pivotal moment in U.S. history, one in which the nation was poised to take on a new role as world leader. Their work would go on to define the discipline of American studies, which, as many contemporary scholars have noted, remains inextricably linked to the exceptionalism, or fundamental belief in the United States' moral superiority to other nations, that was a key feature of the academic movement I refer to as the "beyond innocence" debate.[4] As cultural historian Michael Denning comments, "The notion of 'American exceptionalism' is in many ways the foundation of the 'discipline' of 'American studies'; whether the answers are cast in terms of the 'American mind,' the 'national character,' American 'myths and symbols,' or 'American culture,' the founding question of the discipline remains 'What is American?'" (360).

On the surface, the activities of a small group of white, male intellectuals would seem to have nothing to do with the experiences of the diverse population of the United States, including the women and ethnic minorities that failed to enter into their narrative of national uniqueness. However, as I will go on to show, this particular moment launched a pivotal reimagination of the national myths that defined the United States and made way for the more creative efforts of the literary writers who were similarly responding to the events of the Cold War, from its beginnings in the 1940s to its aftereffects in the decades following the fall of the Berlin Wall. The historical representation of the United States as a "new youth," who was more often than not white, middle class, and male, made way for an adolescent figure who departed from this old set of criteria. In a manner similar to Toni Morrison's reinterpretation of the American literary tradition in *Playing in the Dark* (1992), these writers stripped away the central characteristics of the nation's mythical American hero and revealed the historical tragedies this hero's journey was meant to hide. Through their efforts, the shadows that flitted behind the glimmering image of this youthful figure began to come to the forefront.

In order to chart the importance of the figure of the adolescent in Cold War constructions of national identity, I begin with a reexamination of the foundational work of R. W. B. Lewis, Henry Nash Smith, Perry Miller, and Leo Marx, demonstrating how these

myth and symbol scholars drew on cultural conceptions of childhood and adolescence in order to construct an American literary
tradition that identified the distinguishing features of national
identity. Illustrating what they viewed as the golden past of the nation, including the Puritan era and the frontier days, while warning about the dangers of trying to return to the "innocence" of these
pivotal moments in American history in the turbulent present of
the 1950s, their work was part of a larger cultural turn away from
childhood that I describe as the "beyond innocence" debate. This debate prompted the rise of the adolescent in discussions of the American literary canon that contributed to the national narrative about
progress and power during the Cold War. Although the place of the
adolescent within academic scholarship at this time was tenuous,
I demonstrate how scientific discourses about adolescence, notably
by the leading child psychologist G. Stanley Hall, and popular media depictions of young people as "rebels" led to the utility of the adolescent as a figure for radical reform of existing social structures.
Within the work of the myth and symbol school, the adolescent began to appear as a promising figure for social change. By drawing
attention to the very voices claimed to be silenced by this scholarship, the adolescent provides a radical intervention in these traditional national narratives of westward expansion and creates space
for experiences beyond those of white male explorers. The figure of
the adolescent, as my account reveals, has the potential to revitalize old paradigms in the field of American studies by turning attention to a different marker of identity: age, which has played a key
role in the "growing up" of America.

In my remaining chapters, I demonstrate how the figure of the
adolescent continued to dispel myths that glorified a national past
which was filled with violence and conquest. The myths of the
American Adam, virgin land, errand into the wilderness, and the
machine in the garden were part of what American writer and editor Tom Engelhardt describes as the "free story of America," all
of which contributed to a tale of the pursuit of liberty and freedom, of expansion and progress, and, if violence was present, of
justified rebellion against a threatening power (4). This was a tale
that could not, nor would not, be contained forever, and the Cold
War marks a pivotal moment of counterdiscourse, when contemporary American writers employed the figure of the adolescent to

address the injustices of the past and to empower those previously silenced by these myths. In these chapters, I intentionally combine texts marketed as "adult" and "children's and young adult" literature in order to demonstrate the pervasiveness of the adolescent within cultural debates about national identity, but I refrain from distinguishing between these categories, in large part because too often these distinctions have served as a way to marginalize or diminish the impact of literature for the young. As I demonstrated earlier in my engagement with Beverly Lyon Clark's argument in *Kiddie Lit*, such distinctions were a new invention of the twentieth century and spoke more to the construction of childhood as a position of dependence, vulnerability, and even shame. The rising culture of the adolescent did help ameliorate this in part by finding a youthful figure who had the autonomy to rebel against authority and make positive social changes, gesturing to the potential of the future through these acts of resistance, but this shift was at the expense of the child who came before. Attention to the radical reformation of national identity through the figure of the adolescent has not been addressed before now, nor have the repercussions of this shift for previous images of the nation as a young child. I therefore analyze books marketed for all age categories in order to underscore how the historical events of the Cold War provided the conditions for a new story of America, one that was not only free but freeing.

In chapter 2, "American Adam (and Eve): Rewriting History in an 'Age of Hopelessness,'" I focus on the literary response to the American Adam myth during the Cold War. Understanding the destructive aspects of myths that erased gender and racial conflict from U.S. national narratives, authors responded with literary fiction that exposed the hidden past embedded in the myth of the American Adam, which focuses on the regeneration of male explorers who regain access to the innocence of youth by breaking with their origins. I include three case studies that demonstrate the evolution of the American Adam into a young American Eve between 1945 and 2011, a period that more accurately identifies the cultural tensions that arose in the 1950s with the Cold War. In the *Oxford Handbook of the Cold War* (2013), an edited collection that challenges traditional readings of the Cold War as a struggle between two world powers, contributors insist that the Cold War is just one phase in a much longer movement of globalization, human rights, and decolonization (Iriye 22). The crumbling of the Berlin Wall and the Soviet Union at the end of the 1990s, in Akira Iriye's words, marks just one "important chapter in an *unfinished* story" (27; emphasis mine). Iriye, who is a prominent historian of American diplomatic history, underscores the importance of including the 1990s and early 2000s in scholarship on the Cold War as "both a complement and counter-narrative to the dominant story of cold war confrontations" (Immerman and Goedde 8).

The American Eve that emerges over the course of this period of political conflict is like her male predecessor in that she too is a model of self-reliance and appears to come from nowhere. However, unlike the American Adam, this female figure is haunted by her past and must come to terms with it in order to continue leading an independent life. Due to her need to address this past, she also holds the power not only to understand but also to rewrite this history. In response to issues that include racial segregation, termination (of American Indian reservations), youth suicide, and suburban unrest, among others, the authors of these narratives employ the American Eve in order to reveal the history of U.S. empire and comment on the continued impact of this legacy of conquest in their contemporary moment. The novels I have selected as case studies—Scott O'Dell's *Island of the Blue Dolphins* (1960), Linda Hogan's *Solar Storms* (1995), and Karen Russell's *Swamplandia!* (2011)—seek to dispel the negative aspects of the original American Adam myth by restoring gender and race to the national narrative. Their work, which has received significant critical acclaim in literary circles, underscores the relevance of the American Eve to an American literary tradition.

In my remaining chapters, I take a similar approach and close-read canonical and award-winning novels from across the mid-twentieth and early twenty-first centuries. In chapter 3, "From Virgin Land to Virgin Girl: Nature, Nostalgia, and American Empire," I continue my discussion of race and gender in the context of the virgin land myth. My central argument here is that the adolescent girl became an indispensable figure for novelists interested in critiquing the virgin land myth as a result of the popular interpretation of adolescence as a time of transition. As in nationally sanctioned narratives of U.S. expansion, the girls in these narratives are mythologized by male characters who are attracted by their beauty, and as a result, these girls frequently suffer emotional and physical abuse. The violence in these narratives illustrates the damaging effects of colonialism and brings attention to the absence of empire in the reigning national narrative. I take as my case studies in this chapter Vladimir Nabokov's *Lolita* (1955), Jeffrey Eugenides's *The Virgin Suicides* (1993), and Louise Erdrich's *The Plague of Doves* (2008), which engage heavily with literary tropes and psychological discourses surrounding girlhood in the twentieth century. Through the intersection of female adolescence and American frontier myths, these authors challenge dominant narratives of U.S. expansion by underscoring the violence of the nation's imperialistic agenda.

My fourth chapter considers how critical reception of U.S. national myths expanded from local to global concerns as the United States began a campaign to expand the national "family" through metaphorical acts of adoption. Responding to the father-son theme that undergirds the United States' errand-into-the-wilderness myth, I look at the way that the original errand, perceived as a mission passed on through generations from father to son or from national leader to citizen, serves as the backdrop for the critical reception of this myth among contemporary novelists. Concerned about the nation's foreign policies during the Cold War, these authors turned to father-son bonds as a way of questioning the nation's errand rather than reinforcing loyalty to national leaders. My case studies in this chapter—Meindert DeJong's *The House of Sixty Fathers* (1956), Russell Banks's *Rule of the Bone* (1995), and Sherman Alexie's *Flight* (2007)—use the adoption trope in order to imagine new ties to foreign nations, challenging the popular sentimental rhetoric of familial love that was used to help expand the United States' global power. By employing the figure of the rebellious son, these authors draw attention to the colonial undertones of the paternal relationship through the adoption trope. In doing so, they extend earlier uses of this trope in nineteenth-century American literature, formerly focused on the United States' break from England, by turning this image on its head and putting the United States in the position of the authoritarian father.

My final chapter returns to the figure of the rebellious son, but in this case the boy figure is a response to the dramatic restructuring of the nation's agricultural center, in particular of the loss of rural spaces associated with the frontier and small-town America. I demonstrate how the image of the machine in the garden, and the pastoral literature where it was commonly found, once again held relevance for Cold War Americans. The machine, described as an object that disrupts the peace of the garden (often in a violent manner), serves as a symbol of technological advancement, loss of innocence, and, eventually, of U.S. colonization. In confronting the myth of the machine in the garden, the novels in my case studies—J. D. Salinger's *The Catcher in the Rye* (1951), Leslie Marmon Silko's *Gardens in the Dunes* (1999), and M. T. Anderson's *Feed* (2002)—grapple with the real historical conflicts that are overlooked through nostalgia for an agrarian past. Popular figures of "vanishing" Americans, including the farm and small-town boy as well as the more conventional figure of a lone American Indian who is the last member of his/her tribe, feature prominently in this work. However, rather than simply crafting these vanishing Americans in the same fashion as earlier nineteenth-century authors, postwar writers began to turn their attention to rebellious girls. By including girls in their narrative revisions of the machine-in-the-garden myth, these authors underscore the colonial implications of the foreign machine "invading" the home front and use this adolescent figure to voice dissent about male narratives of conquest, building on previous articulations of frontier myths that depict the American West as a garden by emphasizing how industrialization, and especially technology, is responsible for the downfall of American society.

In closing, I discuss how the destruction imagined in responses to the machine-in-the-garden myth comes to a head with the ending of the "American Century" and what the adolescent's role may be in the reconstruction of U.S. national identity. Though brief, my epilogue reveals the price of maturity for the future of American studies and considers how a closer consideration of youth might inform debates about the "transnational turn" in the field (Pease, *Re-Framing the Transnational Turn* 1).

CHAPTER 1

Beyond Innocence

THE COMING OF AGE OF MYTH
AND SYMBOL CRITICISM

[T]his mood is not without constructive virtue. It reminds us of a significant fact: that instead of recapturing our past, we have got to transcend it. As for a child leaving adolescence, there is no going home again for America.

—**Louis Hartz, *The Liberal Tradition in America***

In 1923 English writer and literary critic D. H. Lawrence suggested that the United States' rebirth as a new youth was the "true myth of America" (60). At the time of its publication, *Studies in Classic American Literature* failed to reverberate with the academic community, in part because American literature was not yet viewed with the same respect as European or world classics; instead, as Lawrence observed, books by American writers were equated to kiddie fare, best read by children (*Studies* 13). While Vernon Louis Parrington's *Main Currents in American Thought* (1927), one of the first substantial critical studies of American literature, was published in the same decade, it wasn't until the release of F. O. Matthiessen's monumental *American Renaissance* in 1941 that interest in the national literature began to emerge. By the 1950s, this interest was in full force, and Lawrence's *Studies* resurfaced as a favorite inspirational source for new scholarship on the unique characteristics of the classics in American literature. Along with this renewed interest in the local creative output of the nation came a hotly contested debate about the ongoing depiction of the United States as an innocent youth. The political scientist and intellectual historian Louis Hartz summed it up best, lamenting that "As for a child who is leaving adolescence, there is no going home again for America" (*Liberal Tradition* 32). In these lines, Hartz underscores the central message of the "beyond innocence" debate, a conversation about the historical association of the United States with an innocent youth that involved myth and symbol scholars, New York Intellectuals, and consensus historians. Beginning in the 1950s and into the early 1960s, those in the "beyond innocence" debate argued that national narratives of youth needed to be discarded in order to support the United States' ability to take up the mantle of global leadership following World War II. As with the case of Hartz, these scholars imagined that they and their fellow Americans were young adolescents on the verge of adulthood. In fact, they insisted that this transition must take place if the United States was to reach full maturity as a nation.

As I began to explain in my introduction, some of the major institutional shifts occurring in the early twentieth century contributed to Cold War critics' adamant refusal to associate with what they deemed "immature" children's books and with childhood more generally. This meant more than simply avoiding children's books in their works of literary criticism; it necessitated an entire rethinking of the canon in search of novels that would resonate with this generation's understanding of their progression from boyhood to manhood. For most of these scholars, World War II represented a loss of innocence that complicated previous notions of a national past, which were defined in relation to the "victory culture" of the 1940s. The frontier, which had long served as an imaginary landscape for staging U.S. triumph, was "effective as a builder of national consciousness because it seemed so natural, so innocent, so nearly childlike and was so little contradicted by the realities of invasion or defeat" (Engelhardt 5). With the emergence of the Soviet Union as a competitor for the position of world leader, and the memory of the potential for global destruction after the dropping of atomic bombs in Hiroshima and Nagasaki, the question of the cost of victory came to the forefront. Victory had stopped the expansion of the Axis powers, but the threat of communism remained and appeared to lurk around every corner (Engelhardt 7).

The members of the myth and symbol school who took part in the beyond innocence debate believed that a position of experience was more appropriate for the postwar generation, even as they found early American myths of returning to a state of innocence appealing. In his overview of their position toward national politics, American historian David Noble claims that "[Henry Nash] Smith joined others of his generation in making a confession that the quest for innocence had destructive consequences" (115). As one of the leaders of the myth and symbol school and a pioneer in American studies, Smith, alongside his contemporaries, grappled with the benefits of clinging to a myth that the nation appeared to have outgrown. The myth of American innocence isolated the nation's citizens by giving them the perception that they were living outside of space and time, apart from the corrupt world of Europe. The luxury of such a vision was not possible at a time when it was glaringly clear that the United States was part of a global community, and it was the goal of the myth and symbol scholars to slowly chip away at this version of American innocence. Following the lead of Protestant theologian Reinhold Niebuhr, many intellectuals would vigorously "denounc[e] an American tradition of 'innocence' and prais[e] a European tradition of 'experience'" (Noble 117). Niebuhr, who favored internationalism, described the entrance of the United States into the world community as a transition requiring the nation to abandon the belief in its innocence, for the United States was "never as innocent as [it] pretended to be, even as a child is not as innocent as is implied in the use of the child as a symbol of innocency" (35).

The intellectual situation of the time, where innocence was pitted against experience, became an ongoing dialogue between historians, novelists, and theologians about the meaning of America. The tension between the prominent theologian Niebuhr, the myth and symbol school, and 1950s novelists that included J. D. Salinger and Vladimir Nabokov, among others, created a charged atmosphere that would help propel the nation out of adolescence and into adulthood. Yet it is rare that the conditions which gave rise to this dialogue are fully described. Due to the myth and symbol school's focus on American myths, their work continues to be a target of criticism among younger scholars of American studies. As American historian Bruce Kuklick famously observed in his 1972 essay, the critical framework of myth and symbol scholars is "suspect" due to its presentist orientation (79). Others have added that the myth and symbol scholars focused on more positive traits of the national character as a way of viewing "culture as a whole" (Noble 107) and that their narratives of national wholeness represented a sort of "myopia" that failed to consider the activism taking place outside of the dominant culture, which tended to be white and male (Tyler May 188–189). The views set out here by second-generation scholars illustrate the desire to shift both the methodology and object of study of American studies, a move that has been highly successful as gender, race, sexuality, and other important markers of identity have moved to the center of critical discussions within the field.

The work of the myth and symbol school continues to be a point of departure in critical reflections on the history of the field and its future, suggesting that the founders maintain an influential presence despite previous criticism of their work. As Amy Kaplan and other prominent voices in the field note in a special edition of *American Literary History*, the 1970s marked the beginning of a cultural turn, a moment when many scholars in American studies were seeking to acknowledge the previously unheard voices in American literature.[1] In the process of discovering these new voices, old ones were silenced on the grounds that they were simply too exclusive, focusing only on those who reflected their own experience as white men (Tyler May 179). While this is one important way to reflect on the legacy of the myth and symbol scholarship, it misses an important aspect of this body of work, namely, the significance of age as a lens for interpreting how myth operated at the beginning of the Cold War and its continued influence up to the present. Without considering the importance of age in the beyond innocence debate, and in particular the strong desire to cast off the innocence of childhood in favor of the experience of adulthood, it is difficult to see how the work of the myth and symbol scholars contributed to the larger cultural changes taking place in regard to national identity. In particular, this debate gave rise to the figure of the adolescent as a symbol of national progress and contradicted the previous national narrative's exclusive focus on white male experience.

The "Beyond Innocence" Debate: A Brief Overview

The mythical narrative of youth that participants in the beyond innocence debate subscribed to can be traced back to D. H. Law-

rence's *Studies in Classic American Literature*. Lawrence's fascination with innocence and experience helped structure the work
of the myth and symbol scholars, in particular, though his influence can be seen elsewhere. As Paul Giles, an international scholar
of American studies, acknowledges, Lawrence's study of American literature "anticipates the epistemology of American studies
in its 'mythic' phase" (89). Like Lawrence, these critics would use
myth to help structure their analysis of the "voices" of American
literature, and they would similarly be turned into "something of
a whipping boy" for doing so (Jenkins 45). The myth and symbol
scholars' tendency to weave their personal narratives into their
scholarship, an approach that mirrors Lawrence's emphasis on
his own movement to maturity, partly engender this criticism. In
Studies, Lawrence's growing pains quickly become a central part
of his story about the development of American literature and are
"evident in the contrasts that he repeatedly draws between the
'innocent' surface meaning of the texts and the infernal 'experience' that smolders beneath" (M. Wynn Thomas and John Turner
46). The dialectic of innocence and experience in Lawrence's work
is shaped by Romantic ideology, in particular the views of William
Blake, whose 1789 collection of poetry, *Songs of Innocence and Experience*, blurred the boundaries between childhood and adulthood. Through his engagement with the dialectic of innocence and
experience, Lawrence led the way toward a preoccupation with the
stages of growing up, especially the awkward in-between state of
adolescence. In his chapter on James Fenimore Cooper's *Leatherstocking* series, for example, Lawrence writes: "That is the true
myth of America. She starts old, old, wrinkled and writhing in an
old skin. And there is a gradual sloughing of the old skin, towards
a new youth. It is the myth of America" (60). Here, Lawrence alludes to the centrality of youth in the formation of American national identity, beginning to trace the historical depiction of the
United States as an innocent youth and paving the way for future
generations to question the benefits of such an association.

The desire to return to a state of youthfulness certainly played
a part in the work of the myth and symbol scholars as well as the
intellectuals and writers who would join in their efforts to unravel
the voices of American literature. Yet it is the crossroads of inno-

cence and experience, the adolescence of one's youth, that most consistently structured their work. This is evident in the cultural climate of the time, when the beyond innocence debate escalated and peaked in the mid-1950s as those involved in the debate argued about the nation's need to "grow up" and move toward a state of maturity. This conversation was at the heart of 1950s American literary and historical criticism, with such notable scholars as Leslie Fiedler, Ihab Hassan, R. W. B. Lewis, and Henry May contributing. Through their publications, contributors to this debate mapped the relationship of innocence to U.S. national identity and considered the implications of what some referred to as the "cult of youth" on present-day American literature (Hassan 315). Fears about the future of America were articulated through such landmark texts as Fiedler's *An End to Innocence* (1955), May's *The End of American Innocence* (1959), and Hassan's *Radical Innocence: Studies in the Contemporary American Novel* (1961). As the titles suggest, there was a sense that innocence was no longer possible in the present age and that something terrifying was part of the nation's future.

The persistence of titles forecasting the close of an "innocent" era for the United States led Jane Knowles and Robert Allen Skotheim to announce that a divide between the "innocence" of the nation's past and attempts to secure a future that would lead "beyond innocence" indicated a growing maturity within the critical scholarship (94). In their 1961 review of the state of the field in *American Quarterly*, Knowles and Skotheim, who both trained at prestigious programs of American studies as graduate students, identified an emerging trend in this scholarship and recognized even at this early stage that there was a shared interest in moving "beyond innocence" among their colleagues in the field of American studies (94). In attempting to come to terms with the nation's frightening future, including the prospect that all life could be snuffed out with a single push of a button, what emerged as a result of this debate was a dizzying exchange of opinions on the benefits and drawbacks of the figure of the adolescent for American culture. Through the lens of adolescence, these scholars attempted to grapple with representations of an innocent past versus those of a more mature, "experienced" present. At times, they would draw on and contribute to these depictions, while in other cases the adolescent represented a rebellion against such distinctions and a symbolic representation of the nation's growing pains.

The postwar consensus about the decline of American innocence that sparked the beyond innocence debate launched a serious consideration of the importance of the figure of the adolescent in the growing-up process for both Americans and their literature. The circumstances that led to this debate can in part be attributed to the sharp increase in birth rates, or midcentury "baby boom," which gave the adolescent greater visibility in postwar American culture. The adolescent's ability to make his/her own consumer choices was nothing unique to this generation (Chinn 4–5; Ringel 4), but the baby boom did lead to the "commercialization of the teenager" as companies responded to higher demand for consumer products from suburban families and their children (Medovoi 35). In responding to these cultural changes, many scholars felt that America must forgo its previous fetishization of innocence if it was ever to mature. These critics generally fell into two broad categories depending on their ideological views on childhood: (1) those who believed that the prominence of the adolescent in contemporary literature, especially the novel, was a beneficial change and (2) those who fiercely opposed the inclusion of this figure on the condition that it risked decreasing the recently established cultural capital of American literature. The lack of consensus about the impact of the adolescent on American literature spoke to larger concerns about this figure's fitness to symbolically represent the national character and underscored the growing discontent with previous definitions of national belonging. The results of this discontent were yet to be decided, but this did not stop those in the beyond innocence debate from grappling with the meaning of innocence, debating its relevance to current Americans, and mapping out their own solution for moving beyond this innocent state.

Those who felt threatened by the increasing presence of adolescence in American culture limited their critiques to the visible changes in contemporary American fiction. The Beats, who rebelled against the conformity of the McCarthy era, took the brunt of the criticism, not surprisingly. Their rejection of traditional middle-class values and laid-back lifestyle meant that those in this pivotal literary movement were associated more with adolescence than adulthood. The Beats' youthful exuberance and adolescent antics made them popular with a burgeoning youth culture but also a prime target for anxious literary critics. An example of this disapproving viewpoint can be found in literary critic James F. Scott's 1962 *American Quarterly* essay, "Beat Literature and the American Teen Cult." In the essay's introduction, Scott remarks, "The Beat conception of the creative process, shot through with inconsistency and naïveté, is an indirect yet almost inevitable result of powerful social forces now active beneath the surface of American life, forces which glorify immaturity and thus obscure an essential distinction between adolescent spontaneity and adult creativity" (151). Scott continues his tirade as he warns readers about the nation's "overblown interest in adolescence" (152). His criticism reflects a subtle yet important change in the beyond innocence debate: by the early 1960s, critics were not only demanding a move beyond innocence, they were genuinely worried about the impact of teen culture on American literature. With over seventy-five million children born between the mid-1940s and 1960s, it was clear that the surge in young people would have both a "remarkable duration and intensity" (Medovoi 35). Teenagers had achieved a significant physical presence as citizens of the nation, and their overwhelming appearance in American culture led to a shift in the symbolic associations with youth. No longer simply serving as a way to represent the growing pains of twentieth-century writers, the adolescent developed into a rebel figure with the potential to radically reconfigure the literary canon.

The heightened anxiety and intensity of the backlash against the American teen reflected in Scott's essay demonstrate the extent to which some critics felt threatened by youth culture. In *Rebels: Youth and the Cold War Origins of Identity* (2005), a cultural history of the importance of "bad" boys and girls in the 1950s generation, American studies scholar Leerom Medovoi attributes some of this anxiety to changes in the book market. The increase in paperback sales meant that librarians and other traditional bastions of literary culture were losing control over the tastes of Americans. Teens in particular embraced the mass-market paperback, which expanded the number of options they had for affordable reading material. As the number of paperbacks marketed to teens increased, these youth quickly gained the power to select for themselves what they deemed worthwhile reading. This power to choose differed from that of previous eras, when young people could purchase dime novels or comics at affordable prices. Medovoi notes that these changes had further ramifications for literary critics, who were equally concerned with the new market trends and the "conformity" they associated with the mass-market paperback (80). These concerns about the massification of literary culture were fueled by the frequent "conflation of mass culture and youth culture" (82), both of which critics tended to view as inferior to canonical works of literature and felt "infantilized" its consumers. While these critics' fears were not entirely unwarranted, the backlash against mass-market paperbacks, and the targeting of the adolescent in particular, were often exaggerated responses to new market trends (82).

The increased visibility of youth cultures in the 1950s is only part of the reason why participants in the beyond innocence debate turned anew to the figure of the adolescent. As the dialectic of innocence and experience suggests, the adolescent was a crucial transitional figure that promised adult maturity in the near future. Younger children, while still central to the argument, were associated more with the America of the past, an "innocent" America that no longer existed or, if it did, had little relevance for the war-shocked scholars participating in the beyond innocence debate. In his summary of the intellectual fascination with adolescence, Medovoi explains that the rebel figure gained cultural capital as a result of changes happening during the Cold War and that Americans viewed this figure as being capable of representing the United States' new position on a global stage (1). Medovoi stresses that the adolescent's association with rebellion and freedom was ideologically useful in the political climate of the early Cold War; however, there were other factors that led to interest in this transitional figure. The adolescent captured Americans' fears that the nation was stuck in a state of arrested development, trapped forever in the pimply, serotonin-ridden body of a teenager. Without some kind of decisive act, those of the 1950s generation felt that the nation might never realize its potential as the leader of the free world.

Such an overview might suggest that participants in the beyond innocence debate saw the adolescent only in a negative light,
but for many the adolescent also provided an opportunity to renew a flagging literary tradition, which in comparison to the nineteenth century produced fewer books capable of contributing to
the growing canon of American literature. In contrast to this predominant view among fellow debate participants, Ihab Hassan, an
Arab American theorist and literary critic, described the adolescent as a complex figure that deserves respect: "The cult of adolescence is not an accident in our time," Hassan contends. "Quite
to the contrary, its history reverts to some of the most basic im-
pulses in American experience. Behind it lies what we used to call
the American Dream, the vision of youth, hope and the open road"
(313). In the most revealing comment in his essay, "The Idea of Adolescence in American Fiction" (1958), Hassan returns to the dialectic of innocence and experience, explaining how the adolescent
fits in it: "What went wrong with the American Dream, we all seem
to be on the verge of asking, and our novelists, perhaps looking
back to their own boyhood, write as if the adolescent knew the answer. And perhaps they are right. The adolescent is no longer simple or ignorant since Innocence has come to be rejected in the favor
of Experience, and the pursuit of happiness has made way for the
greater elegance of damnation" (318). Hassan's commentary may
seem cynical today, but in its own context it expressed enormous
optimism about the potential of the adolescent to open up spaces
for discussion about the fears and anxieties of the current age.

Hassan's optimism can be constructively compared to the attitudes of other participants in the beyond innocence debate, including Leslie Fiedler and Henry May. Both Fiedler and May believed
that the time of innocence was over and that it was necessary to
move to a state of maturity if America was to survive in the second half of the twentieth century. In the conclusion to his 1959
study on early twentieth-century American culture, May remarks
that the end of American innocence was viewed as a terrible loss
for the nation's citizens but that those who fail to acknowledge the
absence of or nostalgically long for a return to this innocent state
have unrealistic expectations, wishing for a "happy ending" as a
child might when listening to a fairy tale (398). May's assertion
that Americans "must get over" a myth of innocence is rooted in

his belief that this fiction of innocence is reductive and counterproductive. May defines innocence as "the absence of guilt and doubt and the complexity that goes with them" (393). Innocence, in May's conception, simply cannot persist because it will leave Americans in a perpetual state of naïveté.

Fiedler joins the choir championing a move beyond innocence in his similarly titled work, *An End to Innocence* (1955), a collection of essays that features his "Come Back to the Raft Ag'in, Huck Honey!" as its crowning achievement. While this essay previews some of Fiedler's concerns about the immaturity of American literature, in "Adolescence and Maturity in the American Novel" he also proclaims that the American writer is an adolescent who "seeks a way toward maturity" (209). Trapped in a state of boyish innocence, these writers strive to attain the maturity that Fiedler associates with Europe. Fiedler's description of the 1950s literary scene revives the Old World/New World divide, positioning those writers in the New World as innocents, and subscribes to a model of growing up that was central to the beyond innocence debate. This model, which Kathryn Bond Stockton critiques in *The Queer Child, or Growing Sideways in the Twentieth Century* (2009), views growth as "[a] vertical movement upward (hence, 'growing up') toward full stature, marriage, work, reproduction, and the *loss of childishness*" (4; emphasis mine). Lee Edelman has similarly argued how children are inextricably linked to the future and attempts to build a queer space that does not depend on "the Child as the emblem of futurity's unquestioned value" (4). These contemporary works of queer theory reveal how, despite some claims that Fiedler was more willing to consider markers of identity excluded by the myth and symbol school (Lavezzo and Stecopoulos 868), that he was equally committed to the narrative of growth that predominated among this generation of scholars.

Even for the more critical beyond innocence participants, the adolescent remained a valuable figure, as he/she enabled them to frame the cultural tensions of the 1950s in terms of a coming-of-age story. Both Fiedler and May, despite their criticisms of innocence, are good examples of this use of the figure. In rejecting innocence, Fiedler and May reached toward what they considered the sophisticated emotional state of maturity or the experience characteristic of adulthood (May 393). One cannot help but think of the

most iconic teenager of American young adult fiction, Holden Caulfield, who embraces these very emotions. Adolescent angst and the
brooding cynical attitude of teen icons like Caulfield embody the
values that advocates of an America beyond innocence embraced.
Pamela Hunt Steinle, an American studies scholar, notes that the
cultural power of adolescent figures like Caulfield stemmed from
their ability to inspire the reader's confidence in their ability to
mature; it is the promise of physical and emotional growth and the
maturity that goes along with it that is imperative (155). The adolescent's power derives from this very promise to transform into a
fully fledged adult. Poised between innocence and experience, the
adolescent exhibits attributes associated with both of these states
and therefore has all the potential, for either success or failure,
that literary critics associated with Cold War America in terms of
both its cultural and political power.

A Childhood Studies Approach to
Myth and Symbol Criticism

The rise of the figure of the adolescent in cultural debates about
American literature marks a critical turning point in American
intellectual thought. In packing away what they viewed as "childish things" (Clark 59), proponents of the beyond innocence debate expressed their disillusion with the present historical moment. This was not just a reaction to increasing birth rates or the
mass production of literature; it was also a response to a political shift in the academy following World War II. Literary critic
Thomas Schaub has described this concern among the 1950s generation as the "liberal narrative," which helped those in the academy grapple with the past events of the previous decade (vii). It
was a move, more importantly, from the radicalism of the 1930s to
the hardened reality of the postwar generation (Schaub viii). Michael Denning, an American cultural historian, indicates in *The
Cultural Front* (1996) that despite the influence of Popular Front
politics through founding figures of American intellectual thought,
"this critical American Studies of the post-war years was scarred
by the intellectual repression of the Cold War, and in many ways
it represented a retreat from the cultural history that had been
pioneered by Popular Front scholars" (446). Godfrey Hodgson, a

British journalist and historian who focuses on twentieth-century American culture, has added that the "liberal consensus" which emerged represented "a grand bargain" between the liberal and conservative values as expressed in domestic and foreign policy (92). The adolescent became key to representing this move toward realism, even if this meant a rejection of the behaviors associated with this stage of life. This figure developed a mythical quality in such notable works as R. W. B. Lewis's *The American Adam* (1955), Henry Nash Smith's *Virgin Land* (1950), Perry Miller's *Errand into the Wilderness* (1956), and Leo Marx's *The Machine in the Garden* (1964) and, in many ways, reflected the psychological dimension of the turn to the liberal narrative, enabling these writers to express their fears about the state of the nation and its politics.

In the major works of the myth and symbol school, the tension that Schaub identifies in the liberal narrative emerges as a pattern where these scholars first celebrate nineteenth-century childhood and the innocence that it represents, only to turn away from this childhood toward the experience of adolescence and (eventually) adulthood. Lewis, Smith, Miller, and Marx, most strongly remembered for their contributions to the development of American studies within the academy in the 1950s, promoted a consensus view of U.S. national identity that predominated in scholarship from this period. Joined by other academics who shared a similar outlook, including Louis Hartz, with whom I began this chapter, the myth and symbol scholars contributed to the celebratory narrative of the West as depicted in Frederick Jackson Turner's "frontier thesis." Turner, who defined the development of the nation in relation to the frontier, had, in 1893, declared that with the end of westward expansion a defining moment in American history had ended as well (1). Patricia Nelson Limerick, best known for her 1987 historical study of the American frontier, attests how the view of the West as an exceptional landscape divorced from the corruption of the Old World made the colonial exploits of the young empire appear innocent: "Innocence of intention placed the course of events [of westward expansion] in a bright and positive light; only over time would the shadows compete for our attention" (36). The scholarship of the myth and symbol school, in part informed by this previous view of the legacy of the frontier, was also influenced by the new American exceptionalism of the 1950s. This ideological support for the United States' rising power in the world was associated with "material prosperity and military power" and was divorced from the exceptionalism of the previous century, which emphasized the ideals "of equality, of opportunity, and of political participation" (Hodgson 92). Fearing the threat of the totalitarian regime of the Soviet Union and haunted by memories of World War II, members of the myth and symbol school advocated for a move beyond innocence.

R. W. B. Lewis, one of the most active members of the myth and symbol school in the beyond innocence debate, embraced childhood innocence most adamantly before forcefully rejecting it. Lewis's interest in the clash between the Old and the New World, first discovered during his military service in World War II, led him to a study of the American Adam myth in nineteenth-century American literature.[2] In his preface to *The American Adam*, Lewis describes his eponymous hero as "a figure of heroic innocence and vast potentialities, poised at the start of a new history" (1). Depicting some of the most famous literary writers of the century as American Adams in their own right, Lewis identifies how the nineteenth-century fascination with innocence led to the cult of the child. Providing the example of Henry David Thoreau, he professes how the author of *Walden; or, Life in the Woods* (1854) urged his fellow Americans to "start life all over again" in the New World, and that "it was in this way that the experience could also appear as a return to childhood, to the scenes and the wonder of that time" (26). Lewis couples this example with another famous literary name, Walt Whitman, noting how innocence was so integral to the nineteenth-century experience that Whitman literally becomes the child that Thoreau celebrated (50). No longer encumbered by the constraints of adult perception, Whitman "begins after [the] recovery" that Thoreau so forcefully insisted upon.[3]

While Whitman embodied the child that was central to some of his key poetic works, such as *Leaves of Grass* (1855), Lewis argues that twentieth-century Americans were barred from this experience of a return to childhood. His presentation of the return to childhood in *The American Adam* is more than an exercise in literary analysis; it is an urgent call to his readers. Lewis wants Americans to return to these prior moments in literary history in order to better grasp "the dangers of innocence," a point he further supports in the conclusion to his study, where he attempts to convince readers that not only is innocence no longer useful but that experience is the preferable option anyway. He provides examples of modern literary Adamic figures, including Ralph Ellison's "invisible man," J. D. Salinger's Holden Caulfield, and Saul Bellow's Augie March. These characters depict the continued fascination with innocence and its inherent dangers, and they are thrust into a perilous world time and again "for [their] own good and for ours" (198). In this respect, they mirror the nineteenth-century figures Lewis identifies through his analysis of canonical literary texts from this period, the most notable of which contain the trope of the "fallen Adam," defined by the hero's loss of innocence as he is forced to endure the harsh realities of experience.

In his examples of the modern Adamic figure, Lewis begins to touch on the very reason for the inaccessibility of innocence for twentieth-century Americans. While the heroes of the nineteenth century were more often than not white, middle class, Protestant, and male, the new heroes he identifies are a decidedly more diverse cast. Ralph Ellison's *Invisible Man* (1952), in particular, hints at the radical potential of the adolescent. When the eponymous protagonist worries about his perception among members of the Brotherhood, an organization working for the rights of the working class and with a predominantly white leadership, his companion points to a poster created by Ellison's protagonist that features a group of children of mixed races and is titled "After the Struggle: The Rainbow of America's Future" (310). The poster also includes marginalized or "dispossessed" groups in the United States, the very people who are absent in the landmark texts of the American Renaissance that feature in Lewis's study of the American Adam. When first entering the Brotherhood, Ellison's unnamed narrator, a black southern man living in Harlem in the 1940s, denounces the powerful authority figures (predominantly wealthy white men) in the organization for stripping the people of their humanity and silencing their voices (277). His speech, described as "dangerous" by members of the Brotherhood, ignites an overwhelming energy among the black community and helps launch positive changes in Harlem (282). Lewis and his colleagues fail to address the radical potential of such youthful figures as Ellison's invisible man, but the promise represented by these literary depictions of adolescence begins to emerge in their work as they grapple with the tension between innocence and experience in American culture.

The figure of the adolescent plays a pivotal role in another famous work of myth and symbol scholarship, Henry Nash Smith's *Virgin Land* (1950). A conscientious objector, Smith did not participate in World War II, and as such his views of the country were not influenced by contact with the Old World like his peers. Instead, he was deeply committed to defining the regional identity of the West, reflected in his intense period of production as coeditor for *Southwest Review*.[4] In his depiction of one of the most notable fictional heroes of the West, James Fenimore Cooper's Leatherstocking, Smith suggests that early pioneers were "presented as children of the ancient mother nature" (73). In his account of Leatherstocking's literary descendants, future heroes become younger and younger and have a striking similarity to Lewis's American Adam. More than once, Smith describes these heroes as "young and handsome." Later heroes such as Buffalo Bill and Kit Carson lacked the spiritual connection with nature of the first wave of frontiersmen but made up for it with their inner sense of moral character and reckless disregard for the rules. These men were the good bad boys popularized in boys' books such as Thomas Bailey Aldrich's *Story of a Bad Boy* (1869) and Mark Twain's *The Adventures of Huckleberry Finn* (1885). Remaining boys at heart, western heroes were "lighthearted, fearless, generous, and 'noble in their treatment of a friend or a fallen foe'" (111).[5] They used their intellect and strength to battle the natural surroundings and Native inhabitants—a prairie fire might be taken just as seriously as an Indian in the dime novels featuring these denizens of the Wild West.

Smith's configuration of the western hero as a "good bad boy" forms another link to the celebratory narrative of innocence popular in the nineteenth century; yet Smith is quick to distance himself from this cult of childhood, a move I earlier indicated was a key feature of the academy in the twentieth century. Smith's chronology of the "Sons of Leatherstocking" demonstrates that the Western hero achieved masculine virility at the price of maturity. Ironically, this hero had to get younger in order to gain the sexual potency lacking in the original Leatherstocking. As Smith explains, Cooper's backwoodsman, while a "noble child of the forest" (64), was also well past his prime, and his age "hindered his transformation into a hero of romance as seriously as did his low social status" (68). Through the redemptive nature of the "virgin land," future variants of the Leatherstocking figure were revitalized; their newfound youth helped resolve the contradictions in the original hero by raising their position in society so that they were not inferior to other characters within the fictional narrative—a shift that fit more neatly with the conventions of the sentimental novel that Cooper draws on in his *Leatherstocking* series (Smith 64). In these young heroes, Smith finds an American that is adaptable, competent, lighthearted, and noble. Spending time in the dirt and the gravel, the muck and the mud, the "sons of Leatherstocking" search for a new self amidst the American wilderness. Yet this promise of renewal, Smith concedes, is responsible for "ma[king] it difficult for Americans to think of themselves as members of a world community because it has affirmed that the destiny of this country leads her away from Europe toward the agricultural interior of the continent" (260).

In his closing remark, Smith makes a similar rhetorical move to that of Lewis, identifying and rejecting the very innocence that he appears to celebrate in *Virgin Land*. In admitting that the myth of the virgin land is a promise that leads Americans inward and away from the maturity associated with adulthood, Smith finds promise in the movement beyond U.S. borders, seeing contact with Europe not as a turn away from the renewal of the New World but instead as an entrance into a much wider space than the western landscape could accommodate. In expanding beyond the frontier, Smith hoped that Americans would be thrust into the realities of a world connected by the shared experiences of World War II. The seeds of this expanded worldview can be found in popular representations of the western hero, where this hero begins to radically alter in response to developments in popular thought. In his discussion of dime novels featuring heroines in disguise, Smith demonstrates the importance of youth to the transformation of gender politics as these young heroines are freed from their role as "genteel women." These gender-bending women are described as being as rough and tough as male heroes in the Leatherstocking tradition and differ "solely by the physical fact of her sex" (119). Smith's suggestion that the western hero could in fact be female

disrupts the traditional depiction of this figure. His notion of progress fits with the promise of the adolescent, which beginning in the
late nineteenth century was already starting to develop its radical
origins, standing in for marginalized groups that included women,
African Americans, and those who identified as queer (Lesko 46).
The emergence of the concept of the adolescent at this time, suggests educational theorist Nancy Lesko, aided in the renegotiation
of power in a patriarchal society: "adolescence—defined as 'becoming'—became an embodiment of and worry about 'progress' and a
site to study, specify, diagnose, and enact the modern ideas for personal and social progress" (21). To be sure, there were those who
subscribed to the belief that children recapitulated the stages of
evolution and that the adolescent was simply at a more advanced,
yet still inferior, stage of development from adults in white, Western (and male) civilization. However, increasingly the adolescent
tested the boundaries of previous divisions between race, class, nationality, and other markers of identity used to categorize and seg-
regate the American people.

If Smith's study of the agricultural interior of the United States
stretched these boundaries in terms of gender, then Perry Miller,
who was actively involved in 1950s politics at home and abroad,
would turn his attention to events occurring outside the United
States' borders and to the relationship between domestic and foreign politics.[6] In ruminating on the U.S. neocolonial presence in Africa and the nation's display of nuclear power in Asia, Miller would
begin to critique the Puritan mission, or errand into the wilderness, drawing on the radical potential of the adolescent in order
to do so. Young people, youth studies scholars Sunaina Maira and
Elisabeth Soep contend in their 2005 study on global trends in adolescent culture, "participate in social relations . . . and formulate
modes of citizenship out of the various ideologies they create, sustain, and *disrupt*" (xvi; emphasis mine). In Miller's introduction to
Errand into the Wilderness, the specter of Africa is present, but it
is the specter of adolescence that most consistently informs Miller's thinking about U.S. imperial power (Kaplan, "Left Alone" 6).
Miller does not consider the adolescent as an isolated figure, as
Lewis and Smith do, but instead positions this figure in a network
of relations that undergird the construction of national identity.
Using the filial relationship between fathers and sons, a classic

metaphor for the colonial relationship, Miller raises his concerns about wielding national power on the global stage.

Miller's preoccupation with the fuel drums in Africa shifts domestic concerns about foreignness and difference abroad, and it also enables him to question U.S. foreign policy in the Cold War by disrupting the Puritan values embedded in the United States' national rhetoric of progress and expansion. Through his focus on the younger generations upon whom these values were bestowed, Miller underscores the fact that the children of the New England Founding Fathers "weren't the men their fathers had been" (2–3). The metaphor of a father/son relationship already begins to appear in these lines and launches Miller's political critique. "[D]isgusted with liberal impotence in the face of fascism," writes American literary and social critic Andrew Delbanco, "he [Miller] developed as a consequence his animating respect for the neo-Calvinism of Reinhold Niebuhr" (345–346). Miller's thesis was rarely interpreted in relation to this agenda (Bozeman 231), despite the popularity of *Errand* in studies of early American literature, with his politics often disappearing into the background. Subsequent scholars of American literature and history, including Randall Fuller, Nicholas Guyatt, and Murray Murphey, pick up on the reading of Miller as a man on his own errand. Fuller describes Miller as a person of action, whose "Cold War anxiety coalesced with his own sense that the study of America had been co-opted by an imperial project that in turn led to intellectual constriction and repression" (104).

Miller's insistence that even an intellectual must put away books in times of war and head out to the battlefield caused him to join the military during World War II, an experience that would shape his reading of the Puritan fathers. Miller saw the fathers as men of action like himself, who fought on metaphorical battlefields for their beliefs and values. As Miller writes in his essay on the Puritan errand, the fathers were "executing a flank attack on the corruptions of Christendom" (11). Miller's Cold War reading of the Puritan errand has led new generations of early American scholars to conclude that "For a famous historian like Miller, the Cold War offered many opportunities for public prominence and even for academic success, but a much narrower space for pure academic 'selfishness,' or for divergent political expression" (Guyatt 127). The pressure to conform did not completely control Miller, who does at moments acknowledge the horror of the destructiveness of U.S. global expansion through the central image of the nuclear bomb. Yet his reverence for the Puritan fathers also fit with the dominant national feeling during the Cold War. By constructing his narrative in relation to father/son bonds, Miller highlights his ambivalence about the future of the nation by casting doubt on the actions of future generations. His disgust at U.S. acts of political aggression is thereby directed at those who have distorted the Founding Fathers' errand into something monstrous and unrecognizable, not with the original errand itself.

These readings of Miller's thesis of the Puritan errand, while important, do not fully unpack the radical potential that the adolescent represents within his text. If we turn instead to the later sections of *Errand into the Wilderness*, there are far more intriguing, though perhaps less read, engagements with the father/son metaphor that connect Miller to the cultural climate of the beyond innocence debate. In his chapter on "Nature and the National Ego," Miller begins to utilize the dialectic of innocence and experience in his commentary on national power by claiming that Nature versus civilization is *"the* American theme.... You can find it in the politics of Andrew Jackson, in the observations of foreign travelers, in the legend of Abraham Lincoln, in Stephen Douglas no less than in Francis Parkman" (205; emphasis in original). For Miller, recognition of the ubiquity of the Nature versus civilization theme is imperative, as it allows readers to see the connection between eighteenth- and nineteenth-century America. The Puritan errand, Miller concludes, was still very much alive in the nineteenth century (205). By tracing the evolution of the Puritan errand, Miller returns to the central theme of father-and-son bonds and positions such nineteenth-century writers as Ralph Waldo Emerson as inheritors of the Puritan errand, distant sons who needed to find ways to complete the founders' original religious mission.

In developing his thesis in the later chapter, Miller cites the common dichotomies associated with the division between Nature and civilization, the most important of which is "the innocent and the debauched" (208). He continues to refer to the saving grace of the wilderness, the setting in which Puritans believed they could best complete their religious mission because it was free from the corruption of the Old World. In this sense, the wilderness provided a layer of protection from the evils associated with civilization. As Miller develops his argument, he invokes phrases commonly associated with childhood innocence, including "tender" (208), "young republic" (211), "simplicity" (212), "young revel" (212), "vigorous youth" (213), and "young empire" (213). The repetition of the term "young," coupled with Miller's description of America as an infant nation making its first "faltering steps" (211), secures the association of the United States with childhood. It is through the American wilderness, Miller concludes, that "America can progress indefinitely into an expanding future" and continue to gain access to the innocence associated with youth.

Miller will ultimately cast doubt on this optimistic prediction of national progress through his concluding remarks, in which he asks: "Can an errand, even an errand into the wilderness, be run indefinitely? To this question, it seems, Americans must constantly revert" (217). Not only must this question continually be asked, Miller warns, but he fears that the threat of the end of the world, particularly in the form of atomic warfare, leaves America with few choices: "What will America do—what *can* America do—with an implacable prophecy that there is a point in time beyond which the very concept of a future becomes meaningless?" (217; emphasis in original). The anxiety that is apparent in these lines fits with the somber topic of his concluding chapter: the millennial belief in Armageddon. To recognize the possibility of an end, Miller notes, means to admit that the errand must also come to a conclusion. This knowledge in turn strains the future generation's sense of duty, making it ever more possible that the Puritan errand, in these moments of crisis, will be abandoned altogether. That the scientific possibility of ultimate annihilation takes away the divine nature of judgment, as well as its promised renewal following destruction, suggests the limits of innocence, which is always already tinged with experience. Here Miller sees the nation not so much as a toddling infant but instead as an adolescent on the verge of adulthood.

Miller's anxiety about the departure from the United States' ideological roots appears like a traumatic rupture in the final pages of *Errand*, a psychological wound that Miller's student and future leader of American studies, Leo Marx, will further explore. Marx's employment of the adolescent in *The Machine in the Garden* fo-

cuses on national progress through technological advancements
and the dislocating effects of the machine. In particular, he uses the
adolescent to consider the traumatic break with childhood that the
entrance into a nuclear age represented. Drawing extensively on
Freudian theory, Marx turned the war against communism into a
"war against nature," one where the fallout from nuclear bombs not
only destroyed lives but also the nature that helped sustain these
lives (he refers to Strontium-90, which made a prominent impact
on Americans much later in 1986 following the Chernobyl disas-
ter). Through his leading image of the machine, Marx argues that
"the sudden appearance of the machine has the effect of irrevocable separation like the cutting of an umbilical cord" (346). Marx illustrates this point in his opening chapter with a detailed reading
of Nathaniel Hawthorne's description of the scenery in the pastoral retreat of Sleepy Hollow, arguing that Hawthorne's notes serve
as a "cocoon of freedom from anxiety, guilt, and conflict—a shrine of
the pleasure principle" (28). In using the concepts from psychoan-
alyst Sigmund Freud's *Beyond the Pleasure Principle* (1922), Marx
aimed to illustrate how the repeated scenes of violent trauma that
occur in American literature, frequently triggered by machines,
represented a "sudden, shocking intruder upon a fantasy of idyllic
satisfaction" (29). While the initial setting of the idyllic scene might
change (an island, a forest, or a raft), Marx saw within this drama
a connection to the anxiety following World War II.

This anxiety, which American literary critic and theorist Donald Pease interprets as a fear of foreign encroachment (*New American Exceptionalism* 163), might be better viewed in relation to
nineteenth- and early twentieth-century constructions of adolescence. In nineteenth-century children's literature, the machine
and budding adolescents were often merged. Frances Hodgson
Burnett, best known for her children's classic *The Secret Garden*
(1911), helped forge this connection in her collection of short stories *Giovanni and the Other* (1892). In "What Use Is the Poet?"
Burnett addresses her young son as the "Electric boy" when he
questions the use of the poet in comparison to the technological
inventions of the nineteenth century (132). L. Frank Baum would
make similar connections between youth and technology in his beloved fantasy, *The Wonderful Wizard of Oz* (1900), where electricity
is alluded to in the magic that pervades the Land of Oz (Wagner

30), including in the silver slippers that help whisk Dorothy back to Kansas.[7] In his chapter "Ethnic Psychology and Pedagogy, or Adolescent Races and Their Treatment" from the second volume of *Adolescence* (1904), G. Stanley Hall usefully comments on the relationship between technological advancements and social progress, which he describes as a modernizing force that has led to global uniformity, a progressive shift with "little charm for the biologist" (717). His curious commentary demonstrates how, for Hall, evolution, in which adolescence represented an important step, "promised that the future would produce not just technological but *psychological* progress" (Arnett 191; emphasis mine).

The colonial mind-set that informs Hall's interpretation of adolescence is not present in *The Machine in the Garden*, but Marx does explore the connection between technology, youth, and national progress. Through the famous American literary hero Huckleberry Finn, Marx demonstrates how the machine violently thrusts those who encounter it into maturity. The destruction of Huck's raft, which represents a safe haven from the corruption of society, becomes a central image for Marx. In his words, "The sudden incursion of the new power [the steamboat] has the effect of a shattering childhood trauma" (319). In Marx's interpretation, Huck's journey toward maturity follows closely Freud's outline of the symptoms that emerge after a traumatic event like a train accident.[8] Huck attempts to recover the damaged raft in a move that may be interpreted in relation to Freud's repetition compulsion, where a victim of trauma repeats the traumatic event in order to work through it. However, though briefly recovered, Huck must eventually let go of this lost object and leave behind the childhood that it represents. This movement away from childhood ultimately turns out to be a fortunate transition. Though Marx does not pick up on this specific connection in his reading, Huck's famous line "All right, then, I'll *go* to hell" does lead to Marx's later discussion of the relationship between youth, power, and rebellion in his epilogue (162; emphasis in original). Turning to the 1964 Berkeley Student Rebellion, in which the movement's leader, Mario Savio, chanted, "You've got to put your bodies upon the [machine] and make it stop" (qtd. in Marx 384), Marx observes how youth protests helped enact widespread social change during the Civil Rights Movement. He expands this point to a global scale through his description of protests about U.S. intervention in Asia, underscoring the adolescent's capability to view the political implications of their actions on an international level.

The potential for social reform that the adolescent represents in Marx's closing remarks may have its limits, however. As Roberta Seelinger Trites argues in her seminal text on young adult literature, the energy of youth rebellion, as it is portrayed in literature, is channeled to help maintain the norms of society rather than upset them. In cases where rebellion does manage to enact social change, the youth leading the movement are viewed as a threat that must be controlled (36). This is certainly true in Twain's novel, where Huck disappears into the western interior in order to escape the civilizing forces represented by his foster parent, Widow Douglass. Despite his friendship with Jim on the raft, Huck does not ultimately disrupt the racial hierarchy in nineteenth-century American culture. His collusion with Tom Sawyer to free Jim is undermined by the fact that Jim has already been set free, a piece of information that Tom fails to impart to his companion. Marx concludes that the smashing of the raft is "extravagant because it is, in a word, unattainable," a point that may well allude to the interracial friendship between Huck and Jim (338). Citing literary critic Lionel Trilling, Marx proposes that the tension represented by the raft and the corrupt banks of the Mississippi River "is nothing if not a dialectic" (qtd. in Marx 342). This quote from Trilling identifies authors as representatives of the dialectic of innocence and experience that was the hallmark of members of the beyond innocence debate, and demonstrates the confidence that American literary critics had in the ability of the national literature to illuminate the cultural tensions of their generation.

The fact that Marx inserts Trilling's observation about nineteenth-century American literature at the close of his reading of *Huckleberry Finn* demonstrates the power he believed novels held, while also suggesting his own part in the making (and remaking) of American national identity. While Marx viewed racial harmony as "unattainable" in the nineteenth century, he found hope in the youth protests of the 1960s. As I suggested in the introduction to this chapter, the project to define the meaning of Amer-

ica was one that would come in stages and would take many generations to successfully complete (Hartz 476). This was not a project
solely relegated to Marx and his fellow myth and symbol colleagues, but rather one that would involve authors who were similarly inspired by the radical potential of the adolescent. Novelists
of the 1950s and of future generations would aid in the process of
finding the "new voices" that were absent in the myth and symbol
works of criticism and, through their creative fiction, would participate in the "aggressive unmasking of the myths of [the myth and
symbol school]" (Fisher xiv). Welcoming a new cast of characters
into the national narrative about innocence and renewal through
this process, these authors would dramatically reshape the answer
to the question, *What does it mean to be an American?*

CHAPTER 2
American Adam (and Eve)

REWRITING HISTORY IN AN "AGE OF HOPELESSNESS"

It has been said that America is always coming of age; but it might be more fairly maintained that America has come of age in sections, here and there—whenever its implicit myth of the American Adam has been a defining part of the writer's consciousness.　　　　　　**—R. W. B. Lewis, *The American Adam***

Buried deep within the pages of his paean to American literature, R. W. B. Lewis departs from his usually male-centered
discussion of the American Adam to briefly acknowledge
the role women play in the literary imaginary. Comparing the "outsider" in European and American fiction, Lewis includes the heroines from two of Henry James's novels, Daisy Miller and Isabel Ar-
cher, alongside the likes of Billy Budd and Huck Finn (128). Both
women are constructed as innocents abroad who are corrupted by
their travels in Europe, particularly through the men they encounter. In *Daisy Miller* (1879), the eponymous heroine is said to look
"extremely innocent" (10), and a similar remark is made in *The
Portrait of a Lady* (1881) when Ralph claims that Isabel is merely
a "young, happy, innocent person," regardless of her protestations
to the contrary (53). Isabel's case is particularly revealing, for in
this same passage the male character denies the young woman's experience, claiming that she has not "suffered" and therefore lacks the knowledge that he possesses (53). While it appears
that Ralph is merely teasing his cousin, since the two have only
just met, their exchange underscores an attitude that has shaped
scholars' understanding of the American national character. Isabel, despite being intelligent, independent, and adventurous, fails

to hold the same charm as literary heroes positioned as American Adams and is not given the same allowances as her male counterparts, whose wide-eyed innocence is viewed as a positive attribute rather than a flaw.

The innocence attributed to Isabel, and her exclusion from the world of experience her male cousin inhabits, reveal some of the important distinctions between early articulations of the American Adam and Eve. During the colonial period, women were often treated as equals to their husbands. Though they may not have held the same legal rights, they were "accepted as sexual, self-sufficient, and active" (McAlexander 252). By the nineteenth century, a new view of women as pious and innocent had set in, which was shaped in part by imported literature, including conduct books for young girls, that positioned women as more suited to the hearth than the homestead (McAlexander 253). The consequence of this view of women as helpless, pious, and domestic was an American Eve who likewise was cast out of the frontier that was believed to hold the power to rejuvenate those who set out to live among the wilderness. American literary critic Leland Person Jr., in his feminist rereading of the American Adam myth, argues that this myth has several weaknesses related to its exclusion of women, including overlooking the feats that female heroines complete in frontier literature and foreclosing the possibility of a myth centered on female experience (670). Person goes on to consider the work of famous nineteenth-century women writers, including Catharine Maria Sedgwick and Lydia Maria Child, who he suggests provide an alternative to the male fantasy of the American Adam, where "an Eden from which Adam rather than Eve has been excluded" is formed.

James's two novels, in the context of this criticism, can be seen as contributing to the traditional view of the American Eve as an outcast from the Garden of Eden, in this case represented by the American wilderness, an interpretation that aligns this frontier myth with the Judeo-Christian creation myth where Eve is viewed as subordinate to Adam. By the mid-twentieth century, when Lewis published his study of the American Adam, this traditional view of the American Eve had radically evolved in response to new cultural concerns stemming from the Cold War conflict. As Lewis himself claimed, the American Adam underwent an aston-

ishing revival in the twentieth century, adapting from the previous
circumstances of the writers of the American Renaissance (1850–
55), who even in their pessimism celebrated the innocence of this
mythical hero, to an age of hopelessness where such innocence no
longer had the same relevance (195). Among this new cast of characters rose a new American Eve who could rival even the most
beloved of Adamic heroes. Both independent and intelligent, this
female figure was deeply familiar with pain and suffering, and
therefore the experience that is denied to James's American Eve.
Through their revisionist efforts, novelists who rejected an all-
male view of the American experience effectively transformed the
pious and innocent American Eve of previous eras into a young
woman who held many of the qualities that had formerly enabled
the American Adam to surpass her, with the exception of this hero's break from his past. In this respect, the Cold War interpretation of the American Eve differs fundamentally from the American
Adam due to this figure's inability to separate herself from history.

The lack of attention to this more resilient American Eve can
be attributed to the overwhelming focus on male interpretations
of the frontier myth among myth and symbol scholars, what feminist literary critic Nina Baym has described as the "melodrama
of beset manhood" (130). Critical reception of the American Eve
within the academy did not really take hold until over twenty-five
years after the publication of Lewis's original interpretation of the
American Adam myth. In her 1975 landmark study, *The Lay of
the Land*, Annette Kolodny suggests that it was not uncommon
for those in the academy to support and reinforce gender binaries
that position men as active and women as passive through their
scholarship, especially in discussions of the frontier myth, where
the western landscape was consistently feminized while men appeared as explorers who came to the New World to conquer the
land. As Kolodny notes in her introduction, "gendering the land as
feminine was nothing new," even as early as the sixteenth century
(8). While I will address the relationship between women and the
land at further length in my next chapter on the virgin land myth,
it is worth noting the relationship here since the American Eve
also has a unique bond with nature. In her interrogation of this relationship, Kolodny brings to light the importance of this gender
binary for early male settlers (and later for male myth and sym-

bol scholars). The American Eden, she writes, "is a realm of nurture, abundance, and unalienated labor within which all men are
truly brothers" (4). The utopian vision of brotherhood in the American Eden, as I earlier suggested in my reading of Ralph Ellison's
Invisible Man, erased difference at the expense of those who most
needed to partake in the freeing power of this landscape. Indeed,
Ellison's novel, celebrated by Lewis for its attention to some of the
most powerful social issues of the mid-twentieth century, underscores how unity can be destructive and how women are left outside of the social experiment of brotherhood, their concerns trivialized and bodies used merely as objects for sexual pleasure.

Lewis's brief nod toward women's involvement in the frontier
can be understood in relation to this history of social subjugation
and disempowerment, which, in the context of the American Adam
myth, positioned women as a mere frame for male exploits. By
turning to the figure of the adolescent girl, contemporary writers
accessed the potential of this figure for radical social reform, unsettling the gender binaries reinforced by the myth of the American Adam. As cultural historians Miriam Forman-Brunell and
Leslie Paris explain in *The Girls' History and Culture Reader:
The Twentieth Century* (2011), the adolescent girl is a powerful
reflection of national social issues: "Twentieth-century girlhood
took many forms, reflecting the nation's diversity, its divisions, social changes, and the particular circumstances of individual girls'
lives" (1). In the case of the American Eve, the female heroines, in
part due to their youth, are able to counter the social expectations
surrounding their eventual growth into womanhood. By acknowledging their place within a history of conquest, they begin to map
a new relation to the land and to their heritage, which reinter-
prets the quintessential American value of self-reliance and even
rewrites this history altogether by bucking cultural tradition; the
young American Eve does not passively accept male expectations
of her place in the world, and if she nurtures anything, it is only
rebellion.

In what follows, I trace the development of a new American Eve
that responded directly to political and cultural conflicts stemming
from the Cold War. In Scott O'Dell's *Island of the Blue Dolphins*
(1960), a classic of children's literature, the shift toward the acknowledgment of women's experiences can be viewed as the lead

character, Karana, survives a series of catastrophic events that leave her isolated on the island of her birth. Previously a part of a patriarchal society, O'Dell's American Eve builds usefully on the qualities of the frontier myth of the American Adam by considering the power that history and memory hold over female experience. The ability to depart from views of women as either temptresses who are responsible for the destruction of man (the banishment of Adam from the Garden of Eden being a classic and apt example) or else as chaste and innocent virgins continued to undergo revision in subsequent work in later decades. In Linda Hogan's *Solar Storms* (1995), men are not completely absent yet are at the very least peripheral to the action and experience of an adolescent girl seeking her family. Drawing strength from her female elders, Angel, whose name is an ironic twist on the image of the "angel in the house," reclaims the history forgotten through the myth of the American Adam by giving voice to the indigenous women who were abused and abandoned at the hands of frontiersmen—the fur trappers, tradesmen, and other entrepreneurs of the wilderness. In contrast to Hogan's heroine, Karen Russell's post-9/11 novel, *Swamplandia!* (2011), expresses tension between a desire to reveal the colonial history of the United States, specifically the entanglement between white settlers and indigenous tribes and freed and escaped black slaves, and nostalgia for the innocence provided by the American Adam's escape from his ancestral history. Through the emergence of these more youthful American Eve figures, a critical turn in the literary discourse surrounding national identity arises, as the silenced history of western expansion comes to the fore, bringing forth not only the voices of women that the American Eve represents but also others marginalized due to their race and ethnicity.

Dreaming Up Eve:
Building a Female-Centered World

In anticipation of the women's rights movement sparked by Betty Friedan's *The Feminine Mystique* (1963), a writer whom most would consider to be nearing the age of retirement began to draft the outline for what would become one of the most beloved works of historical children's fiction, *Island of the Blue Dolphins* (1960). Through this novel, author Scott O'Dell set the stage for more rigorous revisions of the American Adam myth that had for so long silenced women and ethnic minorities, overlooking their essential role in the history of the American frontier. Reflecting on what remains his best-selling work, O'Dell remarked that his choice to craft a strong female character stemmed from his own beliefs about the need for equal rights for women. In an interview with the *New York Times*, the author champions the women's movement, claiming that "I have great admiration for women. They are the repositories of the instinct of preservation. I think they are far superior to men" (qtd. in Wesselhoft). As O'Dell rightly identifies, his writing legacy is often characterized as one bent on inclusion, both of women and ethnic minorities. Yet as Sara Schwebel points out in *Child-Sized History* (2011), this legacy is also troubled by the fact that it draws on other deeply ingrained myths of the frontier, even as it seeks to unravel others (48). Schwebel, who has extensively researched the history behind *Island of the Blue Dolphins*, observes: "In *Island* and other O'Dell books, Native characters function as mediums for exploring moral themes and social practices; having served that purpose, they are then dismissed, folded into Anglo-American myths of tragic disappearance" (49).[1] While it is true that O'Dell would draw heavily on such myths as the "Vanishing American," he would also recast the male explorer as an adolescent girl in a dramatic revision of the American Adam myth. In doing so, he made a modest step forward in literature about the frontier by challenging the dominant belief that the American West was a space intended solely for virile men.

O'Dell's background helped prime him for his ultimate intervention in the American Adam myth. Born in 1898, O'Dell witnessed firsthand the transformation of his California hometown from a small frontier post to a modern industrial city. Such rapid change left a mark on the young O'Dell so that when he finally began writing historical fiction for children at the ripe old age of sixty, he had a thing or two about which to lecture his young audience. O'Dell's fiction is notorious for glamorizing the past, especially the values associated with American pioneers, such as resourcefulness, perseverance, and virtuousness. His personal feelings of alienation—he referred to Californians as "just a bunch of uprooted people" (D. Russell 173)—fueled his fiction and his choice of marginalized

characters. Because of California's geographical location and colonial history, the American Indian girl is one figure that O'Dell returned to at multiple points in his career. *Island of the Blue Dolphins*, which centers on the traumatic experiences of Karana, a
young girl who is a member of the Nicoleño tribe, is no exception.
Describing Karana's struggles to survive on her own after her people are massacred, *Island*'s themes of alienation and loss link to
O'Dell's personal concerns about Californian identity and draw on
the tropes of the American Adam, particularly the "fall from innocence." His inclusion of a courageous and self-sufficient heroine
who survives despite the atrocities she witnesses departs from previous constructions of the American Adam in nineteenth-century
American literature by recasting this figure as a young girl. At the
time, a female protagonist challenged reader expectations about
who could play the role of the frontier hero. O'Dell's literary agent,
who feared that a female heroine would squelch the novel's chances
for success, encouraged O'Dell to change his heroine's gender, but
O'Dell would not budge on the issue (Schwebel, *Island* 35). O'Dell's
disregard for his agent's attitude and the overwhelming success of
the novel, which remains a classic of children's literature and a staple within American classrooms, launched his career as a children's
writer and makes his young American Eve an important contribution to the national literary tradition.

In order to construct Karana as an American Eve, O'Dell drew
on multiple sources to piece together the historical record that inspired the story. Based on the real-life experience of a San Nicolas
woman who was referred to as the "Lone Woman" in the public media, the novel follows the adventures of Karana after she is separated from her brother on a ship with the few surviving members
of her tribe. Leaping from the ship as it departs from her home island in order to rescue her little brother who has been left behind,
Karana is abandoned and must survive to feed and clothe the two
of them. She is quickly isolated even further after her brother is
killed by a pack of wild dogs, and in the remaining chapters in the
book her methods for surviving are described in great detail until,
at the end, she finally returns to society as a grown woman. These
narrative details were shaped primarily by popular and scientific
writings from the 1950s, when O'Dell was conducting research for
his future best seller (Schwebel, *Island* 5). Although he would con-

sult many different accounts of the "Lone Woman" of San Nicolas Island, the work of Clement W. Meighan, an archaeologist remembered for his significant contributions to Californian prehistory, would be particularly influential. Meighan, who published an account of his upcoming fieldwork on San Nicolas Island in *Pacific Discovery*, a magazine published by the California Museum of Sciences, "may well have caught O'Dell's eye" in 1954 (Schwebel, *Island* 12). Similar documents from the 1950s tell a story about the young woman and how she came to find herself isolated on the island. A *Los Angeles Times* article, also from 1954, begins with the provocative claim that "Arthur R. Sanger has a skeleton in his closet" (Sell 1). The skeleton caused a sensation after Sanger claimed they were the remains of the child of the Lone Woman, an assertion that was likely untrue given his penchant for falsifying archaeological findings (Koerper 21). Sanger, like Meighan, was an archaeologist, albeit an amateur one, and it is this scientific approach to digging up the past that most likely shaped O'Dell's construction of not only the San Nicolas woman but also the fictional adolescent version of her.

The research O'Dell conducted explains, in part, the traits he associates with his young American Eve, which emerge from the anthropological turn in scientific studies of adolescence. Cultural anthropologist Margaret Mead's influential *Coming of Age in Samoa: A Psychological Study of Primitive Youth for Western Civilization* (1928) departed from previous disciplinary inquiries into this stage of life, namely in child psychology. Mead asserts, "American conditions challenged the psychologist, the educator, the social philosopher, to offer acceptable explanations of the growing children's plight" (2). For Mead, the period of adolescence had up until then been described by psychologists as one defined by emotional strife, where "idealism flowered and rebellion against authority waxed strong, a period during which difficulties and conflicts were absolutely inevitable" (2). She believed that the anthropologist's ability to observe other cultures made it possible to consider the extent to which "social environment" impacts the experience of adolescence (4). "Were these difficulties due to being adolescent or to being adolescent in America?" Mead questioned in the introduction to her classic study of Samoan girls (5). Elsewhere Mead declared that she spent her life studying cultures abroad so that

Americans could "better understand themselves" (qtd. in Strother 8), a turn of phrase that links her theories of adolescence to child psychologist G. Stanley Hall, whose work she felt she was building upon by moving beyond the limits of psychology. Hall, who also viewed adolescence as a period when budding youth embark on a journey of self-discovery, had ushered in an era during which the adolescent was cast as a rebellious figure, an association that Erik Erikson would secure in the public imagination with the publication of *Childhood and Society* in 1950, which depicted this transitional period of development as a moment of conflict sparked by the adolescent's identity crisis.

Mead's contribution to the long-standing nature-versus-nurture debate, which considers the extent to which environment and biology impact youth, and her focus on female adolescence may well have influenced O'Dell, for whom archaeological studies of past cultures played such an influential role. Mead's belief in the power of environment to shape character, in particular, is shared by O'Dell, who is fascinated by the environment's importance to Karana's story. The island of San Nicolas, which first captured his imagination in his youth when working as part of the crew for the 1937 film *Ebb Tide* (Schwebel, *Island* 12), is depicted as a powerful force in the development of his youthful protagonist's character and helps cultivate the desirable traits he attributes to the American Eve. In the opening passage of the novel, O'Dell first introduces Karana through the following description: "I remember the day the Aleut ship came to our island. At first it seemed like a small shell afloat on the sea. Then it grew larger and was a gull with folded wings. At last in the rising sun it became what it really was—a red ship with two red sails" (1). Here O'Dell resists defining his spunky female protagonist by her gender or race and focuses instead on the approaching invader. The details of the "small shell" and "gull with folded wings" begin to locate Karana within a specific place, which is reinforced as the first chapter continues. Karana quickly reveals that she is twelve years old (1), but it isn't until several pages later that she fully describes the details of her origin. She declares that she is a member of a tribe led by Chief Chowig, that the chief is her father, and that she is known by the name of Won-a-pa-lei or the Girl with the Long Black Hair (5). At this point, O'Dell's protagonist also reveals her "secret name," Karana, which immediately establishes a bond between the young protagonist and the reader. By initially withholding information about Karana's origins, O'Dell emphasizes place, the island for which the novel is named, over markers of identity such as gender or race. His privileging of the environment and attention to origins begin to locate Karana in the American Adam tradition, where noble heroes emerge with little, if any, reference to their personal history. O'Dell's focus on these details also puts the author into the position of the ethnographer. Through his careful recording of each and every detail of the island, O'Dell's style resembles that of the anthropologists he admired.

O'Dell's introduction begins to create a world where female experience trumps male experience, making a space for his young Eve in the American Eden. While the world Karana inhabits is far from idyllic, as suggested in the foreboding tone of the opening lines, the tragedy she faces serves to upset traditional gender binaries. Karana describes her daily life before it is destroyed by the arrival of the ship with the blood-red sails, depicting a tribe that is patriarchal: women gather food, watch children, and provide domestic comforts for men. Her initial tasks as a young female member of the tribe involve gathering roots and watching over her younger brother, Ramo, an indication that such training begins at an early age. O'Dell steadily works up to Karana's isolated existence by first having the foreigners, fur traders led by a Russian, kill most of the men in the tribe, including Chief Chowig. This plot development allows O'Dell to introduce readers to a society where women take on duties traditionally bestowed upon men. In a speech immediately following the murder of the tribesmen, Kimki, the new chief, declares, "The women, who were never asked to do more than stay at home, cook food, and make clothing, now must take the place of the men" (25). Karana explains that one repercussion of this decision is a backlash from the few remaining tribesmen. Feeling that the women have usurped their rightful places in the tribe—and, O'Dell hints, jealous of the phenomenal success the women have achieved as hunters—the men complain to the tribe leader and successfully intervene so that the women must return to their original domestic duties (26). Such a reversal displays the tenuous nature of the newfound responsibilities of the female members of the tribe. Through the power struggles of the tribe, O'Dell acknowledges the difficult position of women and the way that cultural beliefs can often stifle those who are fully capable of carrying out other tasks. His presentation of these early scenes demonstrates empathy for the plight of women and a deep desire to identify alternative social relationships where men and women are treated equally.

The very details that have led many to celebrate *Island* as a children's classic are also what have prompted recent children's literary critics to be more skeptical of O'Dell's feminist agenda. Carol Anita Tarr observes in a 1992 essay how O'Dell's writing is built upon a simple formula, which he uses time and time again, and argues that one of the primary features of this formula is the use of stereotypes about indigenous people ("Fool's Gold"). She expands this claim in a later essay where she asserts that *Island* is successful precisely because of its gaps and failure to fully develop Karana as a character. "What is memorable about Karana's story," Tarr continues, "is not what Karana says, but what she *does not* say" ("Unintentional" 63; emphasis in original).[2] These gaps provide many opportunities for young readers to make of Karana what they will. In terms of challenging gender stereotypes, early reactions mirrored that of O'Dell's literary agent, who insisted that the book would sell better if the protagonist were a boy. As O'Dell's second wife, Elizabeth Hall, reflects, the author often received letters from boys who were astonished that Karana was able to survive on an island alone and expressed their disbelief with exclamations such as, "I don't know if a girl could do all that!" (qtd. in Marcovitz 65). Such questioning appears to indicate that young readers were not as moved as O'Dell might have hoped by Karana's gender-bending activities, but it also adds legitimacy to the reading of *Island* as a feminist work that develops a strong female heroine.[3] While these boys may be left reeling in astonishment after reading *Island*, it at least encouraged them to consider what a girl's abilities might be. Moreover, as the women's rights movement of the 1960s gained strength, these protests began to dwindle and readers more readily accepted a female heroine (qtd. in Marcovitz 65).

While the 1950s are not often remembered as a time of radical social reform for women, the start of the decade was marked by another best seller by Margaret Mead, *Male and Female: The Classic Study of the Sexes* (1949). Based on her ethnographic studies in the South Pacific islands, *Male and Female* focused on the impact of the United States' imperial ventures abroad on domestic issues, especially constructions of the family of which the adolescent was a part (xxv). It also, importantly, linked the period of adolescence to the progression toward national maturity. In her chapter on marriage and family, Mead writes,

> In cultures like ours, there may be a second or third adolescence, and the most complex, the most sensitive, may die still questing, still capable of change, starting like Franz Boas at seventy-seven to re-read the folk-lore of the world in light of new theoretical developments. No one who values civilisation and realises how men have woven the fabric of their lives from their own imaginations as they played over the memory of the past, the experience of the present, and the hope of the future, can count this postponed maturity, this possibility of recurrent adolescent crises and change of life-plan, as anything but gain. (333)

For Mead, the reoccurrence of adolescence is not a hindrance to maturity but instead an opportunity for self-discovery. This particular passage, with its homage to her mentor Franz Boas, is admittedly less concerned with gender; yet this study along with her earlier work positioned Mead as not only a champion of children's and young people's lives but also those of women too. In her reflection on Mead's legacy, anthropologist Nancy Lutkehaus argues that Mead was distinct from other students of Boas for her insistence on "the social, historical, and cultural milieu in which it [adolescence] is experienced," but her emphasis on female experience also positioned her as an innovative figure in anthropology. Mead's "decision to take seriously the lives of women, children, and adolescents" was one of her main contributions and departed from the work of her peers, predominantly men, who failed to include these important members of society in their studies (112).

Another way to view the gaps in *Island*, then, is in terms of how they enable O'Dell to challenge gender binaries, despite some initial reader resistance, a point that is essential for Karana's transformation into an American Eve. As a work of historical fiction, *Island* blends fact and fiction as it draws inspiration from the real-life account of the San Nicolas woman who was brought to Santa Barbara, California, in 1853 by a ship captained by George Nidever. O'Dell selects "the most romantic account" of this woman's survival (Lowry vii), with one noteworthy alteration: instead of leaving her people in order to save her child, O'Dell has his protagonist jump off the ship in order to rescue her younger brother (viii). While it would be easy to say that O'Dell made this change with his child audience in mind, the author did not plan to market *Island* as a children's book until after showing the manuscript to his friend Maud Hart Lovelace, the author of the Betsy-Tacy series (Marcovitz 34), which calls into question his intentions for altering Karana's age from that of a mature woman into a preadolescent girl of twelve. In her 2007 feminist reading of the novel, Diann Baecker offers a plausible alternative, suggesting that as O'Dell crafted Karana's character, he was drawing on the archetype of the young orphaned virgin, who appears in stories that often result in either the rape of the young virgin or her rescue by a paternalistic hero (195). Baecker acknowledges that for many young girls, *Island* is in fact a "story of independence, self-reliance, self-realization, and growth," but that this does not detract from the fact that O'Dell frequently makes choices to maintain Karana's position as a young virgin, both by altering the historical narrative and creating gaps that enable readers to see her as indefinitely young (196). Baecker ultimately concludes that *Island* is what the reader makes of it; that is, it is not incorrect to read the novel as "both a typical female Bildungsroman *and* a feminist manifesto" (200; emphasis in original), a fact that is essential to the novel's ability to fracture the myth of the American Adam and replace the male hero with a female one.

O'Dell's choice to recast the San Nicolas woman as a young girl on the cusp of adolescence can therefore be read as a feminist revision, one, as I have shown, that was rooted in anthropological understandings of female adolescence at the time. O'Dell would apply this feminist perspective in his engagement with the celebratory narrative of the American Adam myth, which suggests that the frontier is a space where the American people can continually renew themselves and return to a state of childhood innocence. O'Dell's choice of a young female protagonist, in light of this definition, is suitable for a novel determined to challenge traditional assumptions about women. O'Dell retains the youthful qualities of the American Adam, especially this figure's resourcefulness and self-sufficiency, and focuses on transforming his heroine into an American Eve. Through the many twists and turns of his plot, O'Dell problematizes the assumption that the New World is a place of fresh starts and encourages readers to consider the contributions of women to the early history of the United States. In the optimistic view of feminist critic Susan Naramore Maher, *Island* functions as a counternarrative to the mythos of the West through its confrontation with the violence of colonization (217), and it enabled O'Dell to challenge the meaning of the male explorer of frontier myths by reinventing what it meant to survive in isolation and suffer at the hands of others.

O'Dell's female character may not be quite as radical as Maher envisions, but the way she is constructed as an isolated hero does depart from traditional representations of the American Adam, whose most important distinguishing feature is his ability to break from history. Much like the male explorer celebrated in American mythology, O'Dell's young female protagonist can hunt, build, and complete other tasks necessary for her survival; but she cannot escape the knowledge that these tasks are traditionally forbidden to women and is haunted by the horrific memory of her tribe's annihilation at the hands of white foreigners, whose actions have forced her to break with tribal tradition in order to survive. Karana's struggles with these memories signal that she cannot be free of the traditions dictated by male leaders despite living completely alone. The guilt Karana feels when completing male tasks differentiates her from the American Adam, as it is precisely her kinship relations that define her. Suffering, an experience previously absent from or trivialized in the lives of former American Eve figures, becomes a defining feature of O'Dell's heroine. His new American Eve departs from the American Adam trope of the "fall from innocence" popularized in the nineteenth century, in which the hero must face a series of "ritualistic trials" where he is "defeated, perhaps even destroyed—in various versions of the recurring anecdote hanged, beaten, shot, betrayed, abandoned— but leaving his mark upon the world" (Lewis 127–128). Karana cannot find redemption in the same way as these fallen heroes, whose departure from history and familial ties frees them to forge their own path in the world. Instead of feeling liberated, the traumatic experiences she faces make it difficult for her to find ways to contribute to society and create her own legacy. Predicated on her

ability to confront and accept her trauma of tribal loss, a task that
O'Dell indicates is deeply challenging for this young survivor, Karana's entrance into maturity is signified by the stormy seas, both
literal and metaphorical, that she encounters during her time on
the island of her birth.

This internal challenge becomes even more apparent in two pivotal events: when Karana decides to burn her village and when
she spends the night in an old barrow. Faced with the reality of her
abandonment, Karana must first decide whether she will continue
to live in her village or find a new home somewhere on the island.
While the village is a place of familiarity and potential comfort,
the violent massacre of her people and her recent abandonment
render it "unhomely."[4] Karana remarks that the village-turned-
gravesite "reminded me of all the people who were dead and those
who were gone. The noise of the surf seemed to be their voices
speaking" (47). Haunted by her memories, Karana destroys one
hut after another until her entire village is nothing more than ash.
The act of burning is cathartic for Karana, but it also recalls the
violence that resulted in her initial isolation. Karana will again
repeat these acts of destruction when she vows to kill the wild
dogs who murdered her brother (46) as well as when she angrily
tosses jewels given in exchange for otter pellets into the sea (51).
These outbursts of anger and violence occur in rapid succession
as Karana works through the grief she experiences as a result of
the recent murder of her father and the massacre of other tribal
members. In foregrounding Karana's grief and rage, O'Dell not
only develops a realistic picture of her suffering but also provides
a means for Karana to break away from old tradition and begin
anew.

This shift in Karana's association with her ancestral past is
clearest in her performance of traditionally male tasks. When Karana begins to consider seriously what she must do to survive,
she quickly realizes that she must make weapons to hunt for food
and protect herself from the wild dogs on the island. Yet the decision to make these tools is a difficult one for Karana, who recalls
that tribal tradition forbids the "making of weapons by women"
(49). More than once, Karana is haunted by this tribal edict and
hesitates to construct or handle a weapon. In an oft-quoted passage, Karana's fears are revealed through an internal monologue:

"Would the four winds blow in from the four directions of the world and smother me as I made the weapons? Or would the earth tremble, as many said, and bury me beneath its falling rocks? Or, as others said, would the sea rise over the island in a terrible flood? Would the weapons break in my hands at the moment when my life was in danger, which is what my father had said?" (52). The final warning from her father, more than the others, is especially meaningful for Karana, who is terrified that her weapon will crumble in her time of need (76, 78). The fact that her father's words haunt Karana is relevant in a narrative that aims to construct a female-centered world. In order for Karana to fully embrace her female power, she must find a means to circumvent tribal tradition while still retaining respect for her ancestors.

This confrontation between present and past reaches its peak when Karana is trapped within a watery cave that serves as a barrow for her ancestors. Faced with these grotesque visions of the past, Karana turns away in fear and huddles in the dark with her dog, Rontu. "I knew that the skeleton who sat on the ledge playing his flute was one of my ancestors," she remarks, "and the others with the glittering eyes, though only images, were too, but still I was sleepless and afraid" (124). The "glittering eyes" of the human images haunt Karana much like the tribal traditions passed down by her father. These eyes seem to her "more alive than the eyes of those who live" (123). While the eyes still emit an aura of power, these effigies are in fact no more than decaying remnants of a lost tribal heritage. These sculpted human figures, meant to represent past tribal leaders, are marked neither as male nor female and are referred to with gender-neutral pronouns such as "its" and "their." These genderless bodies may watch as Karana sleeps in the dark cave, a womblike structure, but they lack the power of the living. With the men of the tribe dead and only these moldering ancestral remains to keep watch over the past, Karana can now set out to construct a new tradition that takes female power into account. Karana's final decision not to look back at the glittering eyes as she leaves the gravesite and her renaming of the cave asserts her power over her situation and her reconciliation of the past with the present (124). Already in love with her island, Karana is now free to make decisions that are not limited by tribal tradition.[5]

O'Dell incorporates many other traits of the American Adam in

Island of the Blue Dolphins, including loneliness, self-sufficiency, compassion, and a sense of betrayal. Yet it is his discussion of origins, specifically in relation to one's responsibility to an ancestral past, that makes his narrative a unique contribution and beneficial critique of previous interpretations of the American Adam myth. Through the figure of the adolescent girl, O'Dell underscores one of the key differences between the American Adam and American Eve: the American Adam has broken with his past while the American Eve is haunted by hers. Despite this contribution, O'Dell does not manage to successfully break from the colonial past bound up in the American Adam myth. His nostalgia for the frontier days represented in his childhood memories of life in California, along with his continual return to the stories of the Native inhabitants of these lands, make it difficult for him to let go of this history. A form of "imperialist nostalgia," which views colonial exploits as "innocent and pure" (Rosaldo 107), O'Dell's desire to return to the frontier days causes his American Eve to lose a bit of her power. Because Karana is shaped by traditional male narratives, she does not completely depart from previous understandings of the defining features of the American Adam, in particular this figure's ability to be self-reliant and survive on his own in the frontier. This flaw would be remedied as the American Eve continued to serve as a means for rethinking the imperial history of the United States, a process of narrative revision that relied on ideas of adolescence in order to gain its political force.

The American Eve in Native Literature

Chickasaw author Linda Hogan returns to many of the concerns articulated in Scott O'Dell's *Island of the Blue Dolphins* in her popular 1995 novel, *Solar Storms*. Following a young American Indian girl's journey to reunite with her biological family, *Solar Storms* addresses the societal traditions that limit female power and the negative impact of colonization. Much like O'Dell, Hogan creates a female protagonist who demonstrates the many traits of the American Adam—self-reliance, isolation, loneliness, and compassion—while also creating a female sanctuary where women can thrive and celebrate their unique skills and gifts. Set in the dreary town of Adam's Rib, *Solar Storms* also parallels O'Dell's fictional world in that it takes place in a society where women are in the dominant role as a result of white interference. Despite their many similarities, however, Hogan's novel departs from *Island* by delving more deeply into the racial issues that set *Island's* plot into motion: the colonization of American Indians. It positions American Indians as a living people, not just a remnant of the past, and engages with issues facing adolescent girls that enable Hogan to "analyze the economic, social, political, and historical factors that construct and institutionalize those gendered, individual experiences" (Hubler 169). Appearing at a moment of heightened attention to female adolescence, *Solar Storms* adds to the conversation about adolescence as a time of "confusion" for girls by acknowledging the deeply traumatic social conditions that led to the silencing of women and the marginalization of female experience.[6]

In large part, Hogan's Native heritage and her firsthand experience of issues that shape the lives of young Native girls allow her to more accurately address racial and gender conflict, effectively avoiding the stereotypes that predominate in O'Dell's classic children's book. Drawing on her experiences as a young girl and as an adoptive mother, Hogan reflects on the repercussions of an "unnamed grief." In her memoir, *The Woman Who Watches Over the World* (2001), Hogan explains that this sorrow caused the girls she grew up with to "cut or hit or [burn] themselves, as if it was a way to kill the self or to trade the pain of what resided within for external pain" (56). Hogan observed this same behavior in her adopted daughter, Marie, a girl who "showed signs of attachment disorder," including hallucinations and physical violence (Vernon 41).[7] Hogan's desire to address the pain associated with colonization, especially as it pertains to young women, inspired her to tell the story of Angela Jensen, an adolescent girl who is removed from her family as a young child and placed into the foster care system.[8] Through the adventures of her female protagonist, Hogan inverts Anglo-American associations with self-reliance in order to expose the negative effects of Euro-American colonization on Native girls. As a result, she brings much-needed attention to the racial and gender issues that are silenced through the myth of the American Adam.

Hogan's fictional fishing town of Adam's Rib is described as "the place where water was broken apart by land, land split open by water so that the maps showed places both bound and, if you knew the way in, boundless"; a land "emptied" by fur traders with lakes "too thin for its fish to survive" (21). The people who inhabit this land are described as an "ill-sorted group," with "homely, work-worn hands" and "accustomed to hard work and . . . familiar with loneliness" (28). The women especially are unhappy, scarred by their experiences with the fur traders who flocked to their land and abandoned them once the natural resources were depleted. As Angel adapts to this desolate environment, she realizes that she is similarly spiritually empty, drained of cultural attachments as a result of her experience in the U.S. foster care system. Her face, scarred by her mother's brutal abuse when she was a small child, reflects her traumatic past and connects her to the black lands of Adam's Rib, a town shaped by the fur trade and the male explorer's desire to conquer.[9] Like the lands drained of their bounty, Angel is also burned, scarred, and emptied of any capacity to love.

What Hogan presents to readers through her descriptions of Adam's Rib is a garden whose inhabitants are destroyed by the greed of white colonizers. By utilizing Adamic imagery, Hogan implies that this destruction is the result of Anglo-American intervention. American literary scholar Christine Jespersen notes that "The moniker *Adam's Rib* mockingly calls attention to colonial tropes of the American Adam" (277; emphasis in original). Jespersen's essay, which focuses on Hogan's resistance to myths of westward expansion such as those found in historian Frederick Jackson Turner's frontier thesis, explains how Hogan's reference to the American Adam addresses the colonization of Native tribes and the destruction of the American landscape. Hogan's selection of the name Adam's Rib also engages with the traits associated with the traditional American Adam. Like O'Dell's Karana, Hogan's female protagonist is weighed down by her history, a history she must confront in order to gain her independence. However, Hogan departs from O'Dell in her definition of independence. While Angel is self-sufficient in the sense that she has the ability to care for herself and survive under harsh conditions, Hogan never indicates that such a lifestyle is preferable. In fact, she encourages readers to understand self-reliance in a way distinct from its traditional American interpretation.

Hogan's protagonist does not immediately achieve this unique form of self-reliance upon arriving at Adam's Rib. Instead, she must transform through a series of renewing experiences that lead to her ultimate development into an American Eve figure. The first transformation occurs at Adam's Rib, where Angel adapts to her new life with her paternal great-grandmother, Agnes Iron, and her great-great-grandmother, Dora-Rouge. Angel declares, "They [Agnes Iron and Dora-Rouge] were blood kin. I had searched with religious fervor to find Agnes Iron, thinking she would help me, would be my salvation, that she would know me and remember all that had fallen away from my own mind, all that had been kept secret by the county workers, that had been contained in their lost records: my story, my life" (27). As she adjusts to a new life with her biological family, Angel learns that simply being with her blood kin is not enough to heal the wounds of the past. Yet she still believes that they are the key to unlocking the history stolen from her by the social workers. In the initial passages from the opening chapter of *Solar Storms*, Angel eagerly devises ways to make herself valuable to her family members, mentally noting that her strength and youthful energy can be used in order to "earn [her] keep" (33). Angel's desperate desire to find a place in Agnes's home derives from her belief that Agnes can help Angel make sense of her past, visually represented by the scars on her face. While Angel knows that her scars have something to do with her mentally disturbed mother, she does not know how she got them or what her life was like before entering the foster care system. Her memories "had fallen away from [her] own mind," and so she must rely on her family members in order to recover them.

Relinquishing her old independent ways and learning to depend on others, especially for emotional love and support, is Angel's first step toward renewal. Angel senses this change even upon arriving in Adam's Rib, believing that this new place constitutes a "beginning" for her: "But I felt that I was at the end of something. Not just my fear and anger, not even forgetfulness, but at the end of a way of living in the world. I was at the end of my life in one America, and a secret part of me knew this end was also a beginning, as if something had shifted right then and there, turned over in me" (25–26). Angel's path toward this new beginning bears some resemblance to the masculine version of the American Adam myth. Angel, much like the youth in Walt Whitman's poetry who are regenerated through the landscape, seeks a new beginning, and this depends on her ability to connect with the natural environment of her tribal land and the people who inhabit it. Whitman's speaker in "Song of Myself" (1855) is so much a part of nature that he likens himself to the grass under one's boot (lines 1339–1340). The speaker's power also comes from his ability to identify with the diverse populations of nineteenth-century America, much as Angel's power is dependent on her ability to reconnect with her tribe.

Hogan further reinforces the path toward renewal espoused in Whitman's poetry when she shows Angel being removed from the town on Adam's Rib in order to live on Fur Island with Bush, the woman who was married to her grandfather and who cared for Angel and her mother for brief periods in their childhood. Angel's removal to the island becomes a way for her to heal from the wounds of the past, one that is instigated by her blood kin, Agnes Iron and Dora-Rouge, who understand the complexity of her pain. On Fur Island, Angel begins to develop the survival skills she earlier lacked by learning to fish, garden, canoe the waterways, and chop the wood needed to survive the harsh winters. With the guidance of her new mother figure, Angel begins to reform herself, growing in spirit as she learns the stories and cultural practices of her tribe from Bush: "I hardly noticed how I grew strong, my hands rough, my arms filled out. It happened gradually. I don't know how it is that people change, or what is required, or how it moves. I know only what it feels like to change; it's in the body, in the stomach, in the heart. They ache and then they open" (89). As Angel embraces her new mode of living, she begins to develop gifts that please her grandmother(s): "I was the only one I knew of who could see inside water. No one else could do this, not even Bush. She approved of my gift" (85). Angel's gift is the result of her openness, her ability to see through the murk of past history. This same openness allows her to penetrate the mystery of her origins and weave together a narrative from the fragmented memories and stories of the past. Angel physically develops alongside her spirit so that each time she returns to Adam's Rib, her great-grandmother Agnes declares that her body is taking on a womanly shape (127, 135).

While these initial events align Hogan's American Eve with some of the American Adam variants in R. W. B. Lewis's 1955 study, Hogan also carefully distinguishes her heroine from her male predecessors. Whitman's romantic notions of communion with nature, for example, have no place in Hogan's narrative. In fact, Hogan stresses again and again that the destruction of the land and wildlife is rooted in male desire for power and wealth. Even the Indian character, LaRue Marks Time, disrespects nature and, as a result, is cursed with bad luck while hunting. LaRue's character is part of Hogan's critique of "frontier tales that celebrate trappers as adventurous men who 'opened' the West" (Jespersen 277). Angel, who is only just growing into her new self, already sees what her mentor, Bush, recognizes in LaRue's abuse of nature: an unsettling echo of the pioneers who similarly ravaged the land. When fishing, Angel notes that she catches fish easily while LaRue fails to get even a bite and that she does so without using "any of the manners, styles, or techniques he insisted I use" (83). Angel further recognizes the difference between her and LaRue's approach to the fish when he guts them before killing them: "I have never forgotten how LaRue left the fish on a slab of stone, without skin or flesh. They were still alive, gill slits moving. Just a reflex, LaRue said. I hated him" (84). LaRue's cold, exploitative view of nature denies the spirit that Angel has learned to see in the world around her, even in inanimate objects like a fishing hook. His outlook, intended to represent the Anglo-American way of viewing the world, is also aligned with the same perspective that male explorers used to justify the colonization of the "virgin lands" of the United States.

In addition to Walt Whitman's variant of the American Adam, Hogan also invokes aspects of Herman Melville's fallen Adam in order to further distinguish between different interpretations of renewal. Angel quickly learns upon arriving at Adam's Rib of a "geological oddity" known as the "Hungry Mouth of Water," a great sucking circular patch in the natural waterways that consumes anything that crosses it (62). Besides the occasional deer or drunk, the Hungry Mouth also once consumed an entire beluga whale dragged from his Arctic home by an exploitative showman. When the whale fails to attract paying customers, the showman sacrifices its body to the Hungry Mouth, "hoist[ing] it up on chains and cast[ing] it outside his boat to die, into that hungry place, until finally it sank in to the open mouth where it remained, an apparition from another world" (63).

Hogan uses the Hungry Mouth's victim and other stories about whales from different cultural traditions to critique the colonial violence of early frontiersmen. In her 1999 study of Hogan's work, Catherine Rainwater, a scholar of American Indian studies, demonstrates how Hogan achieves this effect. She argues that, by inserting the story of Eho, a tale of a woman who falls in love with a whale, within the narrative of *Solar Storms*, Hogan provides an alternative to western tales that depict men trying to conquer nature. Hogan will repeat her reference to this tale, which is told by Angel's great-grandmother Agnes, when Angel dreams of a white whale swimming and singing above her "with something akin to love [in its eyes]" (291). Rainwater's interpretation of the story of Eho suggests that Angel's dream is an inversion of the masculine violence that appears in *Moby-Dick* and gives a new way of understanding Angel's previous preoccupation with the Hungry Mouth's most curious victim. The carcass of the beluga whale, whose body was tortured by its white owner in life, reminds readers of the colonial venture upon which *Moby-Dick* is modeled. Ahab's greed, his desire to possess the whale, results in his ultimate destruction—only Ishmael lives to tell the tale.[10]

These various depictions of the white whale demonstrate that while Angel and her female elders differ in their approach to nature, they are still circumscribed in the history of white masculine violence. Indeed, one of the first things Angel relates in the story of her return to Adam's Rib is that the town is populated by women known as the "Abandoned Ones": "When the land was worn out, the beaver and wolf gone, mostly dead, the men moved on to what hadn't yet been destroyed, leaving their women and children behind, as if they too were used-up animals" (28). Angel identifies with these fallen women: the scars on her face and her mysterious origins also associate her with Adam after the Fall. Since the fallen Adam was a popular trope in Melville's work, Hogan indirectly refers to the American Adam myth through the story of the Abandoned Ones, conjuring up images of Adam and Eve after their exile from the Garden of Eden. It is important to recall that Angel was also once abandoned, lost in the U.S. foster care system. The parallels between the stories that come to define Adam's Rib and the fragmented history of Angel's early life merge to critique the tragic heroes in Melville's work. Melville's heroes, according to Lewis, are innocents lost in a world of sin, redeemers who, despite the obstacles, end up "leaving [their] mark upon the world" (127). Angel will also leave her "mark upon the world," yet she does so in a way that avoids the colonial mind-set that informs Lewis's vision.

Hogan's rejection of male interpretations of the American Adam myth has resulted in readings of her work within an ecofeminist framework. Silvia Schultermandl, a scholar of American studies, contends that Hogan draws on the core ideology of ecofeminism, where the history of the conquest of human and nonhuman beings is placed into dialogue (68). Angel's developing sense of self derives from her ability to connect with her people and the land around her. It is this need to discover a strong identity founded in Native culture that propels Angel on a quest to the land of the Fat Eaters where her ancestors originated, a task initiated when she learns that the lands are now being threatened by a hydroelectric dam project headed by a company named BEEVCO. This plot thread, Schultermandl argues, "adds to a large canon of Native American texts whose characters engage in identity formations that entail negotiations between their native heritages and the impact of dominant society" (67). These plot devices align Hogan's novel with ecofeminist values, where a balance between humans and the natural world is vital. Since Hogan's characters cannot complete their identity quests until they actively fight for their tribal land (Schultermandl 69), their actions provide models for repairing the results of colonial exploitation in addition to providing readers with an alternative model of how to interact with the natural environment.

With her knowledge of the myths that have denied the colonial past of the United States, Hogan provides the context for her protagonist to develop into a strong character with attributes of an American Eve that challenge even the most romantic nineteenth-century account of the American Adam figure. Once Angel departs from Adam's Rib and leaves behind the few men that populate the dying town, she begins to develop even more skills that identify her as a respectable adventurer. For instance, despite her fears about her impending journey to the land of the Fat Eaters, Angel rises to the occasion and carries heavy loads and paddles in turbulent waters. In one of the most riveting scenes on her journey, Angel descends into her canoe and surrenders to the dangerous rapids. Rather than cut through the waters with her paddle, Angel settles into the canoe and lets her hips rock with the constantly changing waters: "We were held in the hands of fighting water. We were at its mercy. Then I remembered John Husk telling me to catch the current and ride it like an animal, and finally, I gave up, giving in to gravity and to the motion of it, allowing my hips to move with it, not against it" (195). As she develops a stronger connection with nature, Angel begins to dream about healing plants and learns that this was also one of her female ancestor's gifts. Angel's second gift, like her ability to see and navigate through water, identifies her as a healer, a nurturer, a giver of life. Rejecting the Judeo-Christian Eve's association with sin, Hogan uses moments such as these to create a positive Americanized Eve.

In order to redefine the American Eve, Hogan must also challenge her non-Native readers' understanding of traditionally lauded traits such as self-reliance. Bush's character parallels the isolated heroes in such nineteenth-century classics as Cooper's *The Last of the Mohicans* (1826) and Twain's *Adventures of Huckleberry Finn* (1885). However, rather than celebrating the male desire to "light out for the Territory" (Twain 220), Hogan stresses the importance of navigating and relating to the land communally. During the early portion of her journey to the Fat Eaters, Angel describes the time alone with her grandmothers as one of healing: "The four of us became like one animal. We heard inside each other in a tribal way. I understood this at once and was easy with it. With my grandmothers, there was no such thing as loneliness. Before, my life had been without all its ears, eyes, without all its knowings. Now we, the four of us, all had the same eyes, and when Dora-Rouge pointed a bony finger and said, 'This way,' we instinctively followed that crooked finger" (177). While Angel still feels pain, grief, and even longing for her boyfriend Tommy, she knows that she no longer has to face the world alone. This differs from simply sharing these feelings with others; Angel does at times consult her grandmothers, but there are other times when she keeps her feelings to herself, including when she cries upon her departure from Adam's Rib (165). Her desire for privacy is respected, and Angel notes that if anyone saw her tears, "she kept silent about it" (165). In this way, Hogan shows that her characters can be together and still retain privacy.

The women's approach to sharing emotion and the burden of defending their land and culture contrasts with traditional U.S. conceptions of self-reliance: to be self-reliant in the nineteenth-century variants invoked in Lewis's work means to be absolutely alone. Characters such as Cooper's Leatherstocking might interact with others, but they are ultimately fated to live their life in isolation. This time alone demonstrates the character's inner strength, his ability to survive outside of the safety net of civilization. It is also the means by which these characters preserve their innocence. Such a desire for innocence is absent in Hogan's work. As Catherine Kunce argues in her 2009 article on *Solar Storms*, Hogan's definition of self-reliance "carries neither Horatio Algerian nor isolationist sentiments" but is instead marked by a person's participation in and contribution to the community (66). Kunce provides the example of Angel's guardian, Bush, who proposes a feast to mourn Angel's loss to her family and the tribe as a whole, an event that is not tribal tradition but rather a method for Bush to grieve communally. The mourning feast enables Bush, a Chickasaw Indian and outsider in Adam's Rib, to interact with others and for them in turn to recognize and share her pain. As the feast participants leave, they feel as if they are carrying away part of Bush's grief (18), which Bush metaphorically passes on as she hands over her material belongings to the visitors. Because the feast occurs in the dead of winter, she must then depend on others to avoid freezing to death. Like the destruction of the "virgin" forests, Hogan's characters are already burdened by the tragic traces of colonialism. Since they cannot escape this past, they must find alternative ways to move forward such as through storytelling, which depends on the interaction of tribal members across generational lines.

As Angel develops she begins to adhere to Hogan's revised definition of self-reliance, which is predicated on her willingness to "relinquish all she possesses, including her self-reliance" (Kunce 66). She does this by listening to the stories told by her elders, including those of her family in the land of the Fat Eaters. When Angel begins to dream about plants, she discusses these dreams with her grandmothers and then follows the advice of Dora-Rouge, who recognizes the dreams as a gift that her mother, Ek, also possessed (171). When Agnes sickens, Angel once again listens to her elders when they ask her to draw pictures of the plants she recently dreamed. These plants are believed to be the herbs needed to cure Agnes's unknown ailment. Angel's receptivity to her grandmothers' request is therefore not simply submission to authority but a way to work together and secure the medicine needed to help the group. Without Angel's dreams, the women would not be able to survive. Angel's quest will ultimately fail since Agnes dies before she returns with the plants, but the act of listening and responding to the needs of the other women, of working together as "one animal" (177), demonstrates that Angel is willing to sacrifice her independence for the sake of the group's survival. In the treacherous waters of the Boundary Region, this collective mentality is the only way that the women can reach their goal of entering the land of the Fat Eaters and fighting the Canadian company, BEEVCO.

The process of forgoing one's self-reliance in order to be self-reliant is best understood within the framework of Hogan's ecofeminist project. Women who fail to integrate into their tribe and establish the kinship relations that will help them overcome their painful history end up being controlled by that history. Angel's mother, Hannah Wing, is one of the many female victims that Hogan presents to readers. Discovered on a log after a heavy storm, Hannah is adopted by Bush and taken into her home. Bush quickly realizes that the child is mentally disturbed, haunted by a traumatic past that has left its traces on her body. When Angel asks to hear stories of her mother's childhood, she first learns of Hannah's scars: *"Beneath all the layers of clothes, her skin was a garment of scars. There were burns and incisions. Like someone had written on her. The signatures of torturers, I call them now. I was overcome. I cried. She looked at me like I was a fool, my tears a sign of weakness. And farther in, I knew, there were violations and invasions of other kinds. What, I could only guess"* (99; emphasis in original). Bush's narrative identifies the physical traces of Hannah's pain and explains how Hannah chose to respond to this pain by retreating from the tribal community. Bush relates how Hannah stole clothing and wore it like body armor (98). Hannah also reenacts scenes of torture, molesting little children and murdering

Bush's dog: *"There were needles in his mouth and nose and ears,
and he'd been cut, the red blood on the fur, matted, one foot cut off"*
(104; emphasis in original).

The repetition of these acts of trauma isolates Hannah from
the rest of her community. As a grown woman, Hannah lives in a
"shabby house" that lies in a remote part of town (241). When Angel visits her mother on her deathbed, she observes how Hannah's
physical state reflects the emotional turmoil inside of her, from the
"white roots" of her hair to the "burn scars on the tops of her feet"
(243, 252). Her aging and damaged body is testament to the pain
she has withstood, but it also speaks to another sickness that pre-
vents Hannah from connecting to those around her, namely her
foul breath and stained teeth with "what looked like dried blood
on them" (243). Hogan describes Hannah's emotional frigidness as
the result of the "naked ice inside her," an allusion to the American Indian myth of the *windigo* popular in northern tribes (104).
The *windigo*, an icy monster that does not have the capacity to feel
emotions such as love, strikes fear into those around him/her due
to their cannibalistic tendency.[11] The *windigo*'s brutality helps explain the coldness of Hannah's heart, which makes it impossible
for her to participate in the healing process that Hogan sees as dependent upon one's ability to see oneself as part of a community
and instead causes her to consume those she loves, including her
own daughter.

Hogan attempts to find a middle path between the cold harsh-
ness of Hannah's life and the dreaming and drifting that dominate
the first leg of Angel's journey to the land of the Fat Eaters. Like
the male and female rain that occupies the narrative at alternating moments,[12] Angel must also become hard at times in order to
defend her way of life and the land that she has come to love. However, she must also avoid becoming so hard that her heart freezes
like her mother's before her. Angel faces several challenges in order
to demonstrate her capacity to balance the hard and soft aspects of
nature, becoming as valiant as any American Adam that came before her and as sensitive and compassionate as her American Eve
predecessors. One of these challenges occurs when Angel must go
and watch over her dying mother. Hardened by years of pain, Angel
wants to remain distant from her mother so that she cannot hurt

her again. Yet the stories told by Bush, Agnes, and Dora-Rouge have taught Angel that there is no benefit in holding in anger, and that it is far better to share and release pain. As Angel watches her dying mother, she reflects: "I would find it in myself to love the woman who had given life to me, the woman a priest had called a miracle in reverse, the one who had opened her legs to men and participated in the same life-creating act as God. Yes, she tried to kill me, swallow me, consume me back into her own body, the way fire burns itself away, uses itself as fuel. But even if she hated me, there had been a moment of something akin to love, back at the creation. Her desperation and loneliness was my beginning" (251). Hogan contrasts this scene with others where Angel must harden herself in order to defend her people and their land. As a group of construction workers threatens to destroy her extended family's home in Two-Town, which is near the dam project that Angel and her grandmothers have come to protest, Angel is sent out into the woods to escape from the imminent danger posed by the men. Angered by this, Angel drives to the local police station and asks for help. Instead of finding aid, she is arrested for driving without a license in an unregistered car that the officer claims is stolen, despite the fact that he knows it belongs to Angel's uncle Tulik (291). Angel learns from this incident that she must emotionally harden herself in order to face the threats to her people and find ways of bringing attention to the dam project and working with the anti-dam activists.

The lessons that Angel learns throughout her journey are predicated on her ability to morph into a heroic figure. Hogan rejects many of the traits associated with the mythic American Adam. These dashing figures are enmeshed in the colonial ventures that "opened up" the land in the West. In order to justify westward expansion, these mythical heroes cover over the wounds suffered by American Indian tribes. Through the story of Angel, Hogan brings attention to this lost history. At the same time, she speaks directly to her Native readers, encouraging them to come together to overcome the trauma of their colonial past. The final lines in *Solar Storms* attest: "Something beautiful lives inside us. You will see. Just believe it. You will see" (351). Hogan is intent on raising awareness of the atrocities of westward expansion, but she also wants her readers to find ways to embrace the future. This desire is represented in Angel's nickname, "Our Future," a name that Angel's family bestows upon Aurora, Angel's baby half-sister (318).[13]

Recovering one's history in order to move beyond it is a defining trait of the American Eve. O'Dell's Karana must let go of her traumatic past in order to move forward and survive on her island alone, but she remains an archetype of the male adventurer as even O'Dell affectionately called her his "girl Robinson Crusoe" (175). As Sara Schwebel argues in her 2011 study of historical children's fiction, this interpretation of Karana's character fails to consider the imperial implications of the situation, where Karana is positioned as victim rather than perpetrator, as in the case of Crusoe (48). Hogan avoids this pitfall by supplementing this imperial interpretation of Native experience with her knowledge of tribal history, culture, and tradition. In her engagement with the tropes of the American Adam, Hogan thus expands beyond the framework O'Dell provides. Her American Eve is not only more fully developed, but the world she creates is also populated by a group of strong women who work together rather than in isolation. By crafting a story about an adolescent who reconnects with her cultural heritage after being wrongfully placed in the U.S. foster care system, Hogan searches for a corrective to the cycles of violence that shape the lives of Native children and their parents as well as the homes that have been lost, damaged, or stolen throughout U.S. history. In doing so, she manages to use the figure of the American Eve to develop her ecofeminist message, which combines her interests in ecological conservation and Native rights.

From the Ashes:
Reviving the Fallen American Eve
for a New Generation

In her debut novel, *Swamplandia!* (2011), Karen Russell returns to the figure of the American Eve and blends the ecofeminist and colonial critique that appears in Hogan's novel in order to comment on the dangers of national myths of progress bound up with the frontier. Shaped in large part by the heavy toll that the 2008 stock market crash had on the American economy, Russell explores the recession following this collapse through the adventures of an adolescent girl, Ava Bigtree, and the slow and steady decline of her family's small business in the Florida Everglades. Ava, whose name is a variation on Eve, tells the story of her family's financial loss and her own traumatic experiences retrospectively, a narrative decision that Russell claims was important as it gives Ava "access to some adult vocabulary but [still shows how she is] really trying to be true to the spirit of that age" ("Karen Russell: Interview"). Drawing heavily on the tropes of Herman Melville's fallen Adam, Ava mourns the loss of innocence brought on by the death of her mother, who was the star of a live alligator-wrestling show on Swamplandia!, the name of their small family-run theme park. Ava views the loss of her mother as the catalyst for the events that have led to the financial demise of Swamplandia!, and in her desperate attempts to recover the glory days of the family business, she embarks on a dangerous mission deep in the heart of the swamplands that nearly causes her death. Through Ava's misguided attempts to recover the past, Russell employs many of the themes that are unique to the American Adam, yet she also underscores the fact that the male tradition of celebrating innocence—commonplace in nineteenth-century representations of this figure—is both problematic and damaging for those marginalized and excluded from these tales. Ava, who is denied the possibility of recovering her lost innocence, learns through the coming-of-age process how to delicately navigate between fact and fiction, turning away from the tropes of male adventurism that originally help shape her understanding of the history of Florida's wetlands and its native inhabitants.

Russell's novel begins deep in the Ten Thousand Islands on the Bigtree's local tourist attraction, Swamplandia!, which was built to take advantage of visitors' interest in the exotic. The island is stocked with alligators that the family advertises as Seths, and the Bigtree family dresses up as Indians in order to attract more tourists to their gator-wrestling show. By beginning with the commercialized island—fake Indians and all—Russell draws attention to several real problems that have shaped the history of the Florida swamplands. Home to the Seminole and Miccosukee Indians, the natural wetlands of Florida and their Native inhabitants were threatened by white settlers during the land rush in the 1930s. Russell inserts many facts regarding this land rush through the youngest member of the Bigtree "tribe," Ava. With extraordinary proficiency, Ava reels off the many legends that constitute the Big-tree family history, including the story of how her Grandpa Saw-tooth and Grandma Risa first arrived on Swamplandia!: "Grandpa Sawtooth and Grandma Risa took the train from Ohio to Florida and then traveled by glade skiff to their new home. When they first docked on the lee side of the island, my grandparents' feet sank a few inches before touching the limestone bedrock. Sawtooth cursed the realtors for the length of an aria. A tiny crab scuttled over Ri-sa's high buttoned shoe—'and when she didn't scream,' Sawtooth liked to say, 'that's when I knew we were staying'" (31). Ava's story describes the hopes and dreams that prompted many northern-ers to settle in the Florida swamplands. Viewing the Everglades as one of the last great frontiers of the United States, men seek-ing adventure and fortune attempted to scratch out a living in the harsh environment of Florida's natural wetlands. In one pop-ular report from 1931, a U.S. government special agent, Roy Nash, describes the difficulties of traversing the land in his Ford truck, relating how he must ultimately abandon the vehicle in order to press farther into the wilderness (Adams 422). The stories of Nash and other Florida settlers served both as a warning about modern technology and as a tribute to the superiority of white masculin-ity, echoing popular narratives from the 1930s such as the *Tarzan* films, which were intended to combat fears about the feminization of boys and men (Adams 422–423).

In their desire to tame an uncivilized land, settlers ultimately led to the rapid destruction of that very wilderness, especially as businesses seeking money began massive projects to make the land arable for prospective farmers. Russell uses her young pro-tagonist to draw attention to these ecological issues, describing how these attempts to urbanize the wetlands ended up destroy-ing the natural cycles of the Everglades. Ava complains about the melaleuca tree, which was planted as part of the massive efforts to drain the swamplands (7–8), and is fascinated by her sister's tale about a young man named Louis Thanksgiving who dies on a dredge deep in the swamp while working on the construction of a superhighway (most likely the Tamiami Trail that runs from Tampa to Miami). Russell builds readers' concern for Florida's natural ecosystem as she describes a metaphorical battle between man and nature. The swamp, Russell explains in a long passage about the natural cycles of the Everglades, is constantly changing in "land-versus-water skirmishes" (23). Ava identifies herself as a savior of this constantly changing landscape—indeed, in addition to being a variation on Eve, her name also derives from the Hebrew word for "life"—which is threatened by the encroachment of mainlanders who seek to control the wild cycles of nature. Calling herself and her sister "tree warriors," Ava is proud of her efforts to return the swamp to its natural state and relishes her power to fell the threatening melaleuca trees with one swoop of her pesticide-coated paintbrush (97).

Russell's concern for the natural environment extends to the marginalized groups who often found refuge in the Florida Everglades, especially the indigenous people that populated the land. Noting how the devastation that impacted the Florida Everglades was also an encroachment on the already shrinking territory of the Seminole and Miccosukee Indians, who originally inhabited areas as far north as Georgia and Alabama before being pushed south by Euro-American settlers (Weisman 224), Ava counters the myth of the white male explorer that predominated in tales of Florida, where white settlers nobly battled Seminole Indians in order to claim their right to the frontier land. Through her accounts of the Seminole Wars (1817–1818; 1835–1842; 1855–1858) and the Calusa Indians, an indigenous Florida tribe that was wiped out in the 1700s by the Spanish, Ava attempts to combat the prejudice of history, "a kind of prehistoric arithmetic . . . in which some people counted and others did not" (250). Ava learns about this history from her grandpa Sawtooth and adopts her grandfather's view of a "true historian," which Ava describes as being able "to mourn amply and well" (250). Her words resemble those of the American Eve, whose task it is to face the history buried by myth and time; but this understanding of the past and her relationship to it is also clouded by an intense imperial nostalgia for the "simpler" times when man and nature could interact more freely together. Passed down to her by male elders that include her grandfather, this longing threatens to unravel Ava's project to restore the historical record, as it has the dangerous effect of glorifying white settlers and appropriating Native cultures in order to regain a sense of connection to the land that has been destroyed through its development.

Throughout her recollection of her last summer living in the
Florida wilderness, Ava repeatedly expresses a desire to return
to a time before the development projects intended to make the
swamplands more habitable destroyed Florida's natural ecosystem, failing to acknowledge her family's and their descendants'
complicity in this transformation—tellingly, Ava claims that she
"cleaned the history" of the Florida Everglades, which may refer to
more than the literal act of dusting off the Swamplandia! museum
artifacts. In addition to the fact that Ava's grandfather would have
been one of the many prospectors benefiting from attempts to ar-
tificially control the natural wetlands, her father's frequent ad-
justments of the "facts" that narrate the meaning behind the artifacts which document these projects and their destructive results
have the underlying intention of increasing business for Swamplandia!, profiting from the shock and horror tourists' experience
when viewing grotesque images such as "bloated [black laborers']
bodies in Taylor Slough, 1935, that floated on our museum wall"
(250). From her father, Ava's understanding of history as nego-
tiable, a lesson previously learned from her grandfather, is reinforced. For Ava and her family, Florida history is just as much a
story as the myths Ava is told about the swamplands surrounding
her home, a fictional account that can be rewritten at will. As Ava
relates, it was a common occurrence for the "facts" in the Swamplandia! museum to be rearranged and edited so that "certain artifacts appeared or vanished [overnight], dates changed and old
events appeared in fresh blue ink on new cards beneath the dusty
exhibits" (32). These changes, she importantly notes, were never
discussed, as if they had not been made at all.

Ava's battle between a desire to set the record straight and
to recover an idealized past is best seen through Russell's use of
the tropes of the fallen Adam. As Lewis attests in his study of the
American Adam, the fallen Adam is characterized by his "ritualistic trials," where he "takes his start outside the world, remote or
on the verges; its power, its fashions, and its history are precisely
the forces he must learn" (127–128). Lewis identifies this variant
of the American Adam as especially significant to U.S. culture, for
whenever it arises it speaks to "the American habit of resistance
to maturity" (129). However, the conscious use of the fallen Adam
can also contribute to "a fresh definition of experience" that is a

sign of an emerging "cultural maturity" (129). A hero that is bat-
tered and bruised until he, too, is tainted by the sin of the world,
the fallen Adam must fight the evil forces of the world in order to
inject a little goodness in the hell that surrounds him. In his analysis of Melville's work, Lewis describes this growing-up process
as one where the hero reaches a "moral maturity" through his encounters with evil (e.g., Ishmael and Ahab, Pierre and Elizabeth,
and so forth) (140). The hardships experienced by the hero enable
him to develop a "durable innocence" that can withstand the trials of life, demonstrating how authors like Melville used the fall of
their heroes to celebrate and reaffirm the value of innocence, even
when it seemed most in peril (146, 148). Characters such as Billy
Budd, the Christ-like adolescent hero from the novella of the same
name, might therefore be destroyed by their innocence, but this innocent state is also necessary to make positive changes in the evil
world: they are, Lewis claims, "redeemer[s]" (151).

Russell follows this pattern in *Swamplandia!* as her heroine is
forced to grow up and face a series of tragic events that eventually lead to her downfall. As the narrator, Ava begins by declaring
that hers is a story of family tragedy, which she sums up in a few
short words (*"we fell"* [9; emphasis in original]), and refers to her
former self as a "child," indicating that her tale ends in the loss of
her childhood and the innocence associated with this stage of life
(8). In a series of flashbacks, Ava reveals her life before the death
of her mother and contrasts it to the hardships she faces after entering the world that "awaits [her]" (Lewis 129). "Back when Mom
was healthy," Ava notes, "we'd see the flash of orange paint behind
the mangroves that meant the ferry had arrived and go scram-
bling for our staff positions" (24). Ava recalls yet another moment
when her mother comforts her after she makes a mistake on one
of her alligator-wrestling moves: "*A-va . . . now you tell me, is that
the octave of a Bigtree wrestler?*" (69; emphasis in original). In contrast, Ava's description of her life following her mother's death is
filled with grief and pain. She calls this period the "Beginning of
the End" (8) and attributes the eventual loss of the family business
and her lifestyle in the swamp to the death of her mother. "Without Mom," Ava declares, "the whole show felt horribly incomplete
to me" (20). Ava's grief is rooted in her feelings that she has lost
her place in the world. Previously an active member of the Swamp-

landia! staff and her mother's understudy, Ava now drifts around
the island without a real sense of purpose.

Russell uses Ava's fall into despair in order to delineate between a life before and after innocence. Much like the biblical creation story, Ava's tale follows the journey of a "young innocent" as
she has her eyes opened to the troubling reality that shapes her
present life. The island of Swamplandia!, which was previously a
safe haven filled with "wood-chip[ped] trail[s]" and special tanks
with "over three hundred thousand gallons of filtered water" to
hold the park's gators (46, 4), is now infested with leery-eyed men.
Ava describes these new invaders as "Red-eyed men with no kids
in tow [who] started showing up at the Saturday shows. Solitaries.
Sometimes they debarked the ferry with perfumed breath, already
drunk" (20). Ava's shock at the behavior of these men reveals how
isolated she has been from society. Growing up in a remote part of
the Florida Everglades allows Ava to preserve her innocence, particularly when it comes to knowledge about sexual desire, but it
also puts her in a vulnerable position. This naïveté is underscored
when Ava makes her first faltering steps into sexuality and flirts
with a mysterious swamp gypsy known as the Bird Man. As her
trust in the Bird Man grows, Ava will often lie in his lap or hold his
hand in order to feel the love that she associates with her parents
(245–246, 248). These behaviors, which she perceives as innocent,
eventually backfire as the Bird Man lures her to a remote part of
the swamp and rapes her, an event that marks Ava's final departure from her innocent state.

Russell's depiction of Ava's budding sexuality engages with popular tropes of sexual innocence in American culture. In a 1975 advertisement for Love's Baby Soft products, the voiceover claims
that "innocence is sexier than you think" while a blonde woman in
a white dress seductively bites and licks a lollipop. The advertisement's linking of innocence and sexuality confirms what Victorian
literary scholar James Kincaid has argued elsewhere about the
eroticization of innocence. Kincaid's work, which is by now a classic in the field of children's literature, reveals how the child came
to be sexually charged: "Our Victorian ancestors managed to make
their concept of the erotic depend on the child, just as their idea
of the child was based on their notions of sexual attraction. We've
been living, not so happily, with the results of their bungling ever

since" (52). Kincaid goes on to explain the ways in which this "bungling" has shaped notions of childhood in the United States, using examples of pedophilia and child stars, among others, to demonstrate how children are framed as sexual beings in the media, and how adult audiences enjoy this. In his own words, "what these stories [of erotic innocence] do for us is keep the subject hot so we can disown it while welcoming it in the back door" (6). Kincaid is not suggesting that all adults are child molesters, but rather that American culture has adopted a discourse that does indeed sexualize children, which has led to widespread panic at times about predators and the need to protect children's innocence.

The obsession that Kincaid observes in his many case studies is supported by the more specific discussion surrounding sexual violence toward young women and rape in particular. Beginning in the 1960s, feminists began to pay an increasing amount of attention to reported rape cases, which led to the initiation of such events as "Take the Night Back" on college campuses (Sielke 367). In her overview of the role feminism has played in the development of rape laws, American literary scholar Sabine Sielke argues that the continued emphasis on rape over all other forms of violence against women has the counterintuitive effect of reasserting gender binaries that were commonplace in the nineteenth century (371), such as the "coquette," who innocently flaunts her sexuality only to have her actions lead to her corruption by a villainous man (375). A figure who was a staple of the popular seduction novel, the coquette served as a cautionary tale for readers who might similarly try to flaunt their sexuality. Within the context of British literature, these lessons in sexual decorum emerged as early as the eighteenth century in conduct books for women, which emphasized the need for young women to preserve their innocence in order to conform to ideals of femininity (Johnston 3–4) or what Barbara Welter has called the "cult of true womanhood." This cult, above all others, idealized a woman's innocence and is one among many mechanisms for infantilizing women, leaving them in a perpetual state of childhood.

Ava's downfall, symbolized by her rape, is thus connected to a long-standing discourse of female sexuality that encompasses both childhood innocence and the vulnerability of young women. Russell begins to reassert the familiar discourse of rape, with the woman as helpless victim, as Ava narrates how she did not "tr[y] to fight this person" and instead compliantly helped him complete the act despite her pain and horror during the process (330). Russell then departs from the trope of the helpless rape victim by repositioning her heroine as an active agent who is capable of defending herself without the aid of anyone else:

> I pulled her [Ava's pet alligator] out and untaped her small jaws and flung her at him in one fluid motion. The Bird Man was surprised into reflex. His naked hands flew out like catcher's mitts; I could see past him to where his falconer's gloves were hanging off the keel. He caught the Seth hard against his chest. There was something almost funny about watching this, hysterically funny, but terrifying, too, a bad hilarity that lights up eel-bright in your belly. A hideous squeal went up through the trees but I don't know what happened next, if the red Seth bit him or clawed at him—I was off. (332–333)

The gator can be read as a reenactment of the rape scene that has just occurred; however, in this case the roles are reversed and Ava is in control. She flings the red gator, a symbol of her sexual innocence, in the face of the Bird Man and thus willingly parts with the thing that separates children from adolescents. Her willingness to place her baby alligator and favorite pet in danger symbolizes her acceptance of the need to disassociate herself from the "childish" behavior that linked her to life on Swamplandia!. The "hideous squeal" that Ava hears further supports the notion that the sacrifice of her alligator represents the loss of innocence. The squeal can be read as both the sound of attack and the squelching, writhing squeal of pain that one might associate with a dying animal.[14]

The escape scene has further ramifications within the context of the economic recession, which frames the entire novel. In a 2009 report from NBC News, the sinking economy following the 2008 financial crisis is directly connected to the sinking of the American family. Citing a marked rise in cases of domestic abuse, both of women and children, the report states that "the American home is becoming more violent, and the ailing economy could be at least partially to blame" ("Domestic Abuse"). Cases of men holding their wives and children hostage are given as examples of the grim state of the family, which is seen as being at risk when placed under financial pressures. In *The Political Economy of Violence against Women* (2012), Jacqui True, a leading expert in international relations and gender studies, explores this link between economic recession and domestic violence, arguing that "recession has the potential to create poverty anew, as well as exacerbate preexisting poverty, and women are most likely to bear the brunt of violent consequences" (105). True cites several surveys to back up her claims, including one from cosmetics company Mary Kay that showed a marked increase in female victims of domestic violence who cited "financial issues" as the leading cause of their abuse. Through these statistics, True demonstrates the severity of the problems that arise in times of economic crisis and the extent to which these problems plague American families (105).

Russell's fallen American Eve feeds into fears about the decline of the American family following the collapse of the housing market in 2008, but her narrative also builds on already existing discourses about domestic violence and child abuse in other ways. Ava's escape, though a momentary victory, leads her deep into the swamp and digs up many traumas of the past. One of these traumas is represented by the female ghost figure, Mama Weeds, who is said to haunt little children and other swamp dwellers. A black woman who fled to the swamp to gain freedom, Mama Weeds was later brutally murdered by the men in the area who were jealous of her success. Ava explains, "Most people believe it [the murder] was the work of several men, owing to the kind of damage that they reputedly did to her. For no other reason than that she'd killed that alligator and let it rot!" (361). Mama Weeds represents the violated female body, a woman wronged by greedy men. Having survived her traumatic sexual encounter with the Bird Man, Ava's confrontation with a woman that she believes is the ghost of this violated female body signals the difficulty of letting go of her pain, her past, and her innocence. Ava clings to a set of clothes in the woman's yard that she recognizes as possessions of her loved ones, including her beloved mother, and "snarl[s]" like a "rabid animal" at the ghostly woman, whose eyes are a portal to "the islands, the saw-grass prairies" of the swamp (363–364). Ava's regression into an animal state links her to the savagery of the feral child. Ava's fighting instinct—her scratching, clawing, and snarling—demonstrate the extent to which she values the memories linked to her childhood. The one scrap of clothing that she rips from the dress of the ghost is thus representative of the lost youth that she turned her back on in her desperate escape from the Bird Man.

While the encounter with Mama Weeds reveals in part Ava's internal state, it also speaks to the often underreported incidents of violence against black women. The reports on increasing domestic violence following the 2008 financial crisis do not mention a specific race that is more at risk, but earlier reports on sexual violence suggest that this may be the case and that the media often overlook such incidents. In her overview of the literary representation of rape, Sielke notes how "black women . . . were assumed to be immune to such violation, their injuries deemed negligible" (376). She further supports this assertion in the comparison of two media reports on rape, one for a white woman and one for a black one. The first is the notorious Central Park jogger rape case, in which a white female jogger was violently raped and killed by a gang of teenagers (later exonerated when serial rapist Matias Reyes confessed to the crime). The second, which occurred a mere week after this first incident, involved a black woman who was brutally raped and murdered, her head nearly decapitated. Yet as Sielke notes, despite the closeness in the dates of these events, the second rape hardly received any notice, in large part because it did not fit the popular narrative of rape in American culture. That is, unlike the jogger case, which involved black and Latino boys violating a white woman, the second case involved the body of a woman already seen to be impervious to such violence, as in the case of earlier antebellum narratives (376).

The lack of concern for black bodies uncovered through Ava's narrative can be traced back to the racial tension that plagued Florida in the 1930s, a time when many freed and fugitive slaves fled to the swamp for refuge. At this time, Florida "led the country in lynchings per capita with twice the rates of Mississippi, Georgia, and Louisiana" (Adams 412). More than a decade before the passage of Jim Crow laws, Florida passed the Black Codes of 1866, which were significantly harsher than similar codes passed in other southern states. Laws making it legal to punish vagrancy with "imprisonment, fine, or being sold to the highest bidder for as much as twelve months" shifted the power of slaveholders to the state and ensured that freed slaves continued to live in a state similar to their previous bondage (Richardson 372, 375). As in many southern states, crimes by blacks and whites were not punished equally, and black women like Mama Weeds were especially susceptible to violence. In one example of the injustice of the system during the period of the black codes, historian Joe Richardson relates how offenses such as rape of a white woman would result in the death of the perpetrator but that "no mention was made of punishment for rape of a Negro woman" (374). The laws were thus conceived as a way of retaining power over the freed black population rather than as a general enforcement of law to ensure the safety of all people. In the case of Mama Weeds, this historical reality is represented through a young black woman who is brutally killed (and likely raped based on Ava's rendition of the tale) and then buried forever in the swamp, only to be remembered through a ghost story meant to scare little children.

Russell continues to explore the traumas buried in Florida's history when Ava encounters her final trial during her miraculous escape from the Bird Man, which involves swimming in a watery cave that is home to a female alligator. The cave is womblike—dark, round, and enclosed—and is connected to the mythology of the local Seminole and Miccosukee tribes that once populated the swamplands. In one particular creation myth shared by these two tribes, the Indian people emerge from a cave similar to the one Ava finds herself in: "The ground shakes and the opening to the cave is exposed—the People slowly walk to the opening and look out onto a strange new place—this is the Mother that had been created for them—but the cave represented security—as a child can not resist the calling of birth the People could not resist the calling of the new place. The cave now gave birth to the People—new life stepped onto the breast of Mother—a beautiful new beginning was at hand" ("Hitchiti-Mikasuki Creation Story"). In Ava's experience, the peaceful entrance into the world that is described in the Native creation myth is inverted, as she struggles to survive her "birth." Nearly drowning and then actually bitten by the nesting gator, Ava is now exposed to a different kind of violence than the one she just escaped. In contrast to the creation myth where the indigenous people hesitantly leave the "security" of the cave in order to enter into a "new life" on the (Mother)land, Ava discovers within the cave the spirit and strength of her mother, whom she has longed for throughout her journey. The fact that in her escape from the Bird Man she has encountered female opponents, first Mama Weeds and then the nesting alligator, sets Ava along a path where she is challenged by women to reject the myths and fictional stories created by men—the Bird Man lured Ava into the swamplands by convincing her it was the "Underworld"—and accept the reality of her circumstances and the historical events shaping women's lives that preceded them.

Russell's choice to batter and bruise her young heroine in this manner may in part be due to Ava's complicity in the continued suppression of Native people, or her acceptance of male myths and "facts" that have shaped her childhood understanding of her world and the history that informs it. Dressing up as an Indian like the rest of her family to increase Swamplandia!'s business, Ava is not completely innocent. Indeed, though Ava will carefully recite facts about the colonization of Native tribes in Florida and even admits that the Seminoles are "the 'real' Indians" (238), she still contributes to the white imagination of this tribe through her narration of a noble Indian past. As historian Mikaëla Adams explains, white settlers "constructed an identity for these Natives in the Anglo-American imagination. This identity was not one that the Seminoles themselves necessarily embraced" (405). While white supporters of Native rights have portrayed and continue to portray the Seminoles in a positive light, which is a far cry from images of the "savage" Indian that previously served to bolster a sense of white superiority, these positive views are still limiting. In her study of cultural shifts among the Seminole tribe, anthropologist Jessica Cattelino reports how the most frequent questions she receives when describing her work are "So are Seminoles losing their culture?" and "Have they sold out?" (67). Furthermore, she adds that mainstream media outlets "worry that native people will become more materialistic, less 'traditional'" (67). Whether this concern stems from a desire for Native tribes to continue to live as they did in the past or from anxiety about the success of tribal-run casinos, these opinions demonstrate the way that even sympathetic supporters pin Natives to the past, preferring them to live up to the white imagination of the "noble savage." This view is reflected in Ava's own speeches about the destruction of Native tribes and the bravery of Seminole wrestlers as well as her pride in her "tribe's" ability to hold out against mainlanders, an association that may well refer to the Seminoles who call themselves the "unconquered people" and whom settlers often admired for their ability to withstand U.S. armies, even as they sought to conquer them (Adams 416).

As her journey unfolds, Ava's desire to reclaim her personal past often gets in the way of her agenda to be a "true historian" who chooses fact over myth, and it is in the final climactic battle scene where this struggle comes to a head and Ava is forced to choose one over the other. As she swims through the den of the nesting alligator, Ava describes how she pushes through a natural obstruction, a "portal, a hole" that she at first believes is a wall (382). This portal can be likened to the birth canal, which Ava desperately seeks to pass through in her efforts to return to the womb of her creation. As she nears her goal, she spies the alligator. "The thing," Ava calmly reflects, "had gotten ahold of my calf" (382–383). Russell inserts vivid visual imagery in the wrestling scene in order to underscore the pain associated with Ava's rebirth: "Dark orange pigment rose everywhere and soon it was too cloudy to see, although I tried—my eyes stung inside a fog that I realized must be plumes of my own blood" (383). Despite the pain she experiences in this passage, Ava still clings desperately to the clothes she found in her encounter with Mama Weeds, which she believes belong to her sister and mother. "The bundle," she recalls, "was becoming so heavy, impossibly heavy," but Ava still holds on to the clothes, claiming that "at no point do I remember wanting to let go" (382). As she swims to the surface of the cave, her old body literally falls apart, and Ava then realizes that she is no longer burdened by the bundle of clothes as she registers that her hands are now free to scoop the water and keep her body afloat (384).

Ava's fears about letting go of the clothes representing her past are partially relieved by her belief that in her fight with the alligator she encountered her mother's spirit, "not her ghost but some vaster portion of her, her self boundlessly recharged beneath the water" (389). While Ava will go on to live a very different life outside of the swamp following her escape from the Bird Man, her continued memory of the spiritual encounter with her mother in the nesting gator's cave is described as being like the sun, or the "yellow inside you that makes you want to live" (389). This interpretation contrasts sharply with the dull and muted colors she will go on to associate with her new life on the mainland, after her family packs up and leaves Swamplandia!, and suggests that despite Ava's nostalgia for her childhood, she accepts that she cannot, and should not, want to return to her prior life. As Sarah Graham explains in her 2013 essay on girlhood, Ava's cautionary tale about male interpretations of frontier myths "serves as a warning against the postfeminist myth that, by the end of the twentieth century, gender equality had been achieved, rendering feminism redundant" (601). Graham's reading suggests that one thing Ava has gained, in a manner similar to Hogan's heroine, is access to a female outlook on the world previously inaccessible to her. This viewpoint is reflected by Ava's claim that only her sister, Ossie, can understand the changes which have occurred in her as well as by her critical account of her rescue by male figures, in which her own heroic efforts to escape are downplayed and she is treated "like a trophy alligator he [the park ranger who rescues her] had just trussed and dropped onto the blond wood of his desk for these hunters' perusal" (385).

The ambiguity surrounding Ava's reflections on the meaning of her journey through the swamplands raises the question of why Russell's American Eve must fall in order to be redeemed. As grown-up Ava concludes, after returning to her family and moving away from Swamplandia!, her life appears to lose its vigor, failing to fulfill the promise of the maternal power she gains in her tussle with the female alligator: "Ossie and I attended a public school in the fall where they made us wear uniforms in the dull sepias and dark crimsons of fall leaves, these colors that were nothing like the fire of my alligator's skin. But things can be over in horizontal time and just beginning in your body, I'm learning. Sometimes the memory of that summer feels like a spore in me, a seed falling through me. Kiwi is sympathetic, but Ossie is the only one who I can really talk to about this particular descent" (395). Ava's description of the memory of her thirteen-year-old self as a living thing inside her might best be understood as a form of embodied memory passed down to her through the generations. In her 2015 study of second-generation memory, Nina Fischer suggests that the body is intrinsically linked to this memory work, which can be both literal and metaphorical (27). "Body memory," Fischer adds, can be both visible and invisible in form: "Family resemblances, scars, or tattoos give memory a physical form, but body memory can also be internal. For instance, a certain trigger can unleash physiological reactions or obsessive behaviors related to the past" (99). The spore, a type of asexually reproducing seed, suggests that the memory of her journey has a life of its own, with the ability to reproduce, multiply, and grow inside her over the years. This reading of her past memory suggests that Ava has two dimensions of body memory—external and internal—represented by the scar left from the bite marks on her leg and invisible marks left by the rape. It also explains the simultaneous obsessive behavior with her mother and sister, whose clothes she desperately clings to while drowning, and the more empowering connection she has shortly thereafter with her mother's spirit when she propels herself away from the attacking alligator.

Ava's inheritance of embodied memory from generations of women living in Florida's wilderness connects her to previous Cold War adaptations of the American Eve myth. In departing from nineteenth-century variations of the American Eve as an innocent woman, divorced from the suffering and experience of frontiersmen, Russell's project is in harmony with Linda Hogan's critical appraisal of race relations and the United States' colonial past. Her modern American Eve also resolves the issues at stake in O'Dell's earlier work by usefully drawing attention to the dangers of applying a male perspective of adventure and survival. In this respect, her work is beneficial in more directly attacking white-male fantasies about the frontier and considering the responsibility of women as storytellers, who bear the burden of passing on the histories untold by these myths. As I will go on to show, the physical manifestations of memory that occur through the American Eve's confrontation with national history take a related but different form in the literary figure of the virgin girl. Rooted in the virgin land myth that was revived by American studies founder Henry Nash Smith during the 1950s, the virgin girl bears a striking resemblance to the American Eve at her lowest point, the moments when she is "beaten, shot, betrayed, [and/or] abandoned" (Lewis, *American Adam* 128). While the physical traces of this abuse are narrated through the body itself, the role of the virgin girl as an active agent in control of her own narrative remains pivotal to these contemporary retellings of a classic myth.

CHAPTER 3

From Virgin Land to Virgin Girl

Eden, Paradise, the Golden Age, and the idyllic garden . . . a resurrection of the lost state of innocence that the adult abandons when he joins the world of competitive self-assertion; and all this possible because, at the deepest psychological level, the move to America was experienced as the daily reality of what has become its single dominating metaphor: regression from the cares of adult life and a return to the primal warmth of womb or breast in a feminine landscape.

—Annette Kolodny, *The Lay of the Land*

The previous chapter discussed how novelists reinvented the American Adam myth in order to recognize the role women played in the formation of the United States. The youthful and daring American Eve figures, unlike their male predecessors, grapple with the history of colonization and must deal with this painful past before securing a space for themselves in the New World. Such struggles set them apart from the happy-go-lucky male youth who set out unaware of this history, and who were indeed created in large part to make it appear as if such a history never existed at all. The female figures that arose from such revisionist efforts complement the much darker narratives that emerged from the virgin land myth. As I will show, both myths inspired feminist narratives that would challenge the white, male orientation of previous versions of these national myths, including the Cold War interpretations popularized by the myth and symbol school. However, the transformation of the virgin land myth into the virgin girl figure would more directly challenge the colonial implications embedded within U.S. national myths, especially the belief that there was a garden awaiting Americans and that this garden would have the power to rejuvenate all those who entered, leaving them in a perpetual state of innocence. The virgin girl figure departs from such an idealized depiction of the American frontier by underscoring the havoc that men have wreaked on the land and returning to many of the same issues that resulted from the United States' expansion policies during the nineteenth century as well as the lasting impact of these policies on Native peoples. As the name "virgin girl" implies, the girls that appear in novels concerned with the virgin land myth draw on the very same ideological constructions that made the original myth so powerful—that is, they understand women as weak and vulnerable, pure and innocent, beautiful and alluring. If a grown woman is perceived to have these traits by the men who desire her, then all the more so for the young girls that populate these narratives. Like the "mother" figure that American literary and feminist critic Annette Kolodny describes in relation to the land (22), these girls are seen as taboo.[1] To desire the virgin and to act on that desire is nothing less than scandalous.

The virgin girl differs from the American Eve in other respects as well. Drawing on the original associations with the virgin land myth, the virgin girl is often connected with nature, imperial conquest, and nostalgia. As Henry Nash Smith suggests in his 1950 study, the virgin land myth revolves around these very same issues. Smith charts the way in which the land beyond the frontier was first imagined as a lush paradise akin to the Garden of Eden and later as a prim and proper garden, perfect for farmers prepared to homestead and make a fortune off the fertile soil. In an effort to further develop these images of the West as a land of opportunity, Americans created tales about explorers, mountaineers, and other male figures who first charted and later settled these sparsely populated areas. Such men emerged as leaders and protectors, who could guide those less capable through the wilderness and past the threats that it harbored. In contrast to the male figures in Smith's study, the virgin girl reveals the perspective of those most deeply impacted by the virgin land myth: American Indians. The virgin land myth, as my brief synopsis demonstrates, is a narrative that contributed to the power of white, male colonizers. Ultimately, it allowed U.S. citizens to justify westward expansion in order to expand their empire and increase the prosperity of the young nation. The primary purpose of the virgin girl figure is to dismantle the very myth that perpetuated the denial of those marginalized through the colonization of Native land. While there is some acknowledgment of the U.S. government's transgression of Native rights and the failure to uphold treaties, these concessions are often limited.

The novels I use as case studies in this chapter demonstrate the way in which the virgin girl figure allowed U.S. citizens from the second half of the twentieth century to the present to unravel the very myth that captured Smith's attention for over a decade. Using Smith's definition and description of the virgin land myth as a guide, I explore the way that nature, empire, and nostalgia—the three defining traits of the virgin land myth according to Smith—converge in this modern female figure. Just like her real-life counterpart, the virgin girl is "off limits" for male adults due to her young age, and it is this very taboo that renders her both desirous and exotic. Drawing on literary, educational, psychological, and political ideas regarding girlhood, the authors examined in this chapter formulate scenarios that parallel the colonizer and colonized relationship between the United States and American Indians, including abusive relationships that involve domestic violence and rape. While these incidents would appear to preclude the virgin girl from the right to her epithet, it is the disparity between the reality of this figure's circumstances and the myths that make her desirable as a body to conquer that are relevant. The virgin girl's frequent inability to speak about these events for herself mimics the position of the colonized. Drawing on the United States' colonial history, authors question the assumptions inherent in the country's national mythology and insist that power dynamics which perpetuate values and narratives which privilege the few while disempowering the many must be abolished. Such counternarratives are not inherently anti-American; rather, they seek to find ways to question past wrongs in search of a better future.

What further relates my examples to one another is a shared investment in the Cold War interpretations of the virgin land myth. As in my previous chapter, each author is responding to the specific political climate that emerged in the 1950s and that continues to impact U.S. citizens in the twenty-first century. It is no coincidence, for example, that Louise Erdrich's *The Plague of Doves* (2008), a novel that engages with post-9/11 desires for vengeance, is set in the 1960s, a time when many American Indians began fighting for civil rights and combating Cold War policies that left them even more disempowered than they had been previously. Nor is it an accident that Jeffrey Eugenides's 1993 best seller, *The Virgin Suicides*, returns to small-town suburbia, a hallmark image of 1950s family life that underwent substantial criticism in later years. These scenarios put the "cold" in Cold War, for they are indeed dark, desperate, and horrifying places for the characters that live in them. While the ability to navigate the cultural expectations and social limitations of these societies varies for each girl, the pattern suggests the depth of each author's political awareness and a shared concern with the United States' rise to a position of global power. The virgin girl therefore becomes a potent figure for those concerned with the United States' former land policies and the continued mistreatment of American Indians, a history that further hints at dark possibilities as the United States rapidly widened its global influence following World War II.

From Virgin Land to Virgin Girl

Vladimir Nabokov's *Lolita* (1955) presents an intriguing case of the emergence of the virgin girl figure with its depiction of incestuous love. A powerful and dark exploration of 1950s American culture, Nabokov does not hold back as he exposes the vices of his adopted nation. Indeed, when Nabokov began sending the manuscript to publishers, he warned one editor of its controversial content by asking, "Would you be interested in publishing a timebomb that I have just finished putting together?" (qtd. in Colapinto). First published in Paris in 1955, the book was indeed like a "time bomb," exploding on the literary scene after its release in the United States in 1958 and shocking those who dared to read it (Colapinto). As journalist Pierre Berton notes in a 1958 interview with Nabokov, critics claimed that *Lolita* was "a joke on our national cant about youth" and "a cutting exposé of chronic American adolescence and shabby materialism."[2] Though some reviewers doubted his motives in depicting American culture, the native Russian was in fact a careful surveyor of the American landscape and the people who populated it thanks to several road trips with his wife, Véra, and drew inspiration from the natural topography of the American West and the myths associated with it when crafting his narrative about a taboo romance between a middle-aged man and an adolescent girl. Protagonist and narrator Humbert Humbert's dream girl is tall, with long brown limbs and dark eyes, and a honey-colored midriff that makes him sizzle with sexual desire. A mere twelve years old when the novel begins, Dolores Haze, or Lolita as she is referred to throughout the narrative, appears for the first time in the backyard garden of Charlotte Haze, her mother and Humbert's soon-to-be second wife. Lolita's placement in the garden links her to Humbert's past love, Annabel, but is also an expression of her grounding in nature, infusing her with sexual potency and making her as desirable as the apple in the story of Adam and Eve. Her status as a young virgin is another connection to the virgin land myth that Smith identifies in his work, and Nabokov frequently alludes to this myth in order to present a critique of 1950s U.S. culture—admittedly a critique he never acknowledged was present in *Lolita*.[3] This myth is both culturally and historically specific, drawing on the same psychological and literary tropes that informed the work of myth and symbol scholars.

Nabokov's focus on the relationship between a grown man and a prepubescent child in *Lolita* immediately associates him with the myth and symbol scholars, particularly those who claimed the United States must "grow up" and mature. In *Love and Death in the American Novel* (1960), a work that contributed to the beyond innocence debate, Leslie Fiedler claims that a "'boyish' theme recurs with especial regularity in American fiction," in which a young male protagonist sets forth in the wilderness with the aid of an older male companion (182). While Fiedler actually spends very little time considering the role of the child in American literature,[4] he does support his thesis that American literature has featured protagonists in a state of arrested development: that, in short, the characters (primarily men) are stuck in a permanent state of boyhood. Fiedler's insistence that American literature is in the midst of a crisis parallels the anxiety present in *Lolita*. Trapped as a result of his unrequited love for Annabel, Humbert is unable to move beyond his adolescent love and continues to be thwarted in his attempts to foster socially sanctioned adult relationships. In this respect, the initial critics of the book were right about the significance of Nabokov's masterpiece, for it was indeed "a cutting exposé of chronic American adolescence and shabby materialism."

While *Lolita*'s discussion of incest is disturbing for many readers, it presents a narrative of maturation, albeit a brutal and forced one, that parallels the concerns of 1950s scholars. Lolita is only twelve when Humbert becomes a lodger at the Haze household, and the novel ends when she is seventeen. During this time, Lolita both physically and mentally matures. When Humbert first meets her, he wonders if she has experienced "the Mystery of the Menarche" (47). The answer to his question is revealed shortly after Humbert has sex with Lolita for the first time: "Presently, making a sizzling sound with her lips, she started complaining of pains, said she could not sit, said I had torn something inside her" (141). As Robert Levine notes, Lolita is experiencing the pains common during a woman's menstrual cycle, an observation supported by the fact that not long after, Humbert purchases "sanitary pads" along with other items for his moody charge (472). In addition to physically maturing, Lolita must also learn how to outwit Humbert in order to extricate herself from her terrible situation. As Lolita matures, she grows increasingly crafty. Not only does she find friends and collaborators like her sexually experienced friend Mona, she finds ways to manipulate Humbert. Money, Lolita (and later Humbert) realizes, is a path toward freedom. Lolita takes advantage of Humbert's dependency on her and manages to turn sexual favors into opportunities for earning money.[5] When Humbert discovers Lolita's cash, she finds better ways to hide her money from her intrusive guardian.

As a consequence of her duplicitous nature, later Nabokov scholars debate the extent of Lolita's culpability for her misfortunes. For instance, in her well-known 1998 essay on *Lolita* and the woman reader, Sarah Herbold suggests that Lolita is not merely a passive participant in the sexual games that occur between her and Humbert but rather an initiator of them: "Lolita . . . is also not only a sexy creature but also as sophisticated and wily as Humbert, and perhaps more so" (80). Herbold scandalously proposes that even before Humbert consummates their relationship, Lolita gains equal amounts of sexual pleasure from their interactions:

"Because she seems to be a mere girl and a mere character, who is 'veiled' by her apparent innocence, she [Lolita] gets to have fun at less risk and cost to herself, and at greater expense to Humbert" (82). Page Stegner, a historian of the American West, is similarly suspect of Lolita's actions, adding that Nabokov's protagonist is a "rather common, unwashed little girl whose interests are entirely plebian, though, in certain respects, precocious" (114). Leland de la Durantaye, a writer and literary critic, challenges the accusations of unsympathetic scholars like Herbold and Stegner, urging readers to recall that Lolita is terribly unhappy during her three-year road trip with Humbert, something that Humbert himself reveals when he confesses that Lolita "sobs in the night—every night, every night—the moment I feigned sleep" (176). De la Durantaye proposes that scholars are able to ignore this quote for two reasons: they insist that Lolita is not innocent; and they turn Lolita into a symbol for something else (180).

De la Durantaye's critique is telling in that it hits upon an important aspect of the narrative: Humbert's dependence on myth. Much invested in the idea of Lolita, it is Humbert far more than Nabokov who wants readers to forget that she is in fact a real child. He often speaks for Lolita and avoids considering her feelings, much more interested in his own desire and his fantasy of their forbidden love. Indeed, his first description of the child turns her into a fantastic mythical creature: the nymphet. Having just bombarded his reader with his academic credentials, Humbert gives a full description of the nymphet: "Between the age limits of nine and fourteen there occur maidens who, to certain bewitched travelers, twice or many times older than they, reveal their true nature which is not human, but nymphic (that is, demoniac); and these chosen creatures I propose to designate as 'nymphets'" (16). Vladimir Alexandrov notes that Humbert's choice of demoniac as a clarification is no accident, as it is meant to refer to the "realm of the daemonic" or "a realm somewhere between the divine and the mortal" (qtd. in Durantaye 191).

Nabokov's construction of a middle-aged European well versed in psychology and literature (Humbert has a degree in English literature) allows him to incorporate popular 1950s myths into his novel. Specifically, the virgin land myth enables Nabokov to complicate an already complex text further by alluding to U.S. impe-

rial power during the Cold War. It was in 1941 that *Life* magazine founder Henry Luce published his famous essay calling for the
United States to intervene in the "European war" (that is, World
War II) and named the twentieth century the "American Century"
(61, 64). Luce's call to his fellow Americans is representative of the
growing belief in American exceptionalism at the time, or the view
of the nation's fundamental difference from the rest of the world,
which would become a staple of Cold War rhetoric. As the U.S. government attempted to remake the world in its own image during
the Cold War, it adopted the popular parent-child metaphor commonly used to justify the imperialistic agenda of powerful nations.
As many postcolonial theorists have noted, this metaphor describes
the relationship between colonizers and the colonized as a paternal one, where the colonizer/father benevolently aids the colonized/
children in the ruling of their nation's domestic affairs. Using this
parent-child metaphor, empires justify the colonization of other nations, since these nations are deemed incapable of governing themselves.

The myth and symbol scholars contributed to the United States'
fight for global dominance in their presentation of a homogeneous
American culture, but they did not wholeheartedly buy into the
American rhetoric popular at the time, as Donald Pease suggests
in *The New American Exceptionalism* (2009). While it is true that
some American studies scholars collaborated with the U.S. government in developing a Cold War rhetoric that supported the
nation's interests abroad, many others stood firm in their critical positions about the nation's actions—indeed, there were numerous examples of academics who were politically aligned with
the left, including the influential scholar F. O. Matthiessen, a dangerous position during the time of McCarthyism. Pease overlooks
this critical activity, instead arguing that most scholars in the field
were willing collaborators in the government's efforts to create "a
mythology of national uniqueness out of whose narrative themes
U.S. citizens constructed imaginary relations to the cold war state"
(11). In a much earlier keynote speech at the American Studies
Association, former association president Elaine Tyler May challenges this long-held assumption about the founders by younger
practitioners in the field, and instead suggests that the myth and
symbol scholars, for the most part, "were not writing a celebratory

scholarship" (188). She uses Smith and Marx as examples, explaining how both depicted national myths about the western frontier in an "extremely negative light" (188).

Nabokov's relationship to the academy suggests the plausibility of reading *Lolita* in relation to this critical backlash against the nation's prevailing national narratives. Nabokov began his teaching career in 1941 at Wellesley College. Hired to teach comparative literature, Nabokov would eventually found the college's Department of Russian Literature, of which he was the only member. In *Vladimir Nabokov: The American Years* (1991), Nabokov biographer Brian Boyd describes this period in the author's life as being plagued with writing challenges. Due to the popularity of his courses, Nabokov often had trouble finding time for his literary pursuits (Boyd 170). In speaking of the long gestation period for *Lolita*, Nabokov asserts, "I found it no longer physically possible to combine scientific research with lectures, belles-lettres, and *Lolita* (for she was on her way—a painful birth, a difficult baby)" (*Speak, Memory* 47). The constant tension between Nabokov's teaching and writing careers reveals the extent to which Nabokov immersed himself in academic culture. Furthermore, his founding of Wellesley's Russian department during the McCarthy era is no mere coincidence; rather, it marks the emerging interest in Russian culture in an effort to protect U.S. interests, a development that might be likened to the increased interest in Arab cultures in the aftermath of the September 11, 2001, terrorist attacks. If Nabokov was not directly working with myth and symbol scholars, he was likely well aware of the nation's political interest in the university and shared some of their concerns about the nation's imperialistic agenda.

Nabokov would return to the original features of Smith's virgin land myth in *Lolita*, only to turn this myth and symbol scholarship on its head. Through the interactions of his characters, he offers a critique of 1950s Cold War culture, mainly by recovering the previously silenced voices of women and American Indians, who only play a small role (if any) in the Cold War articulations of the virgin land myth. He begins by infusing his work with popular psychological beliefs regarding female adolescence and using these as a way to link Lolita to the primitivism Smith originally associated with his male heroes. As noted earlier, Humbert refers to Lolita as "demoniac," reminding readers that psychologists have long considered the teenage girl to be monstrous. A girl's sexual development was an uncomfortable topic for early developmental psychologists such as G. Stanley Hall and Havelock Ellis. Much of this discomfort stemmed from the fact that psychologists traditionally used the girl as a point of reference for male development. While young boys go through various stages, including a "feminine stage" and a "savage stage," girls remain relatively unchanged as they grow into mature womanhood. These myths of development held an enormous amount of power over psychologists, even when there was sufficient evidence to disprove them. Crista DeLuzio, a cultural historian of American childhood and family, notes in her excellent 2007 study that "reconciling the concepts of femininity and adolescence," the latter being a male construct, was the primary difficulty faced by psychologists of the nineteenth and early twentieth centuries (2).

By naming Lolita "demoniac," Humbert attempts to find ways to keep the child in an arrested state of development; but as readers of *Lolita* know, Lolita is constantly changing and moving away from her state of nymphethood. In contrast to psychological myths regarding female development, Nabokov introduces the feral tale in order to draw yet another connection between Lolita and cultural primitivism. Popularized through such famous case studies as the wolf man, the feral tale is about maturation gone awry. More specifically, it is about children who grow up outside of society and the effects this has on their development. One of the earliest cases of a feral child was the "wild child" Victor. First discovered by a local Frenchman in Aveyron, the French government moved Victor to Paris for scientific study and placed him in the custody of Dr. Gaspard Itard, who was charged with the task of determining if the child could be socialized. Victor eventually escaped from his French captors but remained a popular example in the nature-versus-nurture debates. Children's literature scholar Kenneth Kidd explains that cases like Victor are only one of several iterations of the feral tale (87–88). Literary descriptions of wild children, such as Rudyard Kipling's *The Jungle Book* (1894), use the feral tale as a way of defending the colonial project. Kipling and other white authors depict colonized subjects as savage and then suggest that these unruly children need a firm authority figure to oversee them.

The U.S. version of these tales includes the "street rats" of New York City, most of whom were boys. While the girl rarely figures in the feral tale, a few popular cases of feral girls did gain national attention, including the girl called Genie by scientists (Kidd 206–207).

Lolita's appearance and behavior make her a literary descendant of the "wild" street child. In Horatio Alger's *Tattered Tom* (1871), the only book in his series with a female protagonist, the narrator describes the eponymous hero in the following manner: "The child's face was very dark and, as might be expected, dirty; but it was redeemed by a pair of brilliant black eyes, which were fixed upon the young exquisite in an expression half-humorous, half-defiant, as the owner promptly retorted, 'You're another!'" (10). As is typical of Alger's heroes, the child has some physically redeeming features that attract prospective benefactors, in this case her "brilliant black eyes." Yet her poor physical hygiene, coupled with her gender-neutral name, position the child as a tomboy—indeed, the name "Tom" alludes to this aspect of her character. Tom's depiction as a "wild" child is not so different from Lolita. On multiple occasions Humbert comments on Lolita's hygiene, noting, "Although I do love that intoxicating brown fragrance of hers, I really think she should wash her hair once in a while" (43). He declares her speech "vulgar," comprising words that include "revolting," "super," "luscious," "goon," and "drip" (65). Despite the coarseness and the grimy limbs, Humbert cannot resist Lolita's underlying childish beauty. He adds that "all this gets mixed up with the exquisite stainless tenderness seeping through the musk and the mud, through the dirt and the death, oh God, oh God" (44).

The use of psychological myths like the feral tale in an American setting provides a racial undertone to the text. American variants of this myth, namely the popular Horatio Alger dime novels about "street rats" and "city urchins," often cast crude children who were later civilized by a white savior. These children frequently had names that associated them with immigrants who were the target of racism, such as the Irish and Italians, and provide an important connection to the politically charged climate of 1950s America, a time when race was a volatile issue for the U.S. government. Interested in winning over recently decolonized nations to democracy yet still plagued by racism at home, the United

States struggled to present an image of itself that would satisfy its ambitions abroad while still appeasing racist policymakers and citizens back home. The entanglement of the domestic and the foreign in cases such as the U.S. involvement in Vietnam signaled what Amy Kaplan calls in her 2002 study the "anarchy of empire," namely, the "breakdown or defiance of the monolithic system of order that empire aspires to impose on the world, an order reliant on clear divisions between metropolis and colony, colonizer and colonized, national and international spaces, the domestic and the foreign" (*Anarchy of Empire* 13).

While the myth and symbol scholars mostly ignored the topic of race, Nabokov utilizes myth in *Lolita* to address this silence, bringing to the forefront issues regarding domestic and foreign politics debated during the Cold War. Lolita's brown body and her natural aptitude for physical activity, for example, can be read as a reference to the nation's mythical savage: the Vanishing American. A popular figure in early twentieth-century literature, American Indians were often idealized and depicted as the last of a vanishing people in order to represent the kind of "indigenous, masculine Americanism" that was popular in literary works such as James Fenimore Cooper's *Leatherstocking* series (Kidd 101). These novels promoted the myth of the "Vanishing American" in order to suppress the continued disempowerment of American Indians who were the victims of U.S. expansion, a fact that the myth of the virgin land also attempts to repress. Throughout his novel, Nabokov's virgin girl expresses an interest in this "vanishing" culture, first when she begs Humbert to purchase little trinkets from a souvenir shop selling American Indian wares (148) and later on through her preference for a pair of brown moccasins (174, 187, 208).[6] In portraying Lolita first as a marginalized brown body and then as a white, middle-class consumer, Nabokov casts his virgin girl in a double role that troubles the dominant narratives of U.S. empire, especially those popular at a time when the United States was just ascending to a position of world power.

Her guardian, however, subscribes to more conventional assumptions about positions of power and views Lolita as a helpless child who is akin to a colonized subject. In depicting Humbert's relationship with Lolita in this manner, Nabokov draws on the common association between children and colonized subjects. As children's literature scholar Perry Nodelman remarks in his 1992 essay on colonization and children's literature, adults often treat children in this demeaning way (29).[7] Courtney Weikle-Mills, another expert in the field of children's literature, adds that the metaphor of childhood is frequently used to wield power over marginalized groups, including children themselves (4). Precisely because she is aligned with those historically disempowered by the child metaphor, Lolita is rendered silent for much of the narrative. Her identity is mutable as she takes on the roles of orphan, American Indian, and monstrous adolescent. Silence, one of the main techniques that colonizers use to reinforce their beliefs about the other, makes it easier to believe in the radical difference between the other and the self. Yet Nabokov constructs his narrative in such a way that Lolita does manage to express her indignation at her mistreatment. Her cutting remarks about her relationship with Humbert begin to dissolve the fantasy of the romantic couple that Humbert creates as narrator. In one passage, Lolita sarcastically refers to her captor as *"Dad"* (112; emphasis in original), and in another she retorts, "I ought to call the police and tell them you raped me" (141). Since Humbert always filters Lolita's words, often dismissing these attacks by referring to her moody nature, it is easy to ignore these verbal assaults. In order to ensure the reader pays attention to her protests and pleas, Nabokov employs other techniques that lend Lolita the power she needs to counteract Humbert's intoxicating myths, most notably through bodily illness.

Nabokov incorporates scenes of sexual conquest that remind readers of the rape of the natural landscape during U.S. westward expansion and the exploitation of Native peoples. Perhaps the most explicit allusion to U.S. colonization of American Indians is the scene where Lolita develops a serious illness and has to go to the hospital. At first Humbert resists relinquishing his control over her, but he is ultimately unable to ignore the bodily signs of her illness:

> Hysterical little nymphs might, I knew, run up all kinds of temperature—even exceeding a fatal count. And I would have given her a sip of hot spiced wine, and two aspirins, and kissed the fever away, if, upon an examination of her lovely uvula, one of the gems of her body, I had not seen that it was a burning

red. I undressed her. Her breath was bittersweet. Her brown
rose tasted of blood. She was shaking from head to toe. She
complained of a painful stiffness in the upper vertebrae—and I
thought of poliomyelitis as any American parent would. Giving
up all hope of intercourse, I wrapped her up in a laprobe and
carried her into the car. (240)

Humbert presents himself as the concerned parent, but his final
statement that he must "giv[e] up all hope of intercourse" exposes
him as a rapist. Like Humbert's acknowledgment of his real relationship to Lolita, his descriptions of her feverish body also expose
Lolita's suffering. Humbert neglects her pain until it reaches an in-
human level—as Humbert notes, a nymph's fever can often reach
a "fatal count." Moreover, Humbert's selection of "brown rose" to
describe Lolita's genitals is a variation of one of his pet names for
her, "brown flower," referring to Lolita's suntanned skin (151). By
alluding to his earlier use of the pet name, Humbert recalls Lolita's association with American Indian women, who, like Lolita,
suffered at the hands of colonizers. Like the Vanishing American
figure, Lolita disappears shortly after this, but not before revealing the harm done to her by Humbert's repeated violations. The
repetition of the color red and the explicit mention of blood breaks
the spell of Humbert's myth and reveals the violence of his conquest. In this moment, Lolita, the mythical virgin girl, aligns with
the U.S. myth of the virgin land and reveals that both myths are
really shams.

Lolita's vanishing act in the hospital scene is just one of many
moments that instill panic in Humbert, who dreads losing power
over his ward. Yet her vanishing and subsequent reappearance as
a grown woman also compel Humbert to consider the emotions
that the loss of Lolita's childhood awakens for him. "Nostalgia,"
a term that is broken down into its etymological roots of "longing" and "return home," is often associated with a visceral sickness brought on by an individual's yearning for a lost object, especially his or her homeland. While Humbert's longing can easily be
associated with his nostalgia for prewar Europe and his childhood
love, Annabel, scenes of nostalgia are also directed specifically at
Nabokov's U.S. audience. These scenes invoke images of the American landscape in the few places where one might still discover

the beauty of the untamed countryside. Recapturing the allure of
the West, these rural scenes summon Americans' longing for the
shared past of American heroes like Daniel Boone and Leatherstocking. They are spaces, moreover, that sharply contrast with the
material culture that Lolita adores and Humbert despises, a world
of commodities that 1950s Americans would find all too familiar.

Two scenes in particular capture this nostalgia for the American past. The first is when Humbert attempts to make love to Lolita outdoors. This outing is cut short when Humbert discovers a
pair of children with "unblinking dark eyes" observing his and Lolita's naked bodies (169). Humbert nevertheless interprets this moment as one of beauty, worthy of reflection and nostalgia: "The dis-
appointment I must now register . . . should in no wise reflect on
the lyrical, epic, tragic but never Arcadian American wilds. They
are beautiful, heart-rendingly beautiful, those wilds, with a quality of wide-eyed, unsung, innocent surrender that my lacquered,
toy-bright Swiss villages and exhaustively lauded Alps no longer
possess" (168). A few lines later Humbert bemoans the same wild
beauty he has praised, concluding that the combination of "poison-
ous plants," "nameless insects," and "potential snakes" all make
outdoor frolics with Lolita impossible (168). Humbert's land is
therefore identified with his mistress: both are beautiful and dangerous at the same time. Indeed, his first description of the land,
with its "wide-eyed, unsung, innocent surrender," could just as easily be a description of Lolita.

Humbert's display of affection and subsequent disillusionment
with the "American wilds" returns readers to the scenes of the
West made familiar through stories of western heroes. In a time of
revived popular interest in these tales—stories that were valued
for their ability to allegorically allude to the United States' struggle with communism and secure a vision of the world in which
the United States is always victorious (Engelhardt 70–71)—the
reference to the untamed wilderness of the American West would
not be lost on Nabokov's 1950s readers. Nabokov attempts to upset this expectation by inserting the "bad guy" in place of the noble American hero. The substitution of the villain for the hero de-
stabilizes the myth of the virgin land, placing the innocence of
this lauded space into question, an observation that Humbert also
makes by acknowledging the "poison" that peppers the land in the

form of dangerous flora and fauna. This acknowledgment, coupled
with the act of defiling the young Lolita, short-circuits the readers'
fantasy of a preindustrialized America.

The second scene that evokes longing for an innocent America
occurs in the novel's closing, when Humbert attempts to reconcile
with his misdeeds. Humbert claims that he finally understands
how he has wronged Lolita. Yet this revelation only continues to do
violence to the young girl's memory. Humbert passionately cries,
"Reader! What I heard was but the melody of children at play,
nothing but that . . . and then I knew that the hopelessly poignant
thing was not Lolita's absence from my side, but the absence of her
voice from that concord" (308). Humbert laments the fact that Lolita cannot share in the innocent laughter of the children's voices.
His full description of the idyllic scene speaks of "vivid laughter"
and the "clatter of a toy wagon," all of which combine in a musical
symphony at one with the sounds of nature in this small mining
town. Nothing, it seems, is more natural than a child at play, and
nothing more unnatural than a child forced to abandon this play.
Humbert's image of the child at play is deeply sentimental and
recalls Romantic poet William Wordsworth's "Ode: Intimations
of Immortality from Recollections of Early Childhood" (1807), in
which young children frolic and exist for the pleasure of their ador-
ing parents.[8] Such an image is divorced from reality, and not only
that of Lolita; yet it remains powerfully seductive as it invites the
reader to imagine not only a simpler period of life but a simpler
mode of living.

There is no doubt that this seductive image would touch the
hearts of Nabokov's postwar readers. The happy cries of the children form an image of peace and tranquility. This, coupled with
Humbert's lament that Lolita's voice is not among them, is a reminder that America, too, was forced to "grow up." And, like Lolita, the growing up was a painful process. Men went away to war
and grew up because they *had* to do so, and women helped run the
U.S. economy in their absence because they also *had* to do so. Europe "robbed" Americans of their innocence. This is the myth, at
any rate, with which Humbert leaves his readers. The trouble with
this myth is that it forgets the real pain and violence of the little
girl that the entire novel is supposedly about. These moments drift
away into the background as the more seductive image of a hurt

and wronged America comes to the forefront. Yet there is a touch of irony to the image of a vulnerable America—after all, it is the perpetrator who procures the image. Nabokov thus leaves his readers with a final choice: accept the myth given by a man who has committed innumerable crimes, or reject this myth in favor of a less glamorous picture of the nation.

Through his transformation of the virgin land myth into the virgin girl figure, Nabokov manages to counter the image of a unified America. Women and racial minorities, whose stories are often obscured in U.S. national narratives, return in the haunting tale of Lolita's coming-of-age. Nabokov's *Lolita* is therefore best described as an antimythological novel, a story that purges readers of the sickness associated with Cold War conformism and victory culture. This purgation is captured in the closing scene when Humbert becomes ill from "an attack of abominable nausea" (307). Like Humbert, 1950s Americans also burned with a feverish desire—in this case to combat communism and redeem the world in America's image. A reading of *Lolita* could not guarantee a cure of this illness, but it made a heroic effort to draw readers' attention to the negative effects of mythmaking. Nabokov's final message, then, might best be summed up as follows: Americans must indeed "grow up" and mature, but they must first consider the price of innocence and the rural playgrounds—that "heart-rendingly beautiful" American landscape—of the heroes of the American West.

Immaculate Deaths in American Suburbia

Jeffrey Eugenides's debut novel, *The Virgin Suicides* (1993), revisits the American suburbs touched on in *Lolita*, a place Humbert quickly flees when Lolita's mother, Charlotte, dies. Reviewers of the novel declare that it is a "vivid and dreamlike" narrative filled with spellbinding, lyrical prose ("Jeffrey Eugenides: The Art of Fiction"), and some even suggest that Nabokov, the master of style, deeply influenced Eugenides.[9] Traces of this influence can be seen throughout *The Virgin Suicides*. Not only does the novel's narrative structure mirror Humbert's confession about his insidious crime, but the male protagonists also attempt to construct a history of the five Lisbon girls, the virgins of the novel's title, only to end up caught in their own desire. Told in the first-person

plural, *The Virgin Suicides* questions the myth of the American
Dream by using the same mythmaking techniques that made this
dream so alluring to native and prospective citizens. Eugenides
follows in Nabokov's footsteps by critiquing this myth and invit-
ing his reader to make an ethical choice that involves questioning the policies and practices of the U.S. government. The author
takes this critique a step further, though, by addressing domestic
problems that gained international attention during the Cold War:
namely, U.S. racial politics and the policies intended to "contain"
ethnic minorities.

As in *Lolita*, Eugenides's novel transforms the virgin land myth
into a tale about young virgin girls, but it departs from many of
Nabokov's original techniques for alluding to the United States'
imperial power. First, the author does not "darken" his female
characters. In fact, they each have distinct European features—
blonde hair, blue eyes, light skin. Even their surname, Lisbon, de-
notes European origin. Second, Eugenides's selection of Detroit for
his setting, a city notorious for its racial conflict (e.g., the 1943
and 1967 race riots), provides the novel with a racial undertone.
Given the heightened anxiety in regard to ethnic adolescent gangs
and youth violence more generally in the 1990s, the selection of a
Detroit suburb allows Eugenides to address many of the underlying issues erased by such national myths as the virgin land.[10]
Third, and most importantly, Eugenides's graphic descriptions
of the girls' deaths indicate a deep desire for containment. While
"containment culture" is generally associated with the Cold War,
Eugenides demonstrates that similar fears about the stability of
U.S. culture appeared after the fall of the Berlin Wall. Unresolved
issues about race that emerged during the United States' war
against communism returned once again, sparking conversations
about U.S. national narratives that supported the nation's imperial practices. This last point, I argue, is what brings Eugenides's
critique of the United States into direct conversation with issues
underlying the virgin land myth.

Eugenides alludes to the desire to contain violence most explicitly in two contrasting scenes involving the Lisbon girls' bathroom.
The first scene occurs when a dinner guest, Peter Sissen, is forced
to use the upstairs bathroom, which is generally used exclusively

by the girls, because the downstairs one is occupied.[11] As he as-
cends the stairs, Sissen uses this opportunity to thoroughly explore the private space of the girls and observes the mundane objects within the bathroom as if he were a devoted worshipper. One
of the most prized objects in the bathroom shrine is a freshly used
tampon, which Sissen declares "wasn't gross but a beautiful thing"
(10). The narrators' detailed description of the object is charged
with desire, as Sissen emphasizes that the tampon was "like a
modern painting or something" (10). In this passage, the tampon,
a taboo object, transforms into a work of art, a transformation that
is in part due to the fact that it has literally been inside one of the
girls. However, it is also an object of containment. Intended to hide
blood, the tampon can be beautiful only because, as the narrators
relate, it is merely "spotted" with blood rather than soaked with it.
The tampon expresses a desire to contain the blood, and thus the
violence, that the girls expose through their suicides, an act that
becomes a metaphorical stain on the suburban community.

In contrast to this relatively clean and hygienic scene, Eugenides turns to a dramatic suicide attempt involving the youngest Lisbon daughter, Cecilia, that transforms Sissen's dream
world of perfumes, makeup, and other accessories and hygienic
products into a nightmare. When one of the other narrators, Paul
Baldino, first discovers her lifeless body, he is horrified by the spec-
tacle of blood that greets him. Entering the bathroom with the
expectation of finding a naked yet very much alive Lisbon sister,
Baldino instead observes Cecilia's suicide tool, a razor blade, floating in the toilet, and the gruesome evidence of her self-mutilation:
a soaked and stained bathroom mat, walls encrusted with drying
blood, and a barely alive Cecilia floating in warm water meant to
quicken the flow of blood from her body. Horrified, Baldino flees
the scene, later claiming that Cecilia really "sprayed the place"
(15) and that her wrists were still "oozing blood" while she lay un-
conscious in the bathtub (13). Baldino's description of the suicide
places an emphasis on its uncontained violence. By far the most
graphic scene in the novel, Cecilia's suicide attempt exposes her
pain in a vividly visual way that shocks those around her. While
her sisters choose less gruesome ways to take their lives such as
gas or sleeping pills, Cecilia does not shy away from opportuni-

ties to disrupt the community's beliefs and expectations about her
and her sisters, marring an otherwise conventional domestic scene
through her defiant acts of rebellion.

Eugenides links these intimate bathroom scenes to larger issues in the community: one narrator declares that "while the suicides lasted, and for some time after, the Chamber of Commerce
worried less about the influx of black shoppers and more about the
outflux of whites" (99). The narrators' comments indicate an anxiety regarding racial homogeneity in the suburbs and might even
be related to fears of "race suicide." Children's literature scholar
Michelle Abate argues that fears about race suicide emerged
during times of declining birth rates for white women and the increase in the immigrant population (6). Young girls who chose to
buck tradition and forgo marriage and child-rearing were perceived as contributors to the problem. As a result of these decisions, Abate argues, "the nation's patriarchal powers worried that
the New Woman would not only destroy the American social fabric
but bring about the 'race suicide' of Anglo-Americans" (51). Abate
bears out that the decisions of young girls were heavily freighted
with social significance. A girl who chose to reject the promises
of domestic "bliss" was stigmatized, much like Cecilia whose odd
behavior, even before the suicide attempts, mark her as different
from her more socially adjusted siblings.[12]

In the early 1990s, the fears that drove the conversation about
race suicide returned to the forefront of U.S. politics through the
explosive LA race riots. Readers may discern the parallels between
the racial division in the fictional Detroit suburb and this historical event, which ignited discussions about race relations in America. National news stations that covered the original Rodney King
crisis described it as a shocking event that ignited "outrage and
public indignation" (R. Jacobs 85). When the four police officers involved were acquitted on April 29, 1992, the papers turned from
addressing senseless police brutality to the racial biases of the
white jury. In the *New York Times*, the jury members, all of whom
hailed from the affluent Simi Valley suburb, were described as living in a community whose very design revealed racial animosity:
"The very layout of the streets in this well-to-do suburb speaks volumes about how unwelcome strangers are here, about how much
safety means to the 100,000 people, most of them white, who have

crossed the mountain range and then the Ventura County line to escape the chaos and discomfort of the people" (qtd. in R. Jacobs 116). ABC News quoted UCLA sociologist Dr. Melvin Oliver, who claimed that "it's where people who don't want the problems of Los Angeles move, and, of course, they tend to be white" (qtd. in R. Jacobs 116). The repeated referral to the tendency of white, middle-class people to flee the urban center of Los Angeles spoke volumes about the structure and purpose of the American suburb. Indeed, the media coverage following the Rodney King decision made these racial divisions newly visible on a national and international scale.

David Pilgrim, a scholar of African American studies and human rights activist, describes the 1990s as a time when "young black males were portrayed as thugs, gangsters, and menaces to society" (530). The descriptions of the Simi Valley suburb, and later coverage of the riots, troubled this stereotype. While the LA race riots were largely depicted as a "black and white issue" at the time, there were multiple ethnic groups involved, including Latinos and Korean Americans. The mainstream media chose to largely ignore the multiethnic nature of the riots and instead characterized the event as a moment of intensified racial tension between whites and blacks. Social theorist Ronald Jacobs explains that reporters followed a rhetorical pattern that involved "contrast[ing] the optimism and prosperity of the 1960s with the apathy and pessimism of the 1990s" (124). The continued insistence on the failure to address racial tension between white and black Americans led to discussions of how race shapes the way one interprets racial violence. Jacobs reveals the conclusions of a focus group, in which "African-American informants interpreted the television images of the uprisings as legitimate protest against racial and economic injustice; white and Latino informants, by contrast, interpreted the events primarily as criminal activities by anti-civil opportunists" (132).

While the events in Los Angeles reinvigorated discussions of racial division in America, they were not the only events of the early 1990s to spotlight racial issues. The U.S. response to the Iraqi invasion of Kuwait renewed stereotypes of Middle Easterners that paralleled the negative criticism of young blacks. Propaganda surrounding the war described the Iraqis as cruel and callous, most famously in the Nayirah testimony, where a fifteen-year-old Kuwait girl described how the Iraqi soldiers removed twenty-two newborns from their incubators and left them to die on the hospital floor. This testimony has since been questioned, and many agree that it was false information, which President Bush eagerly adopted in an effort to "sell" his war.[13] It is clear that Nayirah's description of the Iraqi soldiers, and Bush's continued reference to this testimony in later speeches regarding the Gulf War, helped revive stereotypes about Middle Eastern men. As Edward Said explains in *Orientalism* (1978), these stereotypes are a "Western style for dominating, restructuring, and having authority over the Orient" (3).

As I noted in my reading of *Lolita*, the virgin land myth was first instituted in order to erase issues related to race and gender, as were other national myths popularized in the 1950s. However, the virgin land myth stands apart from these other myths due to its relation to land loss during the period of U.S. westward expansion. Primary features of the virgin land myth, including an emphasis on the fertility of the land and the abundance of wide-open spaces, allowed Americans to colonize Native tribes without the guilt associated with such actions. These myths remained popular as a way of assuaging white guilt and continued to be invoked to revive American patriotism and instill American values within U.S. citizens. In the Cold War context, the virgin land myth aided in the project of creating a single unified narrative about the United States. Returning to the myth of the wide-open spaces of the American West made it easier to glorify American history and remove troublesome "spots" on the U.S. record—stains akin to those Paul Baldino discovers in the girls' bathroom.

The narrators' comments about racial tension in their Detroit suburb indicate that part of what is at stake is territory, or land perceived as belonging to the white suburbanites. The theme of territorial wars becomes most evident in the reaction of the neighborhood to Cecilia's successful suicide, when an intense desire to contain the violence exposed by her death appears. This desire is made evident when the narrators attempt to re-create the girl's final actions: "First came the sound of wind, a rushing we decided later must have been caused by her wedding dress filling with air. This was brief. A human body falls fast" (30). Flinging herself from her bedroom window and landing on the spiked fence outside, Cecilia ensures that her body will be beyond saving. Her death, the narrators assure us, was quick and painless, but Cecilia's suicide is not without its irony. Her body is ruptured by the phallic symbol of the fence post, which "punctured her left breast, [and] traveled through her inexplicable heart" (30–31). The boys do not catch the irony of Cecilia's death and focus instead on the immaculate nature of her untimely end: "The spike had gone through so fast there was no blood on it. It was *perfectly clean* and Cecilia merely seemed balanced on the pole like a gymnast" (31; my emphasis). The boys' description of Cecilia's lifeless body transforms her into the image of the Virgin that she is found clutching after her first suicide attempt. No longer the monstrous, blood-ridden body encountered earlier by Baldino, Cecilia's body can now be read as the immaculate virgin. What is important about the narrators' description is the way that it inserts Cecilia—a girl who fails to live up to Anglo-American expectations for young women—into a narrative acceptable to white suburbanites. Writing their report in retrospect, the boys censor Cecilia's rebellious act and inscribe it into a neat, clean narrative that retroactively tames her.

Yet Cecilia's inclusion in this narrative is always tenuous. Later, when the boys' fathers all pitch in to remove the "dangerous" fence, the blood that the narrators previously claimed was absent reappears. Like much of the narrative, the discovery of the blood has a mythical quality: "'You can see the blood,' Anthony Turkis said, and we looked to see if the blood that hadn't been there at the time of the suicide had arrived after the fact. Some said it was on the third spike, some said the fourth, but it was as impossible as finding the bloody shovel on the back of *Abbey Road* where all the clues proclaimed that Paul was dead" (54–55). The suburbanites' search for the "blood that hadn't been there at the time of the suicide" is almost comical in the way that it resembles the exaggeration of American tall tales. Much like a description of Paul Bunyan's height, Cecilia's bloody spike changes places depending on who is speaking. This obsession with the blood is telling on a number of levels. First, the fear of blood reappearing suggests an anxiety that the repressed facts of Cecilia's suicide will return to haunt the neighborhood. As the narrators suggest throughout their "report," the suburb might be boring but it is thriving. It is

only with the shocking death of one of the Lisbon daughters that
the entire community is jolted into acknowledging their less than
perfect lifestyle and its deterioration in step with the demise of
the Lisbon family. Second, the obsession with blood indicates that
the suburbanites have their own "spots," which taint the neighborhood, and that it is only with Cecilia's death that these bloody
stains rise to the surface.

Eugenides's portrayal of Cecilia as the catalyst for the cataclys-
mic events that follow has clear parallels with the Cold War situation. Indeed, the fact that Cecilia is the one able to tip the other
girls over into depression and ultimately death is reminiscent of
the "domino theory" that prevailed during this time. This rapid
spread of youth depression is described later by the adults as a
"disease" that is capable of being transmitted from one girl to the
next, an apt metaphor given that the number of teenage suicides
skyrocketed by the 1990s and became one of the leading causes of
death for young people (Gaines 7). Even though the narrators dis-
miss this explanation of the girls' deaths, it is a relationship that
they explore further in the aftermath of the girls' suicides. As the
narrators recall this popular interpretation of the mass suicides,
they remark, "More and more, people forgot about the individual
reasons why the girls may have killed themselves, the stress dis-
orders and insufficient neurotransmitters, and instead put the
deaths down to the girls' foresight in predicting decadence. People saw their clairvoyance in the wiped-out elms, the harsh sun-
light, the continuing decline of our auto industry" (244). As the
narrators indicate here, the community begins to see the girls as a
symbol not only of their declining Detroit suburb but of the nation
at large. The community members attribute the sadness that the
boys can't quite understand to "something sick at the heart of the
country [that] had infected the girls," a symptom of living in what
the older community members recognize as a "dying empire" (231).

Eugenides intensifies the connection between the girls, death,
and U.S. empire through multiple descriptions of a massive city
project to control the Dutch elm disease that is killing suburban
trees. One of the most crucial scenes in the novel occurs when the
girls form a chain around the old oak in their front yard. Using
their bodies, the girls refuse to acquiesce to the state mandate to
cut down all infected trees. The girls recognize the absurdity of

cutting down trees in order to save them, arguing that in so doing, the city destroys them anyway. The girls' prediction proves to
be correct, and the suburb becomes a barren, lifeless place as the
city workers remove all sickly trees. Lisa Kirby, an American literary and women's studies scholar, remarks, "When one investigates
the text, it becomes clear that Eugenides's novel is a document
chronicling the isolation and illusion that exists in the postmodern American suburban community" (51). The illusion that Kirby
identifies is the suburb's imagined immunity to the problems that
plague urban Detroit. Recalling the narrators' earlier claim about
the suburbanites' fears of an increasing black population, the new
scenario of the girls fighting to save diseased trees suggests the
city is partly responsible for its own decline.

Eugenides's insertion of this ethical dilemma highlights a poignant distinction that Sunaina Maira makes in her 2009 study of
Muslim American youth in post-9/11 America. Maira argues that
the word "empire" is often glamorized at the expense of those who
suffer under its power. Speaking specifically about the term's use
in the United States, Maira explains the important difference between "empire" and "imperialism," and why contemporary usage
of the former is problematic. "The discourse of empire has shifted,"
she writes, "and the meanings of empire are rewritten and revised
by political conservatives as well as liberals, not just reintroducing
and normalizing the term, but rehabilitating the concept of empire
as a just, necessary, and benevolent force. 'Imperialism,' however,
has been resistant to this makeover and has retained the taint of
an undesirable form of power" (45). Maira's explanation provides
further insight into the suburbanites' interpretation of the girls'
deaths as "an act of foresight." The community literally sees this
death as foreshadowing the decline of their community, a connection that, as Maira indicates, is often made in relation to youth,
who are seen as tokens of the nation's future (14). In light of Maira's reading, Eugenides's earlier use of the word "empire" gains
further significance, as it attests to the desire to "make over" the
cruel acts of the white members of the community, who go to great
lengths to regulate the influx of urban blacks. In seeing the suburb
as a part of and a figure for a larger U.S. empire, the suburbanites
justify the power that they wield.

Eugenides is able to critique the American Dream by presenting readers with one of its most iconic images: the suburb. His deployment of the tropes of the virgin land myth strengthen this critique. Like Nabokov, Eugenides introduces male narrators who are fascinated with young adolescent girls and who produce an elaborate myth regarding the girls they desire. Through the memories of the narrators, now fully grown men, Eugenides captures the potential consequences of mythmaking. This is most evident in the climax of the novel, when the boys sneak out to go over to the girls' home in the middle of the night. The boys, eager for an adventure and emanating with manly pride, are shocked when they discover that the girls' previous request for help was only a ruse. When they discover the first body—a dangling, lifeless corpse that was once Bonnie Lisbon—they observe, "We had never known her. They had brought us here to find that out" (215). As one by one the boys survey the destruction of the remaining Lisbon girls, they regret their selfish desires and ignorance of the extent of the girls' pain. "We knew them now," they conclude after escaping from the coffin of a house (217). Although the hard lesson of death might seem to cure the narrators of their selfishness, it does not stop them from trying to capture the girls even after they are gone in the mysterious tale of their life and death. As men, they admit that even now they long for the girls and imagine them when they are with other female lovers (147).

Much like the adult members of the community, and like Humbert before them, the boys fail to see the part they play in the girls' pain. Intent on fabricating an elaborate story where they play the role of the knight in shining armor, the narrators distort the facts that they collect in order to create a cohesive narrative that will explain the deaths. The girls, for their part, are acutely aware of the roles given to them by the narrators. Although the girls remove any opportunity for a clandestine union, they do fulfill this role in the end. Each girl chooses a death that is as immaculate as Cecilia's successful suicide. Bonnie kills herself with a rope that she ties to the basement rafter; Mary successfully kills herself with sleeping pills; Lux slowly drifts away into oblivion while breathing the noxious gases from her mother's car; and Therese too causes her demise with sleeping pills. The girls' decisions to fulfill the roles given them by the male narrators reveal their understanding of their position as eroticized virgins. Their violent act preserves the myth the boys create yet does so in a way that is disturbingly grotesque. Bonnie's dangling corpse, with the blood pooling in her face and limbs, shatters any erotic image the boys harbor about her and her sisters. It is through the inclusion of violent acts such as these that Eugenides ultimately unravels the myths used to justify actions such as racial segregation.

Even prior to the mass suicides, Eugenides inserts moments of resistance when the girls voice their opposition to their roles as immaculate virgins. Earlier in the novel, Therese remarks, "We just want to live. If anyone would let us" (132). Later, during their confinement after failing to return as a group by their curfew for the Homecoming dance (it is Lux who sneaks off to have sex with Trip, causing this harsh retribution), the girls send messages to their male admirers using the same picture of the Virgin Mary that the medical team found on Cecilia after her first suicide attempt. In selecting the image of the virgin as a representation of their group identity, the girls at once accept the boys' vision of them and align themselves with Cecilia's more radical subjectivity. On these cards, the girls express their innermost feelings. A card from Lux expresses her anger and resentment toward her former boyfriend, Trip Fontaine: *"Tell Trip I'm over him. He's a creep"* (192; emphasis in original). Other messages range from frustration to anger, from "Remember us?" to "Down with unsavory boys" (192). The girls' final message ends with hopeful words and a desperate plea: "In this dark, there will be light. Will you help us?" (193). Having expressed their grievances, the girls revert to a more subdued tone in order to lure the boys to their home. This shift in tone expresses the conflict between male and female perceptions of the world. The girls understand their position in the community much more than the boys who control the narration, and they ultimately accept that they can only communicate their message through a counter-mythmaking.

The spectacular nature of their final demise guarantees the girls a place in the community's memory, even if that memory is always aligned with myth. In her 2009 essay on *The Virgin Suicides*, Debra Shostak, a scholar of contemporary American literature, elaborates on the relationship between myth and history, an important distinction to make both for an understanding of the novel and for its larger implications for the image of the Ameri-

can West. Shostak argues that the novel contains "conflicting rep-
resentational modes," and these conflicts reveal the boys' discomfort with anything that challenges their vision of the world (810).
Shostak's remarks about the boys' final statements about the girls
explains why history is not a suitable medium for the boys' tale: "to
know, to allow the girls to fall from myth into history, would be to
allow them to move from the status of objects to that of subjects"
(826). Shostak aligns the Lisbon girls with the colonized subject so
that the boys' narrative is interpreted as a violence worse than the
girls' self-inflicted injuries. She concludes that the novel's readers, who must make an ethical choice that involves siding with the
narrators or rejecting their worldview, need not share the hubris
of the boys.

The ethical dilemma of the reader that Shostak identifies is a
familiar one. Moments such as the end of the Cold War and September 11, 2001, shook the very foundations of the nation, putting
into question such foundational myths as the virgin land. In moments of uncertainty such as these, myth works to simplify the
world by presenting an image of unity and harmony that is separate from the real experience of Americans. In the aftermath of
September 11, for example, there was a revival of American myths
that included the "Homeland" and the "Virgin Land," which were
crucial to the recuperation project of the United States' prior vision of itself (Pease, *New American Exceptionalism* 156). Despite
this negative portrayal of myth, these narratives are also potentially empowering, a point that Henry Nash Smith also attempted
to relate to his readers in *Virgin Land* (ix). Although he admitted
that "myths can become dangerous" when they simplify complex
experiences, Smith continued to have faith in the unifying powers
of these stories (*Virgin Land* ix–x). In his definition, myth becomes
as much a way of working through fear and anxiety as it is a tool
for erasing these emotions.

The Virgin Suicides testifies to the anxiety rooted in the instability of periods of war and tragedy, relating how myth pulls those
under its spell in different directions. In the final commemorative
act for the Lisbon girls, the suburbanites memorialize the sadness
they identify as part and parcel of the nation at large. Made of "virgin timber," the simple wooden bench that they place in the town
center bears an inscription claiming that the girls were "*daugh-*

ters of th[e] community" (232; emphasis in original). The girls' connection to nature, especially the dying elm trees, expresses Eugenides's disillusionment with American myths, particularly the foundational myth of the virgin land. The dying land, like the dying girls, signals the decline of the town, a fate that the community comes to accept as inevitable. The author's reference to this land loss underscores the self-destructive behavior of U.S. imperialism, which includes members of the nation as targets (Collado-Rodríguez 38). Through this climactic scene, Eugenides anticipates a long and disastrous tumble for the United States that sets the stage for even darker narratives in the twenty-first century. A crucial contribution to revisionist narratives of the virgin land myth, Eugenides through his novel paves the way for a more active virgin girl who is finally able to speak for herself and escape the tragedy that has historically befallen this literary figure.

A Plague Shall Descend upon Him:
Power, Redemption, and Revenge

In Louise Erdrich's poem "The Strange People" (1984), a female antelope is captured by a male hunter and, in a fantastic turn of events, manages to escape being butchered.[14] As the antelope awaits her fate, she declares, "I wipe the death scum / from my mouth, sit up laughing / and shriek in my speeding grave" (lines 13–15). Shortly thereafter, she manages to confront her attacker and then leaves, wondering who might have the capacity to wound her, not merely in flesh but in spirit. Erdrich's narration in "The Strange People" demonstrates the transformation that overtakes the female speaker when she struggles to escape from her male captor and is but one of many instances where this celebrated author considers the power of women and their capacity to survive tragedy. Yet it is her more recent novel, *The Plague of Doves* (2008), that places her within the tradition of writers attempting to unravel the virgin land myth. Although Erdrich has long considered the impact of the government's expansion policies and modern legal relationship with recognized tribes, she pays special attention in *Plague* to the way that women and the land are tied together. As in the earlier works I have discussed in this tradition, Erdrich features young girls who challenge the authority of their male com-

panions in order to assert their power. It is their ultimate success
in doing so that separates Erdrich's novel from its predecessors.

Plague returns to the familiar landscape of North Dakota,
the setting of many of Erdrich's novels, including *Love Medicine*
(1984), *The Beet Queen* (1986), and *The Master Butchers Singing
Club* (2003). The flatlands of the North Dakotan town of Pluto
serve as the site of a terrible tragedy, where a family is murdered
by a mentally unstable neighbor. The tragedy results in the hanging of four innocent American Indian men who discover the only
survivor—a baby girl—and are then charged with murdering the
family. This local history haunts many of the characters in Pluto,
but it is the depiction of the adolescent girls Evelina Harp and
Marn Wolde that places Erdrich's novel into dialogue with previous critiques of the virgin land myth. Evelina and Marn are both
caught up in the cycle of violence that results in the Pluto murders. Evelina, the granddaughter of one of the men wrongfully ac-
cused (but who survives the hanging), is related by blood to a family who participated in the lynch mob, an ancestry that positions
her in relation to both victim and perpetrator. Marn's family history is similarly complicated. A daughter of German immigrants
whose farm is located on reservation land, she is also the wife of
Billy Peace, a melancholy descendant of one of the American Indian men executed for the murders. While both young women are
connected to the trauma of the murders, it is their ties to the land
and subjection to the power of male figures that constructs them
as virgin girl figures. Erdrich will find ways to subvert the conventions of this female figure, as the two women engage with and gain
control over the town's history: both narrators of their own stories, Evelina and Marn will go to great lengths to regain the power
taken from them by men.

In Erdrich's *Plague*, Evelina and Marn are identified early on
as desired and desiring beings. Evelina begins her first narrative
section with a tale of young love, a childhood romance where she
pursues her classmate and cousin, Corwin Peace. The obsessive
and intense nature of this love is conveyed by Evelina when she
declares, "my fingers obsessively wrote the name of my beloved
up and down my arm or in my hand or on my knee. If I wrote his
name a million times on my body, I believed he would kiss me. I
knew he loved me, and he was safe in the knowledge that I loved

him" (9). Evelina's desire for Corwin is evident in her constant act of writing, which is at once intimate, as it is literally on her body, and sexual, as she writes in places that "changed and warmed in response to the repetition of those letters" (10). While Evelina's love for Corwin is intense, she insists that this love is reciprocated. Evelina is not simply a prepubescent girl with a crush on one of her classmates; she believes that her relationship with Corwin follows a pattern of the great romances that are part of her family's tradition. She provides descriptions of Corwin "trying desperately to catch [her] eye" (14) and turning to her with "a burning glare of anguished passion" (15), feelings that are eventually consummated when the two kiss.

Similarly, Marn is defined by a love affair, in this case with Corwin's uncle Billy. Marn explains that at the age of sixteen, she "was looking at them [men] just to figure, for pure survival, the way a girl does" (138). Yet when Marn meets Billy shortly thereafter, she decides to act on her desires. Marn chases Billy much like Evelina chases Corwin, but differs from Evelina in that she has a host of admirers. After the end of her relationship with Billy, Marn walks into the local restaurant called the 4-B's. Marn is immediately welcomed by the male workers, who we learn are not her only admirers: "You have a crush on her too?" Evelina declares as she observes her coworker staring at Marn (188). And earlier, she concedes, "She was almost beautiful when she smiled and looked into a person's eyes. There was something that drew you. I could see why Billy, I guess, and Earl, had crushes on her. She had a facile, tough, energetic little body" (187).

Erdrich defines the two youngest female characters in *Plague* in terms of passionate and intense love affairs that consume those involved. Like the girls in *Lolita* and *The Virgin Suicides*, this love can become destructive. Evelina, for example, is tortured by Corwin's ploys to win her heart, which take the form of cruel, childish pranks, whereas Marn is enveloped in a physically and emotionally abusive relationship with her husband, whose desire to reclaim Indian land and rights obsess him. The status of victim is a familiar one for the virgin girl, who is often beaten, humiliated, tortured, or stifled by the rules of modern society until she has few options for escape other than death. The death of these tormented female figures is a way for authors to demonstrate the intensity of

the trauma experienced by the girls. It is often in the aftermath
of these deaths that those responsible for their pain begin to consider the depths of the girls' emotional lives. Likewise, readers are
encouraged to consider the social patterns that precipitated these
deaths and are at least in part responsible for them.

The gendered nature of the abuse in *Plague* has led to a number of interpretations of Erdrich's novel within a feminist framework. In a 2011 essay on nationalism and gender, Gina Valentino
argues that Erdrich's novel addresses the tendency for male critics, including those of American Indian descent, to marginalize
women by stereotyping them as "race traitors" (126). In such criticism, women are persecuted due to their perceived tendency to either upset male power or to betray their culture altogether, especially through activities such as writing. Evelina's interest in both
conventional and unconventional forms of writing certainly positions Erdrich's novel as a response to such critical attacks on Native women. However, *Plague* is more than just a critique of male
patriarchy; it is also part of a much longer critical conversation
concerning destructive national myths. While her presentation of
abused girls places Erdrich's novel firmly within the revisionist
tradition of the virgin land myth, the inclusion of historical and
biblical references strengthens this association. Erdrich includes
past historical events such as the lynching of four American Indian men and the rebellion of Louis Riel as a way of representing
the suffering and persecution of American Indian tribes. She likewise includes discussions of ways that the U.S. government has
tried to control Native people, including through blood quantums,
boarding schools, and land removal.

Of these methods of control, land removal figures most prominently in the novel and is strongly associated with the myth that
interests Erdrich. Throughout the narrative, her virgin girl characters decry the loss of land, albeit from radically different perspectives. At one point, Evelina overhears a conversation between her
aunt, Neve Harp, and her grandfather Mooshum in which the latter
angrily cries, "What you are asking is how was it [the land] stolen?"
(84). Evelina explains that the loss of land would "enter me, too"
and remain as a "sorrow" for the rest of her life (84). Evelina's sense
of loss is intergenerational, a pain that is passed down because no
healing takes place. Marn's loss does not have this same sense of

large-scale tragedy. While Marn loves the land, particularly the 888 acres that make up her family's farm, this land is marred by the history of colonization: it was stolen, to use Mooshum's words, from the Native people in the Pluto area. Still, Marn fights to regain control of her land from her husband, Billy: after killing him, she cries that she had "the land deed in my name" (179). The girls are both defined by their love and loss of land, a fact that connects them to a key aspect of the virgin land myth.

Since the main purpose of the virgin land myth was to bolster national pride and to encourage Americans to settle in the western frontier, it was necessary to create an image of this desolate land that would be attractive to prospective settlers. "Virgin" indicated that the land beyond the frontier was unspoiled and more fertile than that of the East. When policies such as the Homestead Act of 1862 encouraged westward expansion, many Americans left their homes in the East in search of property. These settlers, fulfilling Thomas Jefferson's ideal of a yeoman society, were often farmers who believed the propaganda about the unsettled land being the "garden of the world." Erdrich draws on this imagery in order to challenge the myth of the virgin land, making clear that this land was already long occupied before the arrival of white settlers. While reference to historical events in the struggle between Native people and white settlers is part of Erdrich's critique, she also includes references to the images that featured most prominently in the national myth of the virgin land. The garden, in particular, becomes a potent image because it not only refers to the tendency to depict the land as the "garden of the world" but also has roots in Judeo-Christian mythology. Because missionaries were often responsible for the cultural assimilation of Native children, and since the North Dakota area was influenced by French Catholics, Erdrich connects each of her virgin girl figures to this aspect of the virgin land myth.

Evelina's very name connects her to the Judeo-Christian Eve—her family even often shortens her name to "Eve." Like the Eve of this religious myth, Evelina tempts the men around her and encourages them to misbehave. In addition to instigating a series of classroom pranks that are carried out by her male admirer, Evelina encourages her grandfather's riotous behavior, even slipping him alcohol when he is not supposed to have it. As with the biblical Eve's pursuit of the tree of knowledge, Evelina seeks the knowledge denied her by her elders. She ruthlessly attempts to unravel the mystery of the Pluto murders, going so far as to draw up a genealogical chart for the town. Evelina explains that as she develops her complicated chart, which resembles "elaborate spider webs," she encounters resistance from her elders: "I could not erase the questions underneath, and Mooshum was no help. He bore interrogation with a vexed wince and silence. I persisted . . ." (86). Evelina's determination to unravel the myth surrounding the Pluto murders, and ultimately her own family history, marks her as a powerful and potentially threatening figure. Her search for answers threatens to destroy the town of Pluto, since discovering the truth of the murder would challenge the narrative that the town has accepted and used in order to survive this past trauma. This threat extends to her own family, too; the stories she has been told about the murders portray her grandfather as a victim and a hero, even though he had a hand to play in the murders since he betrayed his friends while in a drunken stupor.

Like Evelina, Marn also adopts traits of the biblical Eve. While Marn does not initially have the power to challenge male authority, she engages in alarming rituals with her pet snakes that allow her to regain her sense of power and autonomy. In one such passage, Marn milks her two snakes and then hides the poison behind an apple. The iconography of the snake and the apple links her immediately to the story of Adam and Eve. Other scenes in the novel further cement the connection between Marn and the biblical Eve. Marn allows her snakes to curl around her body while naked, and in one particularly sexualized scene, she invites Billy to join her in bed with the snakes. Similarly, when Marn is bit by one of her snakes, she exclaims, "Let the sickness boil up, and the questions, and the fruit of the tree of power" (162). The snakes, she asserts, are "my way of getting close to spirit" (160). Marn's sacrilegious behavior, particularly in the way she equates her snakes with the Holy Spirit, transform her from a victimized girl into a powerful temptress. Although Erdrich makes it clear that Marn is in an abusive relationship during her entire time with Billy, she also creates scenes where Marn's lust for power and vengeance is horrifying, as when she states that "the hatred was an animal so big I wanted to let it take Billy in its jaw" (177–178).

Erdrich often blurs the boundary between victim and perpetrator, reflecting her investment in issues that arose following
the events of September 11, 2001. In an interview with journalist Jeff Baenen (also available in excerpts in the P.S. section of the
novel),[15] Erdrich reveals that the September 11 terrorist attacks
were an inspiration for the novel: "I think vengeance, rather than
sitting back and allowing justice to be done over time, is really so
much a part of our history. And unfortunately, it's part of our present, as well." Erdrich further notes that this tragic event was one
of those moments when "a terrible thirst for someone to blame, for
someone to be caught and punished right away, and immediately"
emerged. By framing Evelina and Marn as both victim and perpetrator, Erdrich brings past and present together. On one hand, she
frames her book with the murder of the Pluto family, an idea she
developed after coming across a newspaper clipping about a similar incident; on the other hand, she relates this historical incident
to the present of her fictional characters, thereby encouraging her
readers to also draw parallels between the past and the present.
Erdrich's construction of Evelina and Marn as virgin girl figures
aids in this endeavor, as she plays on the virgin girl's traditional
status as victim and then puts this status into question. During
Evelina's childhood romance, for example, Evelina claims that she
"looked on, helpless" as Corwin carries out one of his pranks, and
these same pranks left her feeling like "puking with anxious rage"
(48, 49). Evelina's horror and rage "boil[s] up and rise[s]" in a later
scene as she observes the embarrassment of her beloved teacher,
who is shamed by a class joke that Evelina initiates (53). These
very same comments read in the context of the September 11 terrorist attacks in the United States parallel the growing rage, fear,
and anxiety that emerged after this tragedy. Many U.S. citizens
or residents of Middle Eastern descent or whose skin color might
cause others to incorrectly identify them as Middle Eastern were
often under attack, even suffering bodily harm.[16] This toxic environment, Erdrich suggests throughout her narrative, is caused
when adults let their emotions rule them.

Erdrich continues to develop her theme of "unfettered vengeance" through a variety of scenarios where the line between
victim and perpetrator is blurred. In so doing, she further desta-
bilizes earlier depictions of the virgin girl as victim. If we read

Evelina as a classic virgin girl, she is understood only as a victim of Corwin's malicious pranks and has every right to feel anger and shame. Yet Evelina's hatred for Corwin and her deep pleasure in tormenting him do not allow readers to interpret her character in this way. Evelina's repeated comments regarding her past love interest are downright cruel: "no matter how I tried to humiliate him, Corwin stayed in love with me" (43). This cruelty coupled with her misguided rage directly relate to Erdrich's concern regarding unfettered vengeance. Through the character of Evelina, Erdrich demonstrates the wider implications of impassioned rage. When Evelina reddens after one of Corwin's jokes, it is because her teacher, Sister Mary Anita, is the butt of the children's teasing. Evelina knows that she has had a hand to play in these classroom pranks, as she was the first to compare her teacher with the Japanese monster Godzilla. Evelina's thoughtless ridicule spreads when Corwin invites other children to participate in the taunting of Sister Mary Anita. While Evelina feels shame for her past actions, especially after learning how deeply they hurt Sister Mary Anita, she continues to act impulsively and cruelly, even if she does not perceive her actions as such. In her attempts to protect her teacher, Evelina punches, kicks, and spits insults at Corwin, a tactic that is disturbingly similar to the actions that initiated the class joke in the first place.

Marn similarly breaks down the binary between victim and perpetrator. While Marn does suffer enormously at the hands of her husband, she also plots vengeance in a way that does not leave her free of guilt. As she suffers various forms of mental and physical abuse, Marn begins to develop a "boiling anger" that mirrors Evelina's. As Marn herself describes, she feels both "old, [and] so captured by life already" and also harbors a deep hatred for her husband that prompts her to want to lash out and "not let him breathe . . . [u]ntil I ruled him so that he could hurt no one" (151, 178). Marn's situation is considerably more dire than Evelina's, and she is subjected to forms of physical abuse that are disturbing, including sleep deprivation and bodily mutilation. Marn's decision to transition from victim to perpetrator in response to these forms of abuse is put into question by her pleasure in the ultimate act of revenge—murder. As Marn prepares to stab Billy with a poisoned needle, she remarks, "I would not let him go until I sank through his bones like a wasting disease. Ate him from the inside, devouring his futility" (178). Much like Billy, Marn appears to enjoy power once it is hers, and she wields it in ways that brushes against the norms for women.

Lest one think Erdrich is casting Marn as a modern "fallen woman," Erdrich continually troubles the all-too-easy association between Marn's vengeful acts and evil. Certainly, Marn's abusive husband encourages readers to side with Marn, even as she engages in illegal behavior. This desire to side with Marn is further solidified by Billy's construction as a *windigo* or cannibalistic monster from the mythology of northern Native tribes (153–154, 156–157). This mythological beast, as I explained in my previous chapter, became a cautionary tale for members of the Ojibwe tribe and other indigenous groups in the Great Lakes region in the United States and Canada. In order to deter tribal members from becoming overly selfish or gluttonous, tales of the *windigo* helped ward off any inclination to value the desires of the individual over the well-being of the entire tribe. Erdrich includes many scenarios where Billy's desires are out of control and cause those around him to suffer, and his coldness toward his closest family member, Marn, suggests that he has developed the stereotypical "ice heart" of the *windigo*. His characterization as a ravenous pig (his size grows larger and larger throughout the novel) is another hallmark of the *windigo*, who is known for his insatiable appetite and his desire for human flesh. Billy's transformation into a *windigo* suggests that he is no longer human and that killing him is in fact the only humane thing to do. According to American Indian folklore, those who began to transform into *windigos* would first eat their family members so that many would end up begging to be killed before committing this fateful act (Podruchny 690). By drawing on American Indian mythology, Erdrich indicates that Marn's actions are justified and even necessary, making it difficult for readers to identify her completely as either victim or perpetrator.

Most critics of Erdrich comment on her tendency to blur boundaries in relation to gender and sexuality. However, I would argue that it is the girls' uncertain status as victim and perpetrator that is more relevant here. As unconventional virgin girl figures, Evelina and Marn challenge stereotypes about girls as innocent, pure, and helpless. Historically, goodness has been associated with white, middle-class girlhood, and girls who failed to live up to this standard, as is evidenced in such literary examples as Louisa May Alcott's Jo March, are frequently punished. Girls like Jo are ridiculed for "acting like boys." In her 2008 study of tomboyism in American culture, Michelle Abate explains that for white girls, acting like a boy was acceptable only so long as the girl outgrew this stage in a reasonable amount of time. If she continued to demonstrate masculine behavior, she was chastised and marked as a social deviant. This form of discipline, known as "tomboy taming," gained in popularity during the Civil War period. Abate suggests that this was due to the emergence at that time of a new phase of childhood: adolescence (28). Girls could be tomboys so long as they cast off their boyish behavior by the time they reached adolescence; those who failed to do so would be punished. Abate further explains that the wildness of little girls was often associated with American Indians: girls were described as "wild Indians" when they exhibited boyish behaviors (142).

While Abate reads the white girl as raced due to her activity, this reading does not hold for Evelina, who, despite her white blood, would still be considered an American Indian girl. Evelina is unique because she comes from a family of privilege—her father is a science teacher at the reservation school, and the family lives in Bureau of Indian Affairs housing, along with many modern comforts that go along with town life (36). This allows her to enjoy middle-class status in a town where most girls of her background are significantly less well off. Erdrich's blurring of boundaries thereby shows how race, class, and gender are likewise tied up in these acts of vengeance.

Rather than focus solely on how Evelina's background might limit her ability to challenge dominant narratives about gender and race, Erdrich in fact empowers her by upsetting Anglo-American expectations regarding girlhood. From the beginning, Evelina engages in activities that are coded as masculine: she is outspoken, rambunctious, and bold. Much like the girls in Erdrich's work for children, Evelina's behavior draws on traditional Ojibwe notions of gender, which similarly blur the boundaries between male and female norms. In his reading of the arc of Erdrich's Birchbark series, Don Latham, a library science scholar, insists that girls' engagement in traditional male activities do not necessarily mark them as socially deviant. Girls who act like boys are not pressured to change their behavior because Ojibwe culture accepts the possibility for gender variance, or the ability to choose one's gender, despite one's biological sex. Members of the tribe may even change gender over time, as Sue-Ellen Jacobs, Wesley Thomas, and Sabine Lang attest in their 1997 study of American Indian cultures (4). It is only when the behavior of gender variants threatens the overall welfare of the tribe that they are punished. In the Birchbark series, a young tomboy named "Two Strike" exemplifies this description. Latham explains that Two Strike's boyish behavior is problematic because "her 'gift' is not channeled in consistently productive ways to serve the greater good of the community" (139).

Despite her Ojibwe roots, Evelina is still subject to the social expectations of white culture, a fact that is made evident in the imagery in her stories. Evelina channels her boyish behavior in order to discover answers regarding the Pluto murders. This determination to find answers requires her to rely on more masculine behavior—she does not take "no" for an answer when interviewing town members, even her male elders. Both historian and storyteller, Evelina has the ability to reinterpret history, a power that was never granted to earlier virgin girls. In the fictional town of Pluto, much like in Anglo-American traditions, men tend to be the storytellers and interpreters of historical events. In fact, it is Evelina's Mooshum who is first introduced as storyteller, and these stories play a central role in the childhood portion of her testimony.[17] One of the very first images that Evelina shares is about her grandfather's first meeting with his late wife. In the account originally given by Mooshum, a plague of doves descends on the town and destroys the town's crops. This plague of doves also leads him to his future love: when the town women try to chase the doves away, he is hit in the head by an escaping dove. Upon awakening, he sees his future wife, a young girl dressed in a beautiful white dress: "I saw two beings—the boy shaken, frowning; the girl in white kneeling over him with the sash of her dress gracefully clutched in her hand, then pressing the cloth to the wound on his head, staunching the flow of blood. Most important, I imagined their dark, mutual gaze. The Holy Spirit hovered between them. Her sash reddened. His blood defied gravity and flowed up her arm. Then her mouth opened" (12). Evelina's interpretation of her grandparents' first encounter contains religious and sexual overtones. Evelina's grand-mother, Junesse, a name readers can associate with the French word for "youth" or "young people," performs the role of the sanc-tified young girl. Her frilly white dress, which is completely out of place in the chaos of the dove plague, also associates her with di-vine grace. Unlike the doves who flap around wildly, Junesse is calm and graceful.[18] She also acts in a traditional feminine manner, nurturing the injured boy to health and even overlooking decorum by dirtying her white sash with the boy's blood.

Junesse's actions are in line with conceptions of white middle-class girlhood. Like the "good girls" in Anglo-American novels, Ju-nesse is chaste, loving, and innocent. Her only flaw is that she al-lows her good reputation to be tarnished when she runs away with her future husband. Evelina is clearly captivated by this story of young love, and she interprets her own love with Corwin in terms of it. Evelina breaks from the conventions of romantic love that undergird her stories when she rejects Corwin in favor of her teacher: "As I walked I realized that my body still fought itself. My lungs filled with air like two bags, but every time they did so, a place underneath them squeezed so painfully the truth suddenly came clear. 'I love *her* now,' I blurted out. I stopped on a crack in the earth, stepping on it, then stamped down hard, sickened. 'Oh God, I am *in love*'" (47; emphasis in original). Evelina's horror at loving another woman arises from the fact that it falls outside the narratives she has come to recognize. There is, she later observes, no story about loving another woman (235). While in Ojibwe cul-ture Evelina would be identified as a gender variant, in the town of Pluto she is still subject to Anglo-American norms of female sub-jectivity. It is Evelina's love and her eventual acceptance of her dif-ference that begin to re-mark her so that as she grows into a more mature adolescent she no longer plays the role of the wily, high-strung little girl who torments potential lovers.

Erdrich provides an example of this role reversal when Evelina returns as narrator. After experiencing horrifying hallucinations from a drug slipped to her by her cousin and former love, Cor-win, Evelina volunteers at a mental institution. Once there, she meets a young white girl named Nonette, who becomes her lover. Nonette's name, much like Junesse's, proves to be symbolic, as the first portion translates into the French for "no." Although Nonette invites Evelina to love her, her mental instability makes this love impossible. Nonette taunts Evelina and continually denies their relationship, even in her final goodbye when she checks out of the mental institution. This cat-and-mouse game is strikingly similar to Evelina's childhood romance, except in this instance she becomes the victim of rejection. In her reading of the novel, Valentino argues that Evelina conforms to a "male model of history and not a female one" (129). This is why, during her childhood, Evelina could not understand her love for Sister Mary Anita, and explains why her reaction is one of horror rather than pleasure. Similarly, Evelina is unable to understand how to react to Nonette, who does not follow the narrative patterns in the stories she was told as a girl. While Evelina struggles to develop a new story by conforming to traditional gender roles—Nonette has boyish characteristics while Evelina has girlish ones—her relationship ultimately crumbles.

Evelina's love for Nonette is not simply gendered but raced as well. In her history of the evolution of the tomboy, Abate explains that white tomboys were often "tamed" because of fears about sexuality. This anxiety, according to Abate, was fueled by fear about the decline in white supremacy. Abate cites multiple historical episodes where a girl's decision to be a tomboy appeared as a threat to white culture and even goes so far as to serve as one of the alleged reasons for the "race suicide" of Anglo-Americans. Abate, however, concerns herself with white tomboys who not only desire girls, as in the case of Beebo Brinker in *I Am a Woman* (1959), but also white girls who act like nonwhite ones: Abate repeatedly draws parallels between white tomboys and African American girls and women. For Evelina, race plays a crucial role in the power dynamics between herself and Nonette, and it likewise serves Erdrich's purpose of underscoring how race, gender, and sexuality are tied up in historical acts of vengeance. When Evelina reflects on her relationship with Nonette, the dejected woman remarks, "I was always too backwards, or provincial, or Catholic, or reservation- or family-bound to absorb and pull off [this life]" (241). Later, Evelina will make a direct connection between her Ojibwe heritage and her failure to secure Nonette's love: "I'm just a nothing, half-crazy, half-drugged, half-Chippewa" (244).

Evelina's difference, and her subversiveness as a virgin girl, can
be contrasted with Erdrich's other virgin girl, Marn. The juxtapo-
sition of these two female characters demonstrates the limitations
of white female subjectivity, while simultaneously drawing attention to problems associated with the virgin land myth. If the virgin land myth was intended to make innocent the colonial exploits
of the United States and then bolster national pride during the
1950s, it returned once more following the September 11 terrorist attacks on the World Trade Center and Pentagon. During this
moment, heated debates regarding race emerged as many Americans became suspicious of anyone that even vaguely resembled
the hijackers responsible for the plane crashes in New York, Wash-
ington, D.C., and Pennsylvania. For Erdrich, September 11 presents an opportunity to return to the nation's past treatment of
American Indian people. That Erdrich does not see much difference between the United States' current and past policies, at least
in terms of decisions driven by vengeance rather than justice, is
apparent in the way she contrasts her two virgin girl figures.

This is evident in the way that Marn's tomboyism conforms to
gender, race, and class expectations rather than challenging these
social conventions the way that Evelina does. Marn comes from a
blue-collar immigrant family who struggles to make a profit from
their farm. Because she needs to help on the farm, Marn exhibits behavior that others might interpret as tomboyish. However,
once she no longer has to help with family chores, Marn succumbs
to traditional ideals of femininity. For example, after running off
with Billy Peace, Marn submits to her husband's authority and focuses her energy on caring for her two children. Marn's new life is
far from a model of domestic bliss, as she is constantly subjected to
emotional and physical abuse. Marn cares for her children, washes
clothes, and submits to her husband's wishes. She is even treated
in a nineteenth-century manner when her husband gains rights to
her family farm: "The farm is made over to me now, and through
me to Billy" (154). Billy's ability to own his wife's property harkens
back to the days when women were treated like children, and their
money and property were placed in the care of their "more rational" husbands. Marn's willingness to submit to traditional conceptions of Anglo-American femininity contrasts sharply with Evelina's bucking of tradition.

Erdrich hints early on in the narrative at the role Marn's cultural and racial background plays in her behavior. When Marn determines it is time to return home for a family visit, she persuades her husband to accompany her by referring to her own upbringing: "'Your parents died when you were young,' I tell him. 'Your sister raised you until you went into the army, then she went to the dogs, I guess. So you don't really understand the idea of home, or folks, or a place you grew up in that you want to return to'" (148). Earlier, Marn did not distinguish between her background and Billy's but instead focused on her desire for this mysterious man. As she grows older and develops a sense of duty, Marn begins to refer to these differences and utilizes them to gain a modicum of power over her husband. Marn's reference to Billy's family situation shows little understanding or compassion, as is evident through her use of words such as "I guess" and the didactic nature of her speech: she "tells" Billy why he doesn't understand her position rather than asking. Moreover, despite rifts in her own family, Marn nostalgically writes about her father and mother as they diligently tend to the land, referring to her father as an "overworked German" (150). This work may sap her parents of their vitality, but it is in stark contrast to Billy's alcoholic sister. These contrasting depictions of family demonstrate Marn's sense of racial and cultural superiority, a feeling that will strengthen once she is overcome by rage toward her abusive husband.

Marn's background similarly draws attention to the policies that the virgin land myth was intended to obscure. Despite her family's economic instability, the Wolde family still owns a large plot of land that was obtained at a time when land speculation led many to claim the "free" land in the North Dakota region. This land is described as being "smack up to the reservation boundary," a fact that Marn's husband does not fail to recognize or interpret within the history of land loss: "This was reservation, Billy says, and should be again. This was my family's land, Indian land. Will be again" (152). While Marn's youth and general naïveté seem to exclude her from involvement in this land theft, she is caught up in its history due to her whiteness. Marn's racial background, much like the reddened sash of Junesse, is tainted with blood, and it is this stain that Erdrich encourages her readers to consider within the larger history of U.S. colonization. Marn may be in the right when she is an-

gered by Billy's takeover of her family farm, but his desire for the
land is always cast in terms of the larger history of U.S. colonization. As his speech to Marn indicates, her family's property right-
fully belongs to him and the other members of his tribe since it is
reservation land; it is this history of land theft that drives Billy to
reclaim what Marn sees as her own. Similarly, Marn's determination to get the land deed in her name draws uncanny parallels to
the nineteenth-century frenzy over the "free" land in North Dakota,
a fact that Erdrich reminds her readers of through the narrative
of another local town member named Judge Coutts. In the town of
Pluto, land rights represent a struggle between whites and Indians,
making any reference to them highly racialized.

This struggle over land begins to appear as a driving force in
the violence that defines Marn's relationship with her husband,
especially once Marn begins to imitate the behavior of her uncle
Warren, the man really responsible for the Pluto murders. Despite
Marn's submissive temperament, her family history, much like the
history of U.S. colonization, begins to possess her. The fits of anger that would randomly alter her uncle's behavior begin to af-
flict Marn, which she describes as a "rage" that descends upon her
(151). These rages enable Marn to resist her abusive husband by
physically lashing out. In the scene where she murders Billy, Marn
calmly prepares a poison and places the toxic serum in a needle
that she hides behind an apple. Later, as she flees the religious
commune where she lived with her husband, Marn encounters a
white woman named Bliss who was one of Billy's followers. Marn
tackles the woman and punctures her jacket with a steak knife
that she has hidden in her hand. Such acts starkly contrast with
Marn's earlier naïve country girl persona. Marn's ability to strike
at her enemies seems fueled by a rage that precedes her and is indeed linked to her crazed uncle. Such a genealogical connection
places the conflict between Marn and Billy into dialogue with the
embittered history of the Ojibwe tribe, who likewise suffered at
the hands of French fur trappers and the white immigrants and
settlers who later rushed into the West.

Through her depiction of Evelina's and Marn's maturation, Erdrich captures many of the issues that arose after September 11
and places them into a broader historical context. By subverting

the familiar tropes of the virgin girl figure, she is able to question the atmosphere of vengeance that quickly emerged in the aftermath of this tragic event and to further unravel the U.S. national myths that regained popularity at this moment in time. Erdrich challenges notions of the United States as native land to white settlers by returning to the broken treaties between the U.S. government and American Indians, and by likewise reflecting on the long-term effects of these decisions. She demonstrates that those who partake in acts of violence and vengeance are haunted by them. These acts balloon outward and envelop more than just the immediate victims and perpetrators. They have lasting effects that spread much like the plague of doves that serves as Erdrich's central image in the novel. Just like the doves, whose ordinary associations with peace are inverted when they appear en masse, an act of violence initially committed in the name of justice can later blossom into horrifying acts of vengeance on a massive scale. Such acts, when placed in a global context, reveal much about the American character.

The evolution of the virgin girl figure demonstrates the way that historical events shaped authors' understanding of their present, creating opportunities to add an increasing number of voices to the U.S. national narrative as time passed. Even as the virgin girl becomes stronger and more defiant, refusing to accept a male interpretation of her role, she must still deal with traumatic events that scar her for life. Yet there is a hopeful possibility present in such experiences, as each of the novels that appear in this chapter reveal. The girls that appear in these stories demonstrate that, while beaten, those who suffer most are not necessarily destroyed. Their tales suggest that in order to rectify the wrongs of the past, it is first necessary to shatter the myths created to cover over these wrongs. While the virgin girl figure does not always survive, her acts of defiance allow her to regain control over her life and ultimately dismantle the myths that surround her. It is this dismantling of myths that makes this girl figure so powerful; as she speaks out, challenging readers to question the very narratives that they have come to accept as accounts of national history, the virgin girl offers an alternative to the traditionally male-dominated perspective of U.S. westward expansion.

CHAPTER 4

Extraordinary Boys
on an Errand

RACE AND NATIONAL BELONGING IN
NARRATIVES OF FATHERHOOD

Some historians suggest that the second and third generations suffered a failure of nerve; they weren't the men their fathers had been, and they knew it.

—Perry Miller, *Errand into the Wilderness*

After such fathers, what sons? Indeed, what sons can there be?

—Richard Hofstadter, *The Progressive Historians*

The 1950s marked a growing debate concerning the United States' role on the global stage, with leading scholars in the field of American studies advocating for a move "beyond innocence" in order for the United States to secure its new position as a world leader. At the root of this anxiety about the nation's future, which many felt necessitated a break with the nation's "innocent" past and a move toward the experience associated with maturity, was a concern about national leaders and the continuing mission of the United States in the twentieth century, a feeling effectively captured by Perry Miller's *Errand into the Wilderness* (1956). A guiding national myth that allowed Miller, and those familiar with his work, to reinterpret contemporary political affairs within a longer historical tradition, the errand into the wilderness myth postulated that the Founding Fathers of the nation came to the wilderness of the New World on a divine mission, which they passed onto their sons. As a World War II veteran and respected scholar, Miller had the prestige and social connections (he was friends with the U.S. ambassador to Germany) needed to give his "Puritan thesis" potency and political suasion. Through his thesis, Miller raised awareness about the questionable trajectory of the nation: What would be the logical conclusion of the Puritan errand? Had the nation in fact strayed from the guiding principles that motivated the founders' "errand into the wilderness"? Questions such as these would continue to erupt well into the early twenty-first century, as numerous dissidents took up the pen in order to criticize the U.S. government's political involvement abroad, which, under the guise of benevolence, had bolstered national power and expanded the empire. Supporting a turn to leadership from the younger generation, who had learned from the errors of previous generations, those who opposed the national errand found hope in the figure of the rebellious son, turning attention to both the conflicts of the past and those of the present in an effort to find a path forward that would be more sensitive to the experience of all the nation's citizens.

Just as Miller's Puritan thesis was organized around a father-son theme, so were the critiques of these later writers. Although Miller is primarily remembered as a supporter of the U.S. government, his anxiety regarding nuclear warfare led to a number of statements that suggest his feelings were far more ambiguous. This ambiguity appeared in the work of novelists who, like Miller, questioned the expansionist future of America. Without a secure sense of the United States' political agenda, these authors could only guess about the nation's future prospects. Yet they found reassurance in the familiar theme of the father-son bond. Narratives of fatherhood allowed novelists in later decades, including prominent contemporary writers Russell Banks and Sherman Alexie, to express a mix of patriotic fervor and political anxiety as they explored issues pertinent to their respective generations. During the 1950s, for example, the "loss" of China and the rise of the Nationalist Party in Taiwan led to an active China lobby that kept Sino-American relations at the forefront of U.S. foreign policy. Many Americans were aware of the emerging importance of Asia following the Korean War, as this region became one of the new hotspots for the struggle between the United States and the Soviet Union. In subsequent years, other regions, including the Caribbean (most notably in Cuba with the political rise of Fidel Castro in 1959), gained political importance as the United States' war against communism intensified and fears about national security increased.

By rejecting the nation's "fathers" through the employment of father-son narratives, novelists opened a dialogue regarding the United States' future as a global leader and enabled others to participate in this critical conversation. Issues related to race and national belonging were a common point of contention and became a means for merging domestic and foreign political issues through the metaphors of familial relations. At a time when the United States was urging nonaligned nations to embrace democracy, concerns about who belonged in the national family were central to the nation's political rhetoric. The fact that most nonaligned nations consisted of people of color meant that the United States had to think hard about its own racist policies, including the mistreatment of its American Indian and African American communities. The novels included in this chapter consider the limits of the United States' benevolence toward those outside of the "national family" and demonstrate how narratives of fatherhood were increasingly shaped by anxiety about race. In both Meindert DeJong's *The House of Sixty Fathers* (1956) and Sherman Alexie's *Flight* (2007), white fathers adopt ethnic boys and demand that their new sons assimilate into Euro-American culture. As the boys negotiate these demands, they confront the power not only of their adoptive fathers but also of the U.S. government. In addition, the traditionally white father of privilege is replaced with male figures historically marginalized due to their race. Russell Banks's *Rule of the Bone* (1995) illustrates this inversion of a familiar narrative trope and in doing so challenges white supremacy. Staging struggles of power between fathers and sons in various ways, these novelists put pressure on the myth of the nation's divine errand by taking a critical position toward the leaders responsible for the nation's global mission abroad. In what follows, I explore the implications of these literary interventions and the political context that shaped them.

Failed Adoptions and the
Love/Hate Relationship with China

During the 1950s, Asia emerged as one of the most important arenas for the ideological struggle against communism. The establishment of the People's Republic of China in 1949 significantly undermined the U.S. mission to contain communism, and the national media responded to these developments by describing China's conversion to communism as a tragic "loss" for the United States. Such popular documentaries as the *Why We Fight* series (1942–45), directed by the celebrated Hollywood filmmaker Frank Capra, included films devoted to U.S. activity in China. In the early 1940s, China was presented as a nation much like the United States, with plenty of land and resources to care for its vast population. The Japanese, who were cast as China's greedy and demonic neighbors, needed to be stopped if American ideals were to prevail. China needed U.S. sympathy during World War II, and the United States needed China in order to assert its power. By the time of the Korean War, this rhetoric of loss was abandoned in favor of a more sinister portrait. In the short documentary film *Red Chinese Battle Plan* (1967), made in the midst of the fighting in Vietnam, the U.S. government solidified the image of an evil war-mongering China first developed in the early 1950s, suggesting that the nation, under the leadership of Mao Zedong, was determined to "conquer and enslave" the rest of the world. The negative image of China in propaganda films like *Red Chinese Battle Plan* took time to cultivate, reflecting the shock of China's conversion to communism, but would continue to shape U.S. perceptions of its previous ally for many years to come.

The United States' shifting position in Asia was largely highlighted by the Korean War, which reinforced policymakers' sense of the importance of Asia in the war against communism. In addition, an active China lobby during the 1950s raised awareness in the general public about issues in Asia and urged politicians to take them seriously. While the United States' commitments were often split between democratic experiments in South Korea, Japan, and Taiwan, earlier developments set the tone for future investments in the Pacific region. These began with what Nancy Bernkopf Tucker, an American diplomatic historian, describes as a "growing sense that the Chinese were not doing enough for themselves to merit outside assistance" (10). The United States' shifting attitude toward China was further problematized by the Chinese civil war, which lasted from 1927 until 1950. As China split due to political differences, the United States would also become increasingly divided about its position in Asia. Ultimately, the United States would side with the losing Kuomintang (KMT) forces led by

Chiang Kai-shek and would funnel enormous amounts of financial aid into the Taiwanese economy to steel the island against a possible invasion from mainland China.

Although China was not the only Asian nation of interest to the United States during the 1950s, it remained an integral component of U.S. strategy in the Pacific region. As the rhetoric regarding China evolved, the Chinese were often cast as children in need of help, and the United States as the confident and clever father who could best care for this troubled nation. This was true for mainland Chinese during World War II and then later for Chinese refugees in Taiwan. Father-son rhetoric permeated some of the most popular materials disseminated to U.S. citizens about China—even for the very youngest members of the nation. One novel that received wide acclaim was Meindert DeJong's *The House of Sixty Fathers* (1956). DeJong, a Dutch-born American writer, received the Newbery Honor, the runner-up prize for one of the most prestigious children's literature awards in the United States, for this novel. He would later receive the coveted Hans Christian Andersen Award, an international award given to an author whose entire body of work is seen as making a "lasting contribution to children's literature" ("Hans Christian Andersen Awards"). The first American author to win this award, DeJong's work went on to receive recognition in several foreign countries. In his only recorded interview, DeJong reflects on his literary success, noting that "I've been translated in about 22 languages, so somewhere something is selling" (*A Conversation*).

Of the many books that DeJong wrote during his lifetime, *The House of Sixty Fathers* is the most autobiographical. It recounts the author's experience in China as an American soldier during World War II and his subsequent efforts to adopt a Chinese war orphan. Dedicated to "little, lost Panza," the boy that DeJong's unit cared for and that DeJong himself attempted to adopt officially after returning home, the novel provides a fictional account of the relationship between Panza, named Tien Pao in the novel, and DeJong during the Japanese invasion of China. Most striking about this account is the way that it romanticizes the union between the U.S. military and the Chinese people. DeJong manipulates the real events of little Panza's life, providing a happy ending where he is reunited with his parents through the efforts of a U.S. soldier. In contrast to Tien Pao's happy ending, Panza's fate is significantly darker: abandoned in an orphanage when DeJong's troop returned home, DeJong never contacted the boy again due to growing tensions between the United States and China. DeJong's abrupt termination of his relationship with little Panza haunted the author throughout his life and led him to write *The House of Sixty Fathers* in order to grapple with increasing demands for U.S. citizens to "adopt" Chinese children into the national family. Having personally experienced a failed adoption while being stationed in China, DeJong was poised to comment on the damaging effects of such rhetoric on the real lives of Chinese citizens.

DeJong wrote *The House of Sixty Fathers* while still serving in China in the 1940s, but it wasn't until the mid-1950s that his novel was finally published.[1] This delay enabled DeJong to make correlations between the Cold War atmosphere and his experiences abroad. Having observed firsthand the U.S. military's interactions with the Chinese people and the subsequent breakdown in communications between U.S. citizens and Chinese institutions, DeJong was primed to respond to the wealth of media coverage regarding China's new red status. Most important to his critical reflection was the rhetoric that emerged shortly after the culmination of the Pacific War, when millions of orphaned children became subjects of public sympathy. At this time, organizations that included the Christian Children's Fund encouraged U.S. citizens to provide a loving home for these children. These advertisements informed U.S. citizens that they could "adopt" a Chinese war orphan by donating as little as ten dollars a month (Klein 46). Advertisements such as these, Christina Klein contends in her 2000 essay on U.S.-Asian relations during the Cold War, "make purchasing a political act, and purchasing the idea of the family becomes a mechanism for creating ties between the United States and Asia" (49). "Adopting" a child thus fulfilled the new demand for U.S. citizens to do their part on the world stage, a strategy that would continue during the Korean War in 1950 as waves of transnational adoptions took place with the help of the missionary work of public figures Bertha and Henry Holt and gave greater permanence to the United States' Cold War commitment to Asia (Briggs 153). This approach to adoption, while flawed in many respects, is an example of the United States' shifting approach to international relations in Asia during a time when many believed that Asia had become the new battleground in the war against communism.

The adoption rhetoric that appeared in the 1950s may very well have influenced DeJong. The images of Chinese war orphans that flooded the U.S. media were accompanied by a rhetoric of familial love that tested the limits of national belonging and raised questions about the nation's political mission made familiar through Miller's Puritan thesis. As U.S. citizens were advised to be open to the metaphorical adoption of the Chinese, those critical of this mission considered the nature of the United States' political agenda abroad: What was the relation of this mission to that of the Founding Fathers? Was the United States staying true to its founding principles? And what might be the logical conclusion of the nation's "errand into the wilderness"? In DeJong's novel, these questions led to an engagement with issues of race and national belonging and, in a turn perhaps not surprising based on his personal experiences, a rejection of the familial rhetoric that permeated national media outlets. While not completely abandoning the figure of the benevolent white father who acted as a metaphor for the nation, DeJong would question the role of this figure through his presentation of a rebellious "son" who rejects his entrance into an adopted family in favor of his biological kin.

The House of Sixty Fathers opens with Tien Pao, a young boy perhaps ten or eleven years of age, as he flees with his family from Japanese soldiers when they burn and pillage his hometown in southern China. The family finds refuge in a sampan, a small riverboat with a cabin, and joins other refugees in the river town of Hengyang. Shortly after their arrival, Tien Pao is left home alone as his parents search for work at a nearby American airfield. While waiting for their return, the young boy meets an American airman named Lieutenant Hamsun and volunteers to help him ferry a boat across the rapidly swelling river. His decision to help the airman, an act that, importantly, is in direct violation of his father's orders to remain in the family's sampan while he is away, sets into motion the father-son narrative that structures the novel. This action signifies Tien Pao's division of loyalty between his biological father and this mysterious stranger, who will eventually become his temporary adoptive father. Tien Pao, encouraged by a neighbor woman, believes that his act of defiance will be forgiven once his family sees the money he receives in exchange for his services, but is instead disappointed when he is severely admonished by his father for his disobedience. Despite his own father's admirable actions, including risking his life to keep his family safe from the Japanese soldiers, Tien Pao is more enamored with his new soldier friend, whom he describes as a "river god" and admires for his competence at rowing the sampan and his generosity with money (9).

This first encounter between Tien Pao and the white soldier serves as a modified version of Freud's family romance, where a young child imagines that he is actually adopted and that somewhere a better family awaits him ("Family Romance" 237–238).[2] DeJong's fantasy narrative signals his concern over U.S.-China relations. Even in this first encounter, DeJong casts doubt on the viability of such a happy union. Tien Pao, the preadolescent boy who stands for "innocent" civilians, is caught between loyalties. The arrival of this new white father upsets what had previously been a happy, albeit struggling, family unit. The soldier's good intentions, DeJong shows, result in misfortune for Tien Pao and launch a chain of events that involves both the American soldier and the Chinese boy. As the narrative progresses, the suffering of both parties casts further doubt on the benefit of a union between the United States and China. When the soldier suffers a terrible wound after crash-landing during a Japanese air raid, he must depend on Tien Pao in order to escape from the enemy. Such a reversal of power deflates the image of the once invincible American soldier while also drawing attention to the risks of involving oneself in foreign affairs.

The traumatic experiences of Tien Pao and Lieutenant Hamsun in wartime China propel them into an intimate relationship where Hamsun, even upon first seeing the boy after his crash landing, sits a crying Tien Pao in his lap and "croon[s] like a mother to a little baby" (74). This familial metaphor foreshadows the events to follow, when an American bomb squadron adopts the boy. Adoption, a common trope in American literature, dates back as far as the contact period when the first European settlers considered themselves orphans in a new land. In *Adopting America* (2011), Carol Singley explains how adoption narratives are "rooted in the American migratory experience: they reflect politically and culturally the severed ties to Great Britain and the construction of new forms of so-

cial and governmental organization" (4). Singley provides several
examples of the adoption narrative that span from the Puritan era
to the end of the nineteenth century. Early adoption narratives,
such as Cotton Mather's "Orphanotrophium; or, Orphans well-pro-
vided for" (1711), depict adoption as part of everyday life and encourage parents "to prepare spiritually for the possibility of their
children's orphancy" (Singley 24). Eighteenth-century adoption
narratives, such as Benjamin Franklin's *Autobiography* (1791), began to move away from the more practical advice of the previous
century, raising questions related to roots and national identity, a
trend that continued in the nineteenth century as adoption continued to serve as a central metaphor for the nation. In all these
narratives, a child's successful adoption signified "the resourcefulness of the [child protagonist] and the flexibility of the family in
the context of national expansion" (Singley 152).

Singley demonstrates the way that these various adoption narratives responded to the immediate concerns of the nation, both in
terms of social life and in terms of national politics. Yet, with the
exception of her final chapter, Singley does not explore in much detail the relationship between the adoption narrative and empire-
building practices. Authors, as she notes in passing in chapters on
Louisa May Alcott's *Little Men* (1871) and Harriet Wilson's *Our Nig*
(1859), at times used the adoption trope in order to depict who was
not allowed into the national family. Moreover, narratives from the
early twentieth century, most notably Edith Wharton's *Summer*
(1917), address the limitations of adoption, acknowledging the tension created by turn-of-the-century scientific debates about miscegenation and genealogical inheritance (Singley 173), and include
portraits of unhappy adoptees. The shift in the national adoption
narrative at the beginning of the twentieth century, I would argue,
occurs as a response to the United States' increase in global power.
The adoption trope is adapted to reflect the political and cultural
tension associated with the United States' increasing involvement
with foreign nations. Post–World War II narratives, such as De-
Jong's *The House of Sixty Fathers*, share with prior adoption narratives a concern about the reorganization of social ties and governmental institutions; however, they add to this an awareness of the
United States as a major player in the global scene and attempt to

understand the repercussions of these new ways of relating with the rest of the world.

While much of protagonist Tien Pao's journey in *The House of Sixty Fathers* is devoted to questioning the father-son bond, it is his time in the "House of Sixty Fathers" that best exemplifies DeJong's appropriation of the adoption trope to navigate the growing tension between the United States and China. When Tien Pao is rescued by another American soldier and carried to his base, he happily succumbs to the strength of his new foreign friends. Indeed, he finds it comforting: "When Tien Pao came to again, one of the soldiers was holding him in big, steady arms and carrying him down the steep path. It felt good to be held" (130). DeJong's description of the American soldier supports the United States' new perception of itself as a strong nation with the power to "save" others, building on earlier scenes in the novel where the American soldier is positioned as both a maternal and paternal figure, a pattern that will continue as a way of demonstrating national power through the guise of the nonthreatening figure of the mother, whose love was believed to cross national borders and help "knit together the exemplary America of the white, suburban middle class and the politically contested regions of Asia" (Klein 66). This moment of comfort is disrupted as Tien Pao enters the Air Force base and is overwhelmed by the sights and sounds of the white men. The boy is disturbed by the men's appearance and their voices, but this discomfort is relieved when a Chinese interpreter informs him that the men "feel like fathers to you" (132–133, 136). The boy is giddy, feeling "all of a sudden . . . so light and wonderful—so safe" (137). Believing that "no one could hurt him here—not among sixty white airmen," Tien Pao relaxes.

Although the U.S. airmen feel a special bond with Tien Pao, they are not yet his legal guardians. As the interpreter notes, the airmen only "feel like fathers"—they are not his fathers in actuality. DeJong begins to initiate a dialogue about U.S. intervention even in these early stages of his narrative. The airmen's interest in Tien Pao parallels the United States' rising interest in Asia and the government's desire to bring Asian powers such as China into the national family. Christina Klein argues in her essay on the U.S. government's political discourse regarding Asia during the Cold

War that the 1950s marked a rapid rise in U.S. citizens' interest in
the events taking place in Asian countries. This interest, as Klein
contends, was in part a response to a demand for the United States
to take up the mantle of global leadership. War propaganda such
as Henry Luce's seminal *Life* magazine editorial "The American
Century" (1941) urged American citizens to support U.S. involvement in World War II because it was the nation's duty as a world
leader. Such responsibility was often articulated in terms of family
ties, and U.S. citizens were encouraged to think about Asia as part
of the national family. With the image of the powerful U.S. soldiers
cradling the wounded Tien Pao, DeJong reflects popular attitudes
regarding Asia. His representation of the interaction between soldier and war orphan supports the rhetoric popular at the time and
indicates that the relationship between the two is mutually beneficial: the soldiers are able to fulfill their duty as world leaders,
and Tien Pao is protected from the bullets of the Japanese and the
dangers of starvation.

DeJong contrasts this scene of warmth, safety, and comfort with
the fear and anxiety associated with an unwanted adoption. As the
U.S. soldiers shift from being father figures to adoptive fathers,
the once happy union between the boy and the airmen goes sour.
Tien Pao, although initially thrilled with the idea of having sixty
fathers to care for him, is crushed when he discovers that the men
are no longer "like fathers" but his real adoptive fathers. In a conversation with the U.S. military's interpreter, Tien Pao rejects his
new fathers and the privilege that goes along with being an American adoptee: "'I don't want sixty fathers,' Tien Pao exploded. 'I have
a father and mother. . . . Oh, I'm not ungrateful,' he added hast-
ily. 'But don't you understand? I have a father and mother, and I
must find them and the baby sister. I have to find them!'" (147).
DeJong depicts a situation in which U.S. intervention is in fact
harmful and thereby calls into question the United States' "exceptional" status and the propaganda that declared it was the nation's duty to intervene in conflicts abroad. The bond that Tien Pao
began forming with his new fathers is satisfactory only so long as
it is temporary, only so long as the airmen are just "like fathers."
Once the airmen overstep this boundary and become legal guardians, the child is outraged and defends his birth family ties.

Tien Pao's rejection of his new family hints at the imperial undertones of U.S. involvement in foreign affairs. Tien Pao, the weak and helpless Chinese boy, is dependent in almost every way on his white fathers: they feed, clothe, and shelter him. Moreover, as a child, he has no legal control over his body. On a whim the airmen adopt the boy, with no thought for his real family. Tien Pao's adoption is a disturbing reminder of the relationship between the way children and colonized subjects are treated. Both a child and the citizen of a nation under the influence of a powerful world leader, Tien Pao, in his engagement with the U.S. soldiers, demonstrates the new forms of colonialism taking place as part of the United States' mission to expand its global power. As Tien Pao's experience shows, adoption can at first seem welcome, but once the new adoptee is forced to assimilate, it becomes constricting. The airmen's interpreter underscores this point when he demands that the boy conform to U.S. expectations regarding child behavior: "Now, you are not to run outdoors naked! Your sixty fathers would be horrified" (146). At varying moments, Tien Pao is scolded and told how to eat, dress, and behave. A good American adoptee does not cry or refuse gifts from his new fathers, he is told, nor does he allow his pet pig to sleep inside with him.

Tien Pao's response to his new fathers challenges the national rhetoric about love without boundaries that encouraged U.S. citizens to see those in Asia as family members during the Cold War (Choy and Choy 264). Through the challenges of the airmen's new fatherhood, DeJong demonstrates the difficulty of navigating cultural differences. The airmen must rely on the doctor and the interpreter to communicate with Tien Pao, and even then they often fail to understand the child's emotional needs. At times these incidents provide some much-needed comic relief for the dark narrative, such as when Tien Pao swallows a piece of gum and rubs his belly as a sign of satisfaction despite his confusion about the substance's purpose (128–129).[3] At other times, however, they are heartbreaking: when Tien Pao first wakes up in the barracks of the U.S. military base, he is presented with a tray of food only to have it quickly taken away. The soldier who removes the plate does so because he is unsure whether Tien Pao's malnourished body can handle the rich food, but the child cannot understand and cries hysterically out of rage and frustration (139). These moments of miscommunication show that familial love does indeed have its limits and that it is not always possible to overcome cultural differences through goodwill alone.

DeJong's appropriation of the adoption trope not only provides a critique of U.S. intervention in the Second Sino-Japanese War but also seeks a solution to the political and cultural differences that threatened successful U.S.-China relations. While Tien Pao's adoption fails, DeJong attempts to find a satisfactory alternative to adoption. In a surprising turnabout, the novel ends with Tien Pao being returned to his biological family, while his favorite U.S. soldier, Lieutenant Hamsun, stands happily by the family's side during the reunion: "There sat the lieutenant half turned, and he did not understand what his [Tien Pao's] mother had said. Ah, but he did understand. He understood! The heart understands without words" (189). In a narrative rife with cultural misunderstandings, DeJong's final words convey a hopeful image of Tien Pao's old and new families being brought together. Reflecting on these final words, Judith Hartzell, a friend of DeJong, recalls a conversation she had with the author regarding his conclusion: "Mick loved the last chapter. 'Isn't that something?' he asked me. 'And the last line is perfect. "The heart understands without words." Anything more would have been anticlimactic'" (232–233). The ending evokes the sentimental discourse that DeJong rejected earlier. Rather than finding a rational way to overcome cultural differences, DeJong resorts to a solution that involves the heart.

The ending of *The House of Sixty Fathers* challenges the novel's message in the adoption scene. Taken out of context, the author's change of heart makes little sense. Yet it is important to keep in mind that DeJong is drawing on well-worn patterns of the nineteenth-century adoption narrative, which usually end either in permanent adoption or with the return of the child to his/her birth parents. Even though adoptees in these earlier novels often suffer greatly before finding happiness, they are rewarded in the end. Tien Pao's journey conforms to this narrative trope and draws on the sentimental roots of adoption fiction. Early accounts of adoption in such popular nineteenth-century novels as Susan Warner's *The Wide, Wide World* (1850) and Maria Susanna Cummins's *The Lamplighter* (1854) depict a journey of spiritual renewal that involves the protagonist's suffering: many tears are shed over the loss of the biological family and the painful process of integrating into a new family. Tears become the pretext for spiritual cleansing as the young girls that star in these domestic novels learn to conform to what Barbara Welter has called the "cult of true womanhood." In contrast, boys appearing in tales of uplift and adventure might be aided by an adult patron without the commitment of family ties, setting out on their own after a period of partnership that is mutually beneficial for adult and child (Singley 92). Because Tien Pao is not white or middle class, his happy ending has a very different set of implications from those of the American children in these tales, enabling him to escape the threat of being ripped from the cultural ties represented by his blood kin yet not going quite so far as to give him the power to set out independently on his own. The image of the happy family in DeJong's novel therefore becomes a way to mix old and new literary conventions, suggesting that some middle ground between adoption—a process that appears too similar to colonization in DeJong's depiction of it—and abandonment might be possible.

"Going Native": White Guilt, Illegal Aliens, and the Problem of Black Fatherhood

The consciousness about the United States' responsibility as a world leader that arose in the 1950s continued in the years after the 1989 fall of the Berlin Wall, a period that led to renewed criticism by novelists in the wake of the Reagan administration's zeal to control the spread of communism in regions that extended beyond Asia. Ushering in a new era of Cold War conflict, Reagan ended the period known as "détente" and began making decisions that increased the United States' involvement in global affairs, a move that incited harsh international criticism. For example, after he proposed to invade Grenada in response to the New Jewel Movement, British prime minister Margaret Thatcher remarked, "I cannot conceal that I am deeply disturbed by your latest communication. You asked for my advice. I have set it out and hope that even at this late stage you will take it into account before events are irrevocable" (qtd. in Wapshott 202). Reagan would ignore Thatcher, leading to the invasion of the island on October

25, 1983. His actions were symbolic of the United States' growing power and confidence in controlling world events, an attitude that was also present in earlier conflicts including the 1898
Spanish-American War. These actions marked Reagan's terms as
president as a moment of renewed Cold War rhetoric about the nation's duty to "preserve" democracy in "oppressed" nations and res-
urrected old anxieties about the extent to which the nation's commitment to democracy implied the necessity of U.S. involvement in
international crises.

In *Rule of the Bone* (1995), Russell Banks, one of the most noted
American authors of the 1990s, reflects the growing discontent
with the repercussions of the Reagan administration's actions
abroad in the previous decade with his intricate examination of
the power dynamics at play in the United States' involvement in
the Caribbean. The novel follows the adventures of fourteen-year-
old Chapman Dorset, a troubled youth who runs away from home
and ends up involved in the drug trade in Montego Bay, Jamaica.
In the process of escaping the drudgery of his daily life, Chapman,
aka Chappie and Bone, meets a series of father figures, the most
important of whom is a black Rastaman known as I-Man.[4] By in-
voking the figure of the father, Banks investigates the power associated with fathers in the American tradition. As in the case of
Miller's Puritan thesis, the father not only sets a standard for future generations; he also institutes principles intended to guide
his family and secure its survival, which is dependent on his progeny's ability to carry out the errand bestowed on them. As a figure
often associated with the nation's founders and future leaders, the
father symbolizes the power and authority bestowed on men as a
result of their gender, race, and class. Banks utilizes these associations with the father in his portrayal of the relationship between
Chappie and I-Man to underscore the corruption inherent in white
patriarchy and also to suggest the limits to expanding the national
"family."

By introducing an adolescent boy who questions the authority of
his white fathers, Banks suggests that those in positions of power
are not necessarily qualified to lead. As Chappie relates, "I didn't
exactly have a lot to be thankful for unless you count my real father
taking off on me and my stepfather's sicko visits to my room when

he was drunk" (154). Disgusted with his life, the teenaged Chappie runs away from home and begins participating in criminal activities in order to earn enough money to avoid subjecting himself to the authority of corrupt or irresponsible adults. After several mishaps with his living situation, Chappie searches for a new home and settles on an abandoned yellow school bus in the local junkyard. It is at this point that the young teenager literally trips over the man who will guide him through much of his remaining journey. This father figure emerges, like an American Adam, out of nowhere and introduces himself as a migrant worker who hails from Jamaica and who "walked" when he discovered that he couldn't "practice his religion" on the farm (155–156).[5] Despite his mysterious origins, I-Man quickly becomes a prominent father figure for Chappie, who strongly prefers him to his abusive stepfather, Ken.

Chappie's budding relationship with I-Man enables Banks to subvert the racial connotations associated with fatherhood, which often denigrate the role of black men within the family. Historically described as irresponsible, violent, and hypersexual (Ransaw 2), black men remain a target of public censure in contemporary discussions of fatherhood. In an emotional speech during his campaign for the U.S. presidency, Barack Obama declared, "They [black fathers] have abandoned their responsibilities, acting like boys instead of men. And the foundations of our families are weaker because of it" (qtd. in Bosman). Obama is often cited as a contemporary example of a "good" black father, but many critics still address how contemporary fatherhood movements fail to fully address the underlying reasons for alternative family structures in black families. Moreover, much of the literature that does exist conforms to the media stereotype of the "deadbeat dad," giving little attention to fathers who do subscribe to more traditional models of a loving and responsible father (Connor and White 2). One contemporary fatherhood movement from the 1990s, the "fatherhood responsibility movement" (FRM), demonstrates this split in values, which is divided along lines of race and class. Two main political groups emerged in the FRM, those with conservative values who support fatherhood within the context of the nuclear family ("promarriage wing"), and those who are more open to alternative family structures so long as a father figure is present ("fragile fam-

ilies wing") (Gavanas 250). According to Swedish social anthropologist Anna Gavanas, the fragile families group aims to support
lower-class and minority families, whereas the promarriage group
claims to support "all men," even though this tends to mean white,
middle-class men in reality (250). Despite these differences, both
groups participate in an unsettling trend among the FRM that encourages gender binaries, arguing that "fathers have become marginalized in the family, with catastrophic societal consequences"
(Gavanas 248).

Within the literary sphere, there is a similarly alarming trend
in African American literature, where few black men serve as models of ideal fatherhood, even in the works of such canonical authors as Toni Morrison, Richard Wright, and Ralph Ellison (Moon
64). Instead, an emphasis is placed on men traumatized by slavery or the continued existence of racism and their unhealthy ways
of handling this trauma, including through rape, incest, alcohol-
ism, and infidelity (Moon 68). These representations serve their
purpose in terms of recognizing the many roadblocks black men
might face on their path to fatherhood, but they also present an
overwhelmingly negative portrayal of black men that supports the
pervasive public view of them as fathers. Dating back to such damaging studies as the 1965 "Moynihan Report" or *The Negro Family: The Case for National Action*, which determined that African
American families "were unstable and pathological due to high
levels of divorce, desertion, paternal absenteeism, and black male
unemployment" (Perry, Harmon, and Bright 127), statistics about
crime and unemployment continue to feed the public belief that
black men are incapable fathers and to delegitimize African American families. In his 2017 study of black fatherhood, Theodore Ransaw, an African American studies scholar, claims that "part of the
impetus behind the negative perceptions of African American fathers may lie in false views that are not inclusive of alternative
models [of fatherhood]" (3). With these problems in mind, it is important to note how negative literary portrayals of black fathers
contribute to these perceptions, affecting "how young black male
readers in real life internalize, visualize, and project the distorted
images of black men" and ultimately leading to the whitewashing
of fatherhood (Moon 66).

In a narrative rife with irresponsible white fathers, Banks re-
verses the negative assumptions about black fatherhood by depicting I-Man as a positive role model in Chappie's life. Despite his
limited income as a migrant worker, I-Man is able to combat traditional roadblocks to idealized fatherhood and offers Chappie practical life and spiritual lessons. Like the garden that he grows in
the junkyard, I-Man nurtures the weak and abused boy and helps
him develop into a responsible man by teaching him how to grow
edible plants in the junkyard and scavenge for food in the city. In
addition, he introduces Chappie to the Rastafarian way and the
many rules that followers of Rastafarianism must remember. One
of these rules, I-Man emphasizes, is abstaining from alcoholic bev-
erages "due to the connection between rum and slavery days" (155).
In teaching Chappie how to grow in both body and spirit, I-Man
conforms to many of the overlooked positive attributes of black fathers. These traits, psychologists Michael Connor and Joseph White
argue, include "spirituality, improvisation, resilience, and connect-
edness to others through the extended family and the larger African American community" (2). Connor and White acknowledge that
father substitutes are much more common among African Americans, whose kinship relation model of family derives from their
African roots (3). These substitute fathers are part of a category
of fatherhood named "social fatherhood," which includes any male
figure that provides the "nurturance, moral and ethical guidance,
companionship, emotional support, and financial responsibility" often associated with the biological father's role in the family (3).

While Banks presents alternative attributes of fatherhood, he
also draws on conventional values of white, middle-class fatherhood. I-Man's actions in the school bus portion of the narrative,
particularly his nurturing disposition, depict him as a version of
the ideal father figure that emerged between World Wars I and
II. This "new fatherhood" encouraged fathers to take a more loving approach to parenting and to become more actively involved in
their children's lives (Griswold 88–89). Simply being a breadwin-
ner, under this new logic, was insufficient to make men good fathers. The turn away from more authoritarian models of parenting had a lot to do with the increasing popularity of psychological
theory in the United States, along with the child-study movement

of the early twentieth century. Inspired by the new child "experts," fathers began to accept that their presence in the household was not only important but also necessary for their child's proper emotional development. Drawing on Ernest Burgess's sociological studies of family life, experts insisted that a child's proper emotional development depended on the father's presence, which aided in the child's "interpersonal relations and sex-role socialization" (Griswold 94).

By combining different cultural values of family, Banks is able to trouble the boundary between white and black fatherhood. As the initial events of Chappie's adventures underscore, race has little to do with one's ability to successfully parent. Chappie's stepfather is a lazy alcoholic who takes pleasure in sexually abusing his stepchild; his biological father is a con man who abandoned his young son. Neither of the two white fathers who appear in the novel therefore fulfills middle-class standards of fatherhood, a fact that challenges the racial coding of these standards. In contrast to these white fathers, I-Man meets the criteria of a good father. He listens carefully to Chappie's needs and provides him with skills to survive in a world where corruption is rampant. I-Man provides valuable guidance in areas such as emotional and spiritual development that are seen as imperative to the growth of a well-adjusted child. Under his care, Chappie gains confidence and begins to control his anger and desires. Chappie even notes these changes when he declares how his new chores "made me feel independent" (162), and he views the days he spent with I-Man in the junkyard garden as the happiest ones of his life (164). Chappie's realization parallels that of the reader, who can recognize the deep contrast between Chappie's old and new living situations. Even though Chappie lacks a traditional home, he has the love that his parents failed to provide him in his former life.

In his presentation of the loving bond that Chappie forms with I-Man, Banks suggests the possibility of overcoming the racial issues that dominated during the Cold War. As areas around the world began to rapidly decolonize in the 1960s, a large population of nonwhite people was experiencing the possibility of forming their own governments for the first time. This proved to be an especially jarring change for the United States, whose concerns

about the susceptibility of emerging nations to communism motivated many of its actions abroad. In an effort to prevent the spread
of communism, the United States attempted to woo these nation's
leaders and put them on a path toward democracy. At a time when
fears of the spread of communism were high, rhetoric that promoted familial love and the inclusion of others within the family
circle became critical. Not only was the family a central building
block for smaller relief efforts, it also served as a metaphor for the
nation's grander designs. Just as real families might adopt a war
orphan from impoverished and war-torn nations and pass democratic values onto this child, so too should the U.S. government involve itself in world events that might lead to friendly ties and the
"adoption" of a nation into the expanding U.S. sphere of influence.

The problem with this familial rhetoric was that it overlooked
the fact that race was often a roadblock to national belonging. As
much as the media attempted to present the United States as a
benevolent father who accepts all its "children," there were many
contradictions between the national rhetoric and lived experience.
Historian Thomas Borstelmann notes in *The Cold War and the
Color Line* (2001) that the continuing mistreatment of the African American community was a terrible embarrassment for the
U.S. government, whose authority to intervene in the affairs of
recently decolonized nations was limited because of its racist domestic policies. He provides the example of foreign diplomats of
color who could not even visit the United States without body-
guards, due to the very real possibility of being attacked because of
their skin color (125–126, 165). During World War II, the Axis powers "eagerly brandished every report of racial discrimination in
the United States as evidence of American hypocrisy and the hol-
lowness of Allied rhetoric about democracy and freedom" (Borstelmann 36). Even though the Axis powers committed their own human rights crimes, the propaganda was effective since it "did not
need to enter the realm of fiction to weaken American claims to
moral superiority" (Borstelmann 36). As stories of racism in America reached the ears of the nonwhite majority abroad, suspicion
grew in regard to the United States' motives. For example, following the onset of the Korean War, U.S. policymakers began to
concern themselves more with foreign policy in Asia and Africa,

largely due to "fears that resentment of American racism might
cause Asian and African peoples to seek closer relations with the
Soviet Union" (Von Eschen 113).

The troubles in the United States' domestic and foreign policies
are reflected in the bonds that begin to form between I-Man and
Chappie, and they are further cemented as the characters expand
their makeshift family. While the primary focus of the novel is on
the relationship between Chappie (who now refers to himself as
Bone) and I-Man, the two also include in their family circle a little abused girl named Froggy, whom Chappie/Bone believes to be
about six or seven years old (110).[6] Froggy, sold into the sex trade
by her mother, flourishes under I-Man's care much like Chap-
pie/Bone. However, even in this idyllic picture of racial harmony,
Banks acknowledges the challenges that race poses when forming
alternative kinship bonds, or what Judith Butler has described as
"radical kinship" formations (74).[7] As Chappie/Bone indicates on
multiple occasions, the appearance of a black Jamaican with two
young white children is an unusual sight, especially for the nearly
all-white community of Plattsburgh, New York. Perhaps the most
suggestive of Chappie/Bone's comments is when the boy remarks
that traveling unseen to the local grocery store is "good": "I think
we would've stood out, a little girl and a black Rastafarian with
dreadlocks and a white kid although without my mohawk I wasn't
as obvious as before. Still, it was the combination" (164).

As Banks explores ways to bridge the racial divide that marked
the Cold War period, he relies on the familiar trope of the garden
in order to create a safe space where a new family might form, one
not defined by genealogical bias. I-Man's garden becomes a racially
innocent space, where the white child embraces the black father.
Bone's narrative reaffirms the racial innocence of the garden when
he comments on a memory of I-Man holding hands with Froggy. As
Bone watches the two traverse the garden hand-in-hand, he declares that the pair "made a real nice picture" (160). The picture
that Bone observes is one common in nineteenth-century American literature, a connection that Bone does not fail to make as
he recalls a book he read for a seventh-grade school report. The
book—Harriet Beecher Stowe's *Uncle Tom's Cabin* (1852)—is a
novel whose main characters, Uncle Tom and Little Eva, continue
to be famous examples of interracial friendship. In her analysis

of the novel's nineteenth-century reception and continued influence in twentieth-century American culture, cultural historian
Robin Bernstein argues that Little Eva and Uncle Tom's relationship reaffirms racial division rather than breaking down this bar-
rier. While Stowe herself intended to denounce slavery, the ubiquity of the image of Little Eva and Uncle Tom sitting peacefully
together in a garden, the child's hand upon the knee of the family
slave, supported alternative positions that made slavery appear
innocent. Since innocence has historically been coded white, the
white child became a useful mechanism for nineteenth-century
Americans who were interested in either justifying slavery or ig-
noring it altogether: "What childhood innocence helped Americans
to assert by forgetting, to think about by performing oblivious-
ness, was not only whiteness but also racial difference constructed
against whiteness" (8). The practice of co-opting innocence in order
to forget racial difference, for Bernstein, continued to hold sway in
American culture through the performance of childhood or in the
repetition of "innocent" behavior learned through the circulation
of deeply embedded images such as those of Little Eva and Uncle
Tom. White, middle-class children, because they have yet to grow
up and understand racial difference, can be friends with those who
are racially different through their performance of innocence.

It is this very conceit of racial innocence, or the process by which
"childhood . . . enable[s] divergent political positions each to appear natural, inevitable, and therefore justified" (Bernstein 4),
that Banks objects to and seeks to circumvent in his narrative. He
does this first by rejecting conventional notions of childhood, particularly the belief that children, especially white children, are inherently innocent. Banks has spoken publicly about his views of
childhood innocence. In a 1998 interview for the *Paris Review*, he
remarks how, unlike the author J. D. Salinger, he does not "believe
in innocence": "I have a hard time imagining such a thing, mainly
because I don't think that I believe in innocence. Salinger thinks of
childhood differently than I do, as if the main threat to childhood
is knowledge of adult life. Whereas I think that the main threat to
children has more to do with power, adult power and the misuse
and abuse of it" (66). Banks is quick to call attention to the fragility of the happy family he creates in the garden. Even Bone, who
still wants to believe in childhood innocence, negates his claim that

"I'd found a real home and a real family" with the recognition, "But it wasn't a real family" (167). Bone's statements signal that despite his wish to the contrary, racism will threaten the group's survival, even if this threat comes from the outside world. As Bone later comments, "I was only a kid myself and an outlaw and I-Man was a Jamaican illegal alien trying to get by and eventually get home without getting busted by the American government" (167). As Banks acknowledges in the *Paris Review* interview, it is power that threatens children more than knowledge of the world around them. Even if Bone were innocent enough to be unaware of the government agencies that had power over the bodies of his family, these same agencies would eventually find and break up his family unit.

Bone inadvertently becomes an agent of his new family's destruction when he decides to return home. Before he can do so, however, he must first care for his new family members and, to the best of his ability, secure their safety. His concern for the others, especially Froggy, results in a reversal of power similar to that which occurs in DeJong's *The House of Sixty Fathers*. Because I-Man refuses to assert his authority as adult and father figure, Bone steps up and takes his place as the "father" of the little family. Bone's taking up of the mantle of power will end up being both liberating and destructive. Like his adoptive father, Ken, Bone will make decisions that hurt his family members. Bone's entanglement with the very social forces that he seeks to evade end up jeopardizing his new family's safety—in fact, Froggy and I-Man both die as a result of Bone's decisions. Bone, who insists that Froggy must return to her mother, learns later that the young girl has died of pneumonia, likely a result of neglect from her irresponsible caregiver, while I-Man is murdered by Bone's biological father after Bone, out of a sense of loyalty to his biological parent, reveals that he saw I-Man having sex with his father's girlfriend. Banks uses Bone's failures to further develop his thesis on power. Each time Bone fails and hurts a member of his idealized interracial family, he confronts a system of power that privileges white males. In this system, Bone can grow up to be the authority figure, something neither Froggy nor I-Man can manage to do. This is why, as children's literature scholar Clare Bradford remarks in *Unsettling Narratives* (2007), comparing (white) children to colonized subjects is problematic:

white children grow up and gain power as full citizens, whereas the colonized subject will never have access to this power (7).

Commies in the Caribbean:
A Critique of the Reagan Administration

The first half of *Rule of the Bone* is largely dedicated to dismantling previous American conceptions of family and suggesting that alternative family models, such as those grounded in kinship relations not bound by blood, might be possible. As Banks continues to develop his critique of Cold War America, he draws on associations of power inherent in the figure of the white father. Indeed, the father's association with power and authority are rooted in the complex father-son relationships in the novel. In her 2010 study of early American childhood, Anna Mae Duane provides some contextualization for the multiple meanings of fatherhood in the Anglo-American tradition. She explains that early literature such as English philosopher Robert Filmer's *Patriarcha* (1680) defended "the long-standing hypothesis that equated fathers with rulers and children with subjects" (*Suffering Childhood* 29). Other forms of literature, including the popular captivity narrative, "reenact[ed] the confrontation between the rigid father figure and the rebellious, but overpowered, child" (39). Enlightenment philosopher John Locke also weighed in on the issue, "insist[ing] that fathers must watch over their offspring" in order to ensure the child's safe entrance into maturity, a view intended to recognize the brevity of the child's dependency and the parent's role in helping the child reach the more autonomous state of adulthood (*Suffering Childhood* 130). Duane suggests that Locke's position differed from other representations of fatherhood in that he actually "empowers the child—making the patriarch more guardian than ruler" (130).

Much like the more authoritarian and overbearing father in early American literature, the white father in Banks's narrative serves as a site of resistance for his offspring. Upon arriving in Jamaica, Bone discovers his biological father, a development that will challenge his sense of loyalty to his father substitute, I-Man. As he struggles with his sense of obligation to his biological father and his fondness for his friend and guardian, Bone unveils a system of power that privileges white male authority. Bone learns that a few rich white men rule the island and that white tourists similarly have power over impoverished locals. One of the leaders of this ring of power is Bone's father, an American expatriate named Doc. Americans like Doc assert their authority over the locals due to their affluence and their sense of racial superiority. As a biological descendant of Doc, Bone must decide whether he wants to continue his father's errand and grow up to be as ruthless and corrupt as this man or align himself with the compassion that he has come to associate with his black father substitute. This situation parallels the similarly divided loyalties that emerged during the Cold War. As many were divided on the subject of "the color line" at home and its ramifications abroad, the nation's mission to expand its family by "adopting" nonaligned nations came under question.

By returning to the controversies over race in Cold War America, Banks highlights the interrelationship between domestic and foreign affairs. A blot on the U.S. government in its initiatives in recently decolonized areas of the world such as Africa, the race question conflicts with the United States' errand of freedom and democracy for all. Historian Penny Von Eschen explains that "fabricating an image of American racial harmony, and of simultaneously not wanting to embarrass its white supremacist allies by pretending to believe in this very fabrication" was of chief importance to U.S. policymakers (120). Banks's empathetic portrayal of I-Man allows readers to identify with a character that is ultimately crushed by a system of power that privileges whiteness. The presentation of whiteness in *Bone* is rooted in the domestic issues surrounding racial inequality in the United States and illustrates its effects on a global stage. Modern forms of U.S. imperialism, particularly neocolonial activities such as tourism and the drug trade, highlight the negative impact U.S. involvement can have on other nations. Contrary to the U.S. rhetoric of familial love, this involvement does not always benefit the local population. By presenting a black rather than a white father as Bone's role model, Banks questions the authority that has long been associated with racial superiority. Whiteness in his narrative is not a guarantee of sound decision making; rather, it is a sign of corruption.

In order to confront the system of power associated with fatherhood, Bone must first learn what it feels like to be part of a racial minority. In Jamaica, Bone finds himself in a world where his whiteness makes him more visible; at the same time, his status as adolescent contributes to his continuing invisibility. Stuck in this in-between state, a product of his age, race, and legal status (he is an illegal alien during his stay in Jamaica), Bone searches for a way to transform himself into a "brand-new beggar" so that he might make a home in Jamaica (241). He initially believes that such a transformation depends on his ability to physically blend in. Indeed, as he works on the ganja plantation with I-Man, Bone notes that his labors have physically changed him: "I was standing alone dribbling water from a pail onto the plants like I-Man'd showed me and I flipped my head to chase off a mosquito and saw dreadlocks swirling through the air in my shadow. Then I looked down at my arms and hands which were like coffee-colored and when I saw I didn't look like a regular white kid anymore I put down the bucket and did a little Rasta dance right there in the sunshine" (313). Bone's reaction to this physical transformation reveals his belief in the power of external changes to shape internal ones. In his interpretation of this passage, literary scholar Jim O'Loughlin argues that Bone's desire to physically transform himself is indicative of his current understanding of subjectivity, which he views as mutable based on superficial changes like appearance (39). Such a belief is grounded in Bone's belief that it is possible to "transcend the limitations of his given subject position and construct an identity of his own, on his own terms" (39).

O'Loughlin's argument about the role of whiteness in *Rule of the Bone* neglects the fact that Bone's age contributes significantly to his understanding of subjectivity. The fact that he is an adolescent, on the cusp of solidifying his subjectivity as a white male, plays a role in his belief that subjectivity is fluid, a belief, O'Loughlin points out, that is later revised based on Bone's experiences on the island. Karen Sánchez-Eppler, in her 2005 study of the historical treatment of children and childhood in the United States, explains that children are frequently seen "not as selves, but as stages in the process of making an adult identity" (*Dependent States* xvi). Children are taught to understand their own position as fluid and to interpret their existence as one dominated by change. Bone accepts this notion of childhood and believes that if he tries hard enough, he can reform himself physically as well as spiritually.

The limitation of Bone's understanding of his subjectivity is that he fails to account for the fact that he cannot transform himself without the aid of an adult, I-Man, whose authority allows him to "pass" as black. If we return to the passage where Bone experiences his physical transformation, it is evident that it is prompted by I-Man in every respect: Bone's skin tans because I-Man allows him to work in his ganja fields, and he manages to grow dreadlocks because I-Man rubs a liquid concoction in his hair. Bone's experience on the island will eventually lead him to reassess his previous beliefs about race and about the fluidity of one's subjectivity; however, before he can do so, he must first accept his inclusion in the system of power that is predicated on whiteness.

Bone's sense of a fluid subjectivity is first tested when he learns that his biological father, "Doc," is living a few miles away from him. A rich white man who deals in hard drugs, Doc introduces Bone to a lifestyle that highlights racial difference. At the plantation where his father lives, there is a group of black men whom Bone refers to as "natties" or "Rent-a-Rastas" (the latter a term he learns from I-Man) because they hang out with white women and are willing to have sex with them in order to share in the women's upscale lifestyle. Bone admits that "No actual money changed hands," but he believes that what the natties and white women are doing is wrong: "People who have to sell themselves ought to be paid in cash" (287). Despite his strong words, Bone initially overlooks the hierarchy on the plantation because he is so taken with his biological father. In their very first encounter, Bone races after his father's car, yelling like a small child, "Daddy! Daddy! Over here, it's me, your son Chappie!" (271). Bone's fascination with his biological father has a lot to do with his memories of life with his mother and stepfather. Blaming his failed relationship with his mother on his stepfather and harboring understandable feelings of rage as a result of his stepfather's sexual abuse, Bone wonders if "things would've been different if I'd've had my real father to go to when I was seven and Ken first started in" (222). "With my real father to help me," Bone further reflects, "I wouldn't have been scared to tell like I was with my mom who I couldn't go to or didn't think I could because Ken was her husband and she loved him supposedly and never let me complain about him" (222). As Bone separates from his mother and stepfather, he builds up a fantasy image of his biological father, be-

lieving that "things would've been different" if his father had been
there to shelter him.

Bone's belief in his father, along with his desire for his protection, initially enables him to ignore the treatment of the black men
on the plantation. Owned and run by Doc's girlfriend, Evening Star,
the plantation is a site for wealthy elites from the United States
who are interested in having a good time. Drugs swap hands as
quickly as sexual partners, and food and liquor seem to appear
from nowhere. While Bone sees Evening Star as the source of the
sexual energy in the house, it is his father who underscores the
system of ownership. Bone learns this lesson when he discovers
Evening Star and I-Man having sex: disturbed by this primal encounter, Bone runs to his "real" father and confesses what he has
witnessed. Bone's need to confess is prompted by his fear that he
is not loved by his biological father and will be abandoned: "I don't
know what I'm pissed at. It's everything I guess. The no birthday
cake and I-Man banging Evening Star and my father gone without
even saying goodbye" (300). Bone hopes that confessing to his father will make him feel better and strengthen their bond; instead,
it results in his father's decision to kill I-Man. The conversation between biological father and son shatters Bone's ideal image of his
white father, who at last transforms into his true monstrous self:

> Well, Bone, I'm going to have to kill him.
>
> Jeez. How come?
>
> Why? Because what's mine is mine. That's the rule *I* live by,
> Bone. And when some little nigger comes into my house and
> takes what's mine, he has to pay. He has to pay and pay, many
> times over. And the only thing that nigger owns is his worth-
> less life, so that's what he'll have to pay with. (302; emphasis in
> original)

Doc reveals the extent of the racial divide at Starport, on the island more generally, and in the contemporary world system. His
belief in ownership, and in a system of exchange where bodies
function as currency, is one with which Bone is already well familiar. However, the conversation with his father forces Bone to confront the system of power in place in Starport and to make a decision concerning his future.

These narrative developments return readers to questions of fatherhood that Banks raises from the beginning of the novel. At the novel's opening, Bone's maternal grandmother declares, "You don't *have* a father, Chappie. Forget him" (4; emphasis in original). It seems at this point that his grandmother's words are correct since all his fathers have failed him. Drugs and hatred consume his biological father, whereas business and sexual pleasure preoccupy his black father substitute. While Bone tries to fit into his two fathers' worlds, he cannot manage it. Such concerns about fatherhood and its ability to survive in the late twentieth century are, in children's literature scholar Claudia Nelson's opinion, testament to the belief that "fatherhood is something that doesn't always come naturally, something that may require peculiar circumstances if it is to flourish" (99). Nelson gives the example of a Merlin story in which the wizard of legend is his own father, literally birthing himself. Banks's protagonist appears to follow a similar course. Like Merlin, Bone must also "father himself" in the sense that he must first choose his own father and then decide to change his position from son to father. As in the garden scene, Bone must act quickly in order to survive and resolves to betray both his fathers, at once rendering him the "bad" son and aligning him with the guilt and shame associated with white fatherhood.

Bone experiences this guilt and shame most strongly when he discovers I-Man's corpse. The death of his father figure makes Bone realize that his attempts to protect his family and play father have failed. I-Man's mutilated body, with "his skinny little legs sticking out and his eyes and mouth open" and a "jagged hole in the center of his forehead," is a disturbing image of the potential violence of fatherhood (339–340). As critics of fatherhood have noted, the power of fathers remains a constant source of interest. Citing several examples where fathers either abuse their wives or children or else abandon them completely, Claudia Nelson concludes that "clearly our culture feels considerable anxiety about fatherhood—an anxiety that long predates the supermarket self-help book and the network talk show" (98). Historian Robert Griswold shares Nelson's view, remarking that "Today, fatherhood has become politicized: its terms are contested, its significance fragmented, its meaning unstable" (9). These anxieties about fatherhood extend to metaphors related to the making and breaking of national ties. As I noted previously, Carol Singley argues that the adoption trope served as a way to work through anxieties about the United States' break from Great Britain. Familial relations, particularly the parent-child bond, also prevail in historical representations of colonial conquest, where a paternalistic colonizer is said to protect his weak and innocent children. Such rhetoric is dangerous because it legitimates forms of oppression and dependency; however, it remains instructive as it constitutes yet another way in which fatherhood is used to think through the power dynamics of social ties, at once on an individual, national, and international scale. Through questions related to family loyalty and genealogical roots, Bone as father upsets traditional power hierarchies due to his age while reinforcing others through his compliance in a system that privileges white male power.

Bone's declaration upon seeing I-Man's body that "somehow the whole terrible thing felt like it was my fault and there was no way left for me now to make it right" serves as one of the many instances where Bone is used to comment on white guilt (340). This guilt is related not just to the slave trade but also to the neocolonial practices of wealthier nations that are powerfully on display in Banks's novel. Bone's need to narrate this history is rooted in the very origins of "nation" and in the United States more specifically. In the landmark collection *Nation and Narration* (1990), Homi Bhabha begins by claiming that nations are like narratives, which "lose their origins in the myths of time and only fully realize their horizons in the mind's eye." It is through this process of narration that "the nation emerges as a powerful historical idea in the west" (1).

Bhabha's identification of the nation as narration is instructive within the American context. Cold War scholars, including Lewis and Miller, traveled to distant countries in order to gain the perspective needed to narrate their version of "America," an experience that Amy Kaplan captures nicely in her 1993 critique of Miller's preface to *Errand into the Wilderness*: "Miller's expedition did for his intellectual development what he claims the Puritan errand did for American history; it founded the 'beginning of a beginning' that gives coherence to all that follows. From the remote vantage of the Congo Miller discovered himself at home with a coherent national identity; there, like the Puritans in the wilderness, he found himself 'left alone with America'" (4). Much like Miller before him, Bone travels to Jamaica in order to know "I-self," to grasp his individual as well as a national identity—or, to use Bhabha's words, to "narrate" his national self. This process of narration depends on notions of family, and in particular on the social construct of fatherhood, since it is fatherhood that has often been employed to narrate the colonial projects of Western nations.

Bone's desire to separate himself from this national history, a history that stares him in the face in I-Man's postmortem gaze, leads him to conclude, "I was definitely not into fatherhood" (367). Bone's refusal of fatherhood is linked to his experiences on the island,[8] which solidify his suspicion of white fatherhood in all its past incarnations. The novel's final scene is most telling in this regard as it provides a potential solution to the problems raised by Bone's journey for self-understanding. Having completed his journey and realigned himself with his black father by betraying Doc, Bone feels that he now understands what it means to be part of a family, as both a father and a son. Watching the stars above him, Bone realizes that each constellation is like its own special family unit: "The biggest stars or at least the brightest ones were related like in a family and you could connect the dots so to speak and make a picture if you wanted" (388). Bone's realization prompts him to search the sky for his adopted family, an act that ultimately empowers him. Bone is now able to create rather than destroy in the final moment of his journey. The shift suggests that perhaps he has at last escaped the system of power that he loathes. Yet even in this moment of triumph, Bone must also keep in mind his failures. The constellations that he forms are of those who died because of him, including his recently deceased father figure.

The comfort of gazing up at those who served as positive influences in his life enables Bone to better understand his past and to come to terms with his origins. As he observes a constellation that represents I-Man, Bone is comforted by the fact that his father substitute will be watching and guiding him with the simple words, "Up to you, Bone!" (390). Such an ending rejects traditional conceptions of childhood and empowers the adolescent protagonist. Yet such empowerment comes at a cost: Bone is stripped of his family ties and returns home as an orphan and survivor of tragic events, a pattern common in adventure stories featuring young boys and men in American literature, including Herman

Melville's *Moby-Dick*, upon which Bone's journey is modeled. Having drifted out to sea after surveying the consequences of racial divisions and neocolonialism, Bone returns to mainstream American society. Even in the post–Cold War society of the 1990s, Banks suggests, crossing racial boundaries has its risks, and national belonging is still largely dictated by the color of one's skin. Such a conclusion challenges the Cold War rhetoric of familial love, which proposes that one's race does not define one's ability to belong in the U.S. family.

Native Fathers, Oriental Others, and American Discontent after September 11

In his novel *Flight* (2007), Sherman Alexie expands on previous critiques of U.S. policy, once more merging the domestic and the foreign. Focused primarily with policies that developed in response to the September 11, 2001, attacks on the World Trade Center and Pentagon, Alexie returns to the figure of the father to question the decisions of U.S. leaders. Rejecting the image of the father as an upright and infallible character, Alexie inverts the power relations that underwrite the errand into the wilderness myth. For Miller, fathers appear as strong, authoritarian figures that determine the future destiny of their progeny. The role of the son, in contrast, is to fulfill the mission set down by his father. A novel that revolves around the exploits of a troubled American Indian adoptee, *Flight* rejects this model of father-son bonds. Alexie acknowledges the complicated nature of the father-son bond by demonstrating that sons do not always admire their fathers, nor do they always follow the orders set down by their guardians. The son's doubts, in ways not envisioned by Miller's Puritan thesis, are given credibility, demonstrating how in many cases fathers fail to fulfill the role of the ideal father and creating scenarios where the son must override the father's authority in order to make decisions about his life trajectory. In *Errand into the Wilderness*, Miller initially proposes that it is the son's inability to live up to his father's high standards that creates a problem for the future of America, a position he will later question and that Alexie more fully negates through his view that it is in fact fathers who are at fault.

Flight is not the first novel in which Alexie turns to the figure of the father in order to criticize U.S. government actions. Ralph Armbruster-Sandoval, a scholar of race studies, points out that Alexie's constant obsession with fatherhood enables the author to develop critiques of national leaders. In works such as his 1998 film *Smoke Signals*, Alexie creates fictional fathers whose actions parallel those of the Founding Fathers and recent government officials, including former president George W. Bush and his defense secretary, Donald Rumsfeld. By having these fictional fathers "make up stories or lies to cover up or rationalize their actions," Armbruster-Sandoval believes that Alexie is able to comment on historical actions of the United States that continue in the present through the behavior of men who bear the metaphorical title of "father" (129).[9] The similarities that Alexie identifies between these fictional and real-life "fathers" extend beyond the desire to run away from or deny one's problems. Zits, the protagonist of *Flight*, is troubled because of his inability to find a replacement for his drunken father who abandoned him as a child. In *Flight*, much as in *Smoke Signals*, the narrative is not so much about reforming the father as it is about forgiving and transcending the father's limitations. This requires a confrontation with one's history and cleaning of the proverbial attic. Much like Bone's need to relinquish his fantasies about his biological father, Alexie's protagonist must come to terms with his father's inability to fulfill the role of a loving guardian.

Flight marks a break from the common pattern of absent, drunken fathers who fail to redeem themselves in Alexie's work. In *Smoke Signals*, for example, Victor's father, Arnold, abandons his son after accidentally setting Thomas Builds-the-Fire's house on fire.[10] While he is able to save baby Thomas, Thomas's parents end up perishing in the flames, leaving him to grow up as an orphan. In narratives such as these, fathers and sons do come to some understanding of each other, but this empathy is limited, as the ending of *Smoke Signals* suggests. When Thomas recites Dick Lourie's famous poem "Forgiving Our Fathers" (1998), he asks, "If we forgive our Fathers what is left?" Alexie returns to this question in *Flight* and adds a new perspective that can be attributed to the shock of the September 11 events, something he attests to in a 2008 interview in the *Guardian*. In his words, the terrorist attacks "changed him . . . by revealing the lethal 'end game of tribalism—when you become so identified with only one thing, one tribe, that other people are just metaphors to you'" (Jaggi n.p.). American literary scholar Jennifer Ladino adds that after September 11, 2001, Alexie's writing, with its emphasis on "multitribal identity categories" and universal suffering, demonstrates the author's embrace of humanism (28). In order to express this all-embracing empathy, Alexie uses a "historiographic metafiction[al]" approach as a way of turning history on its head (Ibarrola-Armendariz and Vivanco 32), challenging previous representations of violent moments of history that include the Battle of Little Big Horn and the American Indian Movement of the 1960s and 1970s. This attempt to return to and revise past historical narratives includes father-son bonds, reviving deeply embedded beliefs about fatherhood among American Indians through Alexie's depictions of the narrator's own broken bonds.

Alexie's transformation as a writer participates in a wider trend to revise history after the turn of the twenty-first century, when a surge of biographical sketches about the United States' Founding Fathers emerged and became known as the "Founders Chic" movement among historians. A term first coined by a *Newsweek* journalist on July 8, 2001, to describe the nation's "nostalgic [desire] for an earlier era of genuine statesmen" (E. Thomas), the term took on greater significance following the September 11 terrorist attacks as this breach in national security led to the revival of national myths, including those about the nation's founders. The goal of the Founders Chic historians was to make the founders seem extraordinary by emphasizing what made them ordinary, an appealing transformation at a time when the nation's belief in its greatness was shattered and there was a strong desire to recover this national strength and power.[11] According to historian Ray Raphael, the members of the Founders Chic movement created a level of historical analysis that is frivolous at best (163). He further claims, "Like modern celebrities, the founders have been humanized, personalized, and made accessible to the masses" (161). In the aftermath of the September 11 terrorist attacks it was precisely the ordinary that was celebrated, as can be attested through the outpouring of support by the general public for everyday heroes that included police and firemen, helping fuel the Founders Chic movement. Those who participated in the movement worked to carefully balance the ordinariness and greatness of their famous historical subjects, moving between facts about mundane daily activities and influential political actions. As the historian Gordon Wood remarks in *Revolutionary Characters* (2006), "despite all the criticism and debunking of these founders, they still seem to remain for most Americans, if not for most academic historians, an extraordinary elite, their achievements scarcely matched by those of any other generation in American history" (9). Wood's comment attests to the continued potency of the figure of the father. No matter their flaws, these leaders appear as models of moral superiority; indeed, part of what has made the Founders Chic movement so popular is its ability to capitalize on such flaws in order to make these early statesmen more accessible to a general public.

The Founders Chic movement testifies to the desire to recover positive images of fathers and make them accessible to a general public in times of national tragedy. Although focused on the nation's founders, these biographical sketches demonstrate how in times of crisis the traditional associations of fathers as strong, wise, and capable leaders return as sources of comfort. As the head of the traditional nuclear family, the father is the one who brings the respective members of his family together. He gives a sense of unity to the family, and he also makes the hard decisions that will determine the family's future. This view of the father's role is integral to national mythology surrounding the nation's leaders. Since fathers have historically occupied positions of leadership, be it in the family or the broader community, they are subjected to standards that match their level of authority. In the case of the Founding Fathers, their high position of authority means that they are required to be flawless—intelligent, compassionate, morally upright, and, above all, devoted and loving fathers, be it to their biological children or the children of the nation. Should a founder fail to live up to these standards, the national narrative requires that this history be revised in order to comply with the expectations for the leader's role. In the case of Thomas Jefferson, one of the most famous of the Founding Fathers, historians have uncovered many blots on his reputation, namely his sexual relationship with one of his slaves, Sally Hemings; yet a walk through Jefferson's large estate overshadows this moral stain, instead drawing visitors' attention to the man as an inventor, farmer, and statesman. In times of crisis, the mission to preserve the image of the founders is even more imperative, and great efforts are made to build up the "greatness" of these national leaders in order to preserve the image of a healthy, thriving nation.

In *Flight*, Alexie breaks with the tradition of celebrating fathers and chooses instead to recuperate the son, who is often overshadowed by the myth of the infallible father. Zits's father, a drunken man who has abandoned his son, is portrayed as beyond saving, but Zits himself, a fifteen-year-old boy who recently shot several people, is not. Zits's journey is one of redemption: in bearing witness to the crimes of the men who came before him, the troubled teenager can break a historical cycle of violence. Like the new "fathers" that Armbruster-Sandoval identifies in his analysis of *Smoke Signals*, Zits can either repeat his father's mistakes or begin anew. Zits surpasses his father by learning from mistakes made in the past. He witnesses firsthand how those thrust into positions of authority can let anger drive their decisions and in so doing hurt those least capable of defending themselves. As Alexie's protagonist learns from these experiences, he develops into a figure far stronger than the various fathers that populate the narrative. It is through this transformation of the lost, vengeful son that Alexie ultimately challenges the myth of the superiority of the father. Sons are capable of overcoming, and even of surpassing, the damage done to them by negligent fathers. By touting the son as the heroic figure, Alexie negates the national myth that upholds the belief in the father's unquestionable ability to lead and direct the course of his family. With the father figure's association with national leaders, such a critique suggests that those currently in power in the United States are similarly unqualified to lead.

Sins of the Father: Zits's Flight through Time

Even before opening the cover of *Flight*, readers are reminded of recent events that challenged the ability of U.S. fathers to lead the nation. The novel's title invariably conjures up images of Flights 11 and 175 crashing into the World Trade Center, a connection that is emphasized further by the book's cover. The shooting target on the front, along with a darkened figure, presumably Zits, raising two guns in the air, hints at impending terrorism.[12] The terrorist, described as an unknowable force of evil in post-9/11 propaganda, became a pretext for racial exclusions from the national family. In an interview with CNN on September 17, 2001, President George W. Bush declared that the Al-Qaeda terrorists were an enemy unlike any the United States had ever faced before. Bush claimed that the terrorists were "a different type of enemy . . . [one] that likes to hide . . . [and] slit throats of women on airplanes in order to achieve an objective that is beyond comprehension." The title and cover page thus work together to remind readers about this rhetoric regarding terrorism and the response of national leaders to the recent threats to national security.

In an effort to defeat "the enemy," many residents in the United States, even citizens, came under surveillance simply because of their skin color. Because they looked similar to a terrorist, or because they originated from the Middle East, their right to belong came into question. Through the adventures of his protagonist, Alexie suggests that the inability of nonwhite characters to fit into white society is the result of a much longer cycle of vengeance and pain. While Alexie indicates that the pain of his nonwhite characters is partly due to their participation in this cycle, primarily through the commitment of acts of terrorism, he also suggests that national leaders, or "fathers," are to blame. The decisions of past leaders, for example, led to the decimation of Native peoples, an act with long-term consequences. By expertly drawing on Anglo-American associations with fatherhood, Alexie launches a full-scale critique of these national leaders' actions.

In order to achieve his goals, Alexie encourages his readers to identify with the son rather than the father. An orphan who finds it difficult to live with foster families, Zits is filled with anger toward his father. His mother died when he was six, and his father abandoned him before he was born. His loss is compounded by the fact that he is left adrift in the social system for Indian orphans: "There's this law called the Indian Child Welfare Act that's supposed to protect half-breed orphans like me. I'm only supposed to be placed with Indian foster parents and families. But I'm not an official Indian. My Indian daddy gave me his looks, but he was never legally established as my father" (8–9). The Indian Child Welfare Act (ICWA) was passed by Congress in 1978 "in response to the alarmingly high number of Indian children being removed from their homes by both public and private agencies" ("Indian Child Welfare Act"). The intent of ICWA is to prevent children from being removed from their tribes so that they can maintain their cultural identity. However, because his father never claimed him, Zits is not protected by the law and becomes an outcast from tribal culture. Zits similarly feels alienated from his mother's Irish culture. He identifies primarily as Indian although he loves and misses his mother more than his father. Zits's identification with Indian culture has to do with his orphan status as well as the fact that his physical appearance reminds him of his father. He feels he has no home, an experience common to Native peoples forced to live on reservations and one that drives his own father to the streets.

Zits's feelings of alienation have especially troubling ramifications in a post-9/11 context. Svetlana Boym, a comparative literature scholar, argues in *The Future of Nostalgia* (2001) that Americans possess a strong desire for roots: "Americans are supposed to be antihistorical, yet the souvenirization of the past and obsession with roots and identity here are ubiquitous" (38). Boym refers to the American tendency to shore up what little history is available or, in the words of historian Richard Hofstadter, "to make remarkably intense demands upon their history" (4). The need to collect and preserve history, a need driven by the search for roots, returned with a fierce passion in the aftermath of September 11. Books memorializing the Twin Towers began pouring out of publishing houses before the year was over. Museum curators began collecting debris, biological material, and anything once owned by victims of the attacks. Clothes, shoes, backpacks, steel girders, cell phones—nothing was considered too mundane for these collections. Oral history archives were also established so that the families of victims could record their experiences, and these collections also collected the messages left by victims in their final moments. The desire to remember a contemporary historical tragedy thus launched an enormous effort to preserve history for future generations.

Such a move is not surprising considering the patriotic fervor that struck many in the nation in the aftermath of the attacks. However, these acts of national remembering excluded others based on racial difference. In her 2009 study of the effects of post-9/11 rhetoric on Muslim American youth, Sunaina Maira explains that young Muslim children faced harsh racism from other Americans. In one of Maira's interviews, a teenage girl named "Sara" (a pseudonym given to protect the girl's identity) reflects on the racially charged environment of post-9/11 America: *"I wish that thing did not happen on September 11, and I wish they* [the terrorists] *did not kill those people in the buildings. But I wish America did not send the bombs over there, to Afghanistan. My father told me that I should not say these things outside, because people think that the Muslims had something to do with that thing on September 11. What did we do? I don't understand"* (3; emphasis in original). Other children in Maira's study make similar remarks, attesting to the difficulties of being racially different at this moment in American history. Maira considers the important role that family bonds play for these children, who are often sponsored by parents, siblings, or even more distant relations already based in the United States as they attempt to gain citizenship. Although she does not extensively address the part national leaders play in the problems that plague Muslim American youth, Maira does hint at the long-term impact of decisions made by these "fathers." She writes, "the post-9/11 moment is not exceptional, but part of a longer history of U.S. imperialism and political repression that has generally been evaded or erased" (6). In Alexie's novel, political (and cultural) repression is directly related to the decisions made by fathers. While Alexie does not include any political leaders in *Flight*, he does invite his readers to think about the connections between the fictional male characters and those responsible for historical U.S. government actions.

In one particular scene, Alexie combines the ubiquitous image of crashing planes following the events of September 11 with his assessment of the cyclical nature of damaging father-son bonds. After finally being placed in an Indian foster family, Zits quickly realizes that his foster father is no better than the cruel and malicious white fathers with whom he has previously lived. After gifting him with an expensive remote-control airplane, Zits's Indian father figure loses his temper when Zits repeatedly beats him at an airplane race, leading Zits to declare that Indian foster fathers "were bigger jerks than any of my eighteen white foster fathers" (9). As he relates the story of this traumatic incident, Zits solemnly recounts how his vision of the ideal Indian father went crashing down with his model airplane:

> Yes, Edgar had forgotten we switched planes. But I suppose it didn't matter because he flew the other plane into a tree, too.
> *Crash.*
> He didn't yell or cuss or get all crazy. Edgar calmly destroyed six hundred dollars' worth of model airplane.
> *Crash, crash.* (11)

The repetition of the word "crash" in Zits's narration of this event recalls the planes crashing into the two World Trade Center towers. Although Zits focuses on the economic loss, the readers recognize that it is not the planes that really matter. Zits's recollection of the event, of handling the broken wings, bent rudders, and the missing head of the miniature pilot, confirms the emotional and psychological damage done in this moment (10). Like the little plastic pilot in the plane, Zits has "lost his head" due to a lifetime of emotional wounds at the hands of temporary father figures. He recounts numerous stories where his foster fathers abuse him emotionally and physically, as well as the moment when he snaps and resists this abuse for the first time: "When I was nine, I poured lighter fluid on my aunt's boyfriend and tried to set him on fire" (161). While Zits fails to murder this father figure, his desire to burn the man's body symbolizes his pent-up rage and returns readers to the trope of the burning home, one that Alexie uses in earlier work such as *Smoke Signals* (1998) in order to signal discontent with the American family.[13]

The damaging effects of the father's actions, especially in relation to indigenous adoptees, can be traced back to the historical mistreatment of American Indians. In *Somebody's Children: The Politics of Transracial and Transnational Adoption* (2012), Laura Briggs, a feminist critic and noted American historian, describes the terrifying ordeals that Native families underwent with relocation and termination programs as well as the wildly unjust social-service practices on reservations. Although many families were continually haunted by the prospect of having their children removed to boarding schools for "reeducation," a more pernicious alternative emerged in the 1950s as government agents sought to

permanently remove children from their families in an effort to
stop what they believed was a cycle of poverty particular to American Indians. Out of the issues that arose for Native tribes in the
twentieth century, Briggs argues that sovereignty rights were the
foremost concern and that "the most fundamental question about
sovereignty was whether Native nations had control over their children" (66). Children, torn from the arms of their mothers, would be
placed into the care of white, middle-class families deemed more
suitable caregivers, and families often spent years trying to recover their lost children. In one particularly heart-wrenching account, a Chippewa woman testifies how a government agent forced
a Native woman to agree to sterilization by using her children as
a bargaining chip: "an unmarried mother . . . was told by a welfare
worker that she could keep her four children only if she consented
to sterilization; she agreed, under duress, and they took her children anyway" (Briggs 89). These and other testimonies eventually
led to the passage of ICWA, but as Zits's situation underscores,
the bill failed to protect all children since its definition of what
counted as "Indian" was extremely limited.

The horrific tales of adoption used in welfare trials, which often focus primarily on the lack of rights given to Indian mothers,
also speak to a situation that left fathers equally impotent, unable to secure the most basic rights of citizenship. In one case, a
young toddler named Benita Rowland was taken from the Pine
Ridge reservation in South Dakota in 1972. Her father's lawyer,
who helped the family regain custody of the child, claimed, "there
was not only no adoption, their [sic] was no *pretense* of adoption,
no color of law. These people had absolutely no legal right to take
that little girl" (qtd. in Briggs 82; emphasis in original). As the case
gained attention from the human rights organization American
Association of Indian Affairs (AAIA), the situation become even
more complicated as legal consultants learned that Rowland's father was seeking to regain not one but two daughters (Briggs 82).
His long, drawn-out fight and his need to prove that white families
had disregarded his parental rights underscores the pain many fathers had to undergo in order to perform their traditional role as
head of the family. One can imagine how humiliating such trials
were for these men, bringing to the surface painful memories of

other transgressions such as the violations of the sovereign tribal rights of Native tribes.

In her important contribution to the topic of childhood and national identity, Anna Mae Duane explains how, prior to the humiliating events that led to the breakdown of Native families, early Anglo-American settlers recorded the devotion of Indian fathers to their children, frequently remarking how these fathers put their child's needs above their own. It was this loving bond that settlers first identified as the key to their "predatory colonialism" (Johnson 343), as they attempted to manipulate tribal leaders through their children. In the famous example of Chief Powhatan and his daughter, Pocahontas, the English boasted that "paternal affection [w]as the gateway into successful colonization" (Duane, *Suffering Childhood* 24). The effects of such emotional manipulation transformed the Native father, turning his devotion into anger, a transformation that can also be seen in earlier literary examples, in particular Catharine Maria Sedgwick's *Hope Leslie* (1827), in which an American Indian father slaughters a white family in order to rescue his captive children and later attempts to sacrifice a young white boy in retribution for his son's death in the Pequot War. When Zits enters the body of a small American Indian boy living in the nineteenth century, he witnesses this emotional transformation as a once loving father is embittered by rage after his child is disabled from a wound to the throat. This father, a man built "like the Arnold Schwarzenegger of Indian warriors" and so devoted to his son that he affectionately sings to him, immediately instills within Zits a sense of respect, making him feel "like I'm going to explode [with joy]" (63–65). However, when Zits is asked to cut the throat of a teenage soldier captured during the Battle of Little Bighorn, Zits begins to question the morality of the man's actions. Noticing that his new father has "little hands war-painted on his chest," he understands that the man simply wants revenge for the damage done to his son, but he also is disturbed by the man's transformation from a tender father to a hard-hearted warrior (76). This transformation leads him to ruminate on father-son bonds, wondering how, whether "good" or "bad," a father's mandate for his son to fulfill his errand may perpetuate and compound violent actions.

Alexie uses Zits's transformation into the Indian boy to critique
the violence associated with colonization. Mirroring the destructive father-son bonds in Zits's present-day life, the failed ties between two nations competing for the same land result in the dis-
solution of the loving relationship between the Indian father and
his young son. The internal conflicts for land ownership during
the colonial period influenced the concept of childhood, shifting its
meaning until the understanding of it changed altogether (*Suffering Childhood* 11). For early Americans, childhood was a metaphor
for the changes associated with the violent process of nation making so that the vulnerable, suffering child came to represent both
the "infant nation" and its colonized subjects (*Suffering Childhood*
13). In his comprehensive 1984 study of the relations between the
U.S. government and American Indian tribes, historian Francis
Paul Prucha contends that the relationship between these competing nations, like many other colonial relationships, was rooted
in paternalism. The U.S. government treated grown Indian men
and women like children, so much so that the indigenous people
commonly referred to the president as the "Great Father." "The
Great Father rhetoric," writes Prucha, "largely disappeared after
1880, but paternalism continued and sometimes increased" (xx-
viii). Although Alexie does not ruminate at length on the Great
Father rhetoric, this narrative, like the Indian motif more generally, is addressed obliquely (Salaita 34). Fathers like the unnamed
Indian warrior from the Battle of Little Bighorn compete to gain
the power and authority associated with fatherhood, and the ability to obtain this power depends on the father's willingness to assert his authority over his children. This process is illustrated in
the scene where the warrior insists that his son gain revenge by
cutting the throat of a young soldier, continually pushing the boy
to act by yelling and reminding his son of the loss of his voice, the
result of damage done to his vocal chords by a white soldier in an
earlier attack on the tribe (75).

In this respect, the situation of Native fathers parallels that of
African American fathers, who similarly have been described as
absent, drunk, and otherwise irresponsible. Due to repeated historical events that left tribes humiliated and disenfranchised, Native men had limited abilities to be the affectionate fathers that
early Americans had once witnessed. Alexie addresses this long-

term impact on American Indian men's ability to father in Zits's final transformation, when he enters the body of his own father. Once in his father's body, Zits is able to discover the source of his inner pain and to recognize its parallels with his father's troubles. It is when Zits forces his father to remember why he left that Zits comes to this realization, seeing in his father's childhood the same patterns of father-son abuse. Zits's father's father stands over his son and forces him to repeat over and over again the phrase "I ain't worth shit" (155–156). The father's words recall a previous scene where Zits jokes that the Indian tribe at the Battle of Little Bighorn smells "like the Devil dropped a shit right here in the middle of this camp" (61). These repeated references to shit pick up a motif that is woven throughout the narrative. Indians not only smell like shit, they are treated like it as well. Zits's emotionally abused father is part of this intergenerational trauma, a fact that leads Zits to declare "my father cannot be a participant. He cannot be a witness. He cannot be a father" (156). This series of negations, of what the father *cannot* become, speaks to the decline of fatherhood within American Indian culture. Indeed, "one of the more puzzling and disconcerting features of recent American Indian fiction," claims Robyn Johnson, a scholar of American Indian literature, "is the veritable disappearance of nurturing father figures within American Indian families" (342). However, it also addresses a deeper flaw in the U.S. national narrative, where some fathers not only get to count more than others but are also able to be forgiven again and again.

The inequality of some members of the national family based on race or ethnicity is tested to the extreme in the only transformation where Alexie departs from his preoccupation with fatherhood. When Zits enters the body of a white flight instructor named Jimmy, he learns that Jimmy is haunted by visions of his dead friend, Abbad, an Ethiopian immigrant who died while committing an act of terrorism. Jimmy's narrative dwells on the betrayal of his "brother," whom he took in when no other flight instructor would work with him. Jimmy continually repeats the phrase, "*Oh, Abbad, you are a murderer. Oh, Abbad, you are a betrayer*" (127; emphasis in original), a lament that is both touching and disturbing. The phrase signals Jimmy's affection for his lost friend; its repetition becomes chantlike, giving it religious undertones that some might

associate with Muslim prayer. Such words recall the stereotypical nature of Abbad and other similar Muslim characters in Alexie's fiction. Steven Salaita argues in his 2010 essay that in this
way, "Alexie reinforces the sanctification of American suffering at
the hands of Muslim terrorists, but he simultaneously endeavors
to undermine the causal fusion of Islam and terrorism" (34). The
combination of events such as Abbad's act of terrorism, which vin-
dicates U.S. citizens' fears about the Muslim other, combined with
his character's "clichéd attitudes," appear to undermine Alexie's efforts to achieve this goal; however, he always combines the actions
and behavior of his Muslim characters with instances of anti-Mus-
lim racism so that the guilt associated with acts of vengeance is
equally distributed.

Alexie's distribution of guilt and his inclusion of ethical questions in the Jimmy and Abbad passages depend on the fraternal
metaphor. The usefulness of the fraternal metaphor, as historian
David Waldstreicher attests in his 2001 review of Founder Chic
historian Joseph Ellis's *Founding Brothers*, is that it connotes
"commonality, rivalry, reconciliation" (198). Jimmy, while treating
Abbad like a younger brother, cannot openly claim Abbad as family because of his betrayal. He refers to Abbad as his "best friend,"
while Abbad replies, "You are my brother" (130). Jimmy commits
many brotherly acts, reassuring Abbad when he is scared and celebrating his triumphs. Even his grief over Abbad's betrayal is the
emotion that an older brother might feel. Jimmy feels responsibility for Abbad and his actions, and it is this feeling of responsibility,
of brotherhood, that drives his pain. Yet Jimmy's ability to accept
Abbad as brother is limited by his perception of his friend as an
absolute other. Abbad is referred to as Jimmy's "brown friend," and
his presence in Jimmy's memory is antagonistic. Abbad's rivalry
with Jimmy is rooted in their perceived differences. Abbad lectures
Jimmy on masculinity, declaring that Muslim men don't let their
women control them, only to retract this statement a few minutes
later when he sheepishly admits that he is in trouble for forgetting to purchase a bottle of milk (114). Moments such as these occur frequently so that readers can never trust the apparent differences between the two characters. Indeed, the fraternal metaphor
encourages readers not to forget that Jimmy and Abbad have a
commonality that overrides any conflict between them.

Alexie's approach to the brotherly bond of Jimmy and Abbad is an example of what Steven Salaita calls "liberal Orientalism," by which he means "a representation of Islam and the East more broadly rooted in the liberal principles of American multicultural-ism" (22). Salaita explains how this orientation applies to Alexie's post-9/11 literature and to *Flight* more specifically: "His [Alexie's] post-9/11 fiction renders Natives customary to American national identity by evoking the specter of Islamic terrorism as a standard marker of inalterable difference. Alexie complicates this simplis-tic formula by retaining a type of Indigenous autonomy through nominal comparison of Indians with brown-skinned Muslims, but those comparisons never allow Muslims into the same philosophi-cal or national polity, and so he ultimately leaves that formula fun-damentally intact" (37). Salaita's recognition of the Muslim other's inability to enter the national family is consistent with Alexie's portrayal of family throughout *Flight*. As I mentioned previously, the scene with Jimmy and Abbad is unique not only because it is the only one that does not deal with Indian-white relationships but also because it replaces the paternal metaphor with a frater-nal one. These changes encourage readers to compare Abbad to the Indian characters in other sections, and this comparison touches on the liberal Orientalism that Salaita identifies in the novel. The Indian characters, while persecuted, are still part of the national family, even if they are presented as a disowned or orphaned child like Zits. However, Abbad's position as family member is always tenuous. He is "like a brother," yet this relationship is deemed dan-gerous because Abbad is so volatile. While some rivalry is normal in a fraternal relationship, Abbad's penchant for destruction is presented as confusing and irrational. In a later scene where Jim-my's marital infidelity is discovered, the pilot's thoughts return to Abbad, and he remembers observing that his former friend has lived in the United States for fifteen years, a fact that he brings up presumably because it should prove that Abbad has had time to become a part of the American family. However, Abbad retorts that he is only in the United States because his home has been de-stroyed (121).

The scene with Abbad and Jimmy is important because it sup-plies readers with a point of comparison for the many scenes of family rivalry that fill the pages of *Flight*. It attests to the limits of multiculturalism and how some bodies are able to count more than others. As the story of Zits's fantastic flight through time comes to an end, Alexie turns to tropes of the adoption narrative to reinforce this message. Zits, after months of therapy, is welcomed into the family of his friend, Officer Dave, whose brother has agreed to offer Zits a new, and possibly permanent, home. While the story of Zits ends with the promise of adoption, this adoption is contingent on Zits's willingness to assimilate his white family's values. This need to change is apparent when Zits's new foster mother enters the bathroom and hands Zits some acne medicine, teaching him how to wash his face so that it will finally be clean. At this seemingly motherly act, Zits responds with a swell of emotion, even crying and hugging the woman like a small child. As he clings to the woman's body, Zits softly murmurs, "Please, call me Michael," offering his new mother the one secret that he has kept from others throughout the narrative—his given name (181).

Some critics have read Zits's willingness to abandon his nickname as a sign of his acceptance of his past trauma and willingness to embrace his identity (Ibarrola-Armendariz and Vivanco 42; Johnson 364–365); yet given the historical backdrop of the narrative in Zits's flight through time, there remain unsettling implications of the white foster mother's desire to help Zits "clean" himself, a request that metonymically positions Zits as an infection to be cured through the acne on his face. In her 2015 analysis of the novel, Kerry Boland concurs with this view, claiming that "Zits is still—perhaps even more than initially—an unrecognized Indigenous body that the settler state may move as it pleases" (86). Lydia Cooper, a specialist in American Indian literature, concurs, adding that "to read Zits as 'brand-new' is irresponsible if that reading does not recognize that he is still a sexual abuse victim, still an adolescent with a criminal record, and still the inheritor of intergenerational trauma" (139). By abandoning his chosen name, Zits demonstrates that he accepts his position in white culture, not necessarily that he has come to terms with his Indian identity. The ending is thus one of loss since Zits must discard his ethnic identity in order to gain his foster family's acceptance. While such themes of loss and identity are present in Alexie's previous novels, the message here is altered by *Flight*'s persistent engagement with questions raised by the September 11 attacks, in particular the price of integration into the national family.

In tracing first the bonds between fathers and sons, and then those between brothers, Alexie questions the nation's errand, altering the Puritan belief that it is a son's duty to carry on the mission of his father. From the earliest days of settlement, the Puritans "were particularly invested in seeing their own authenticity and sense of purpose mirrored in their flourishing offspring" (Duane, *Suffering Childhood* 28). At that time, fathers raised children not so much for the pleasure of it—that wouldn't come until centuries later—but rather for the ability to secure their own legacy. A child's most important role was to live up to this legacy and to carry on the mission of his or her father. Despite the many transformations of the meaning of childhood, the desire to make children in their father's image has not completely disappeared in our present moment, as the emergence of the Founders Chic movement indicates. An image of a strong, authoritarian-type father who inspires his children to carry on his legacy remains in vogue, regardless of the fact that this figure has historically served as a means of disenfranchising ethnic minorities. In the next chapter, I show how the role of the son continues to serve an important function, and not just as a means of paying tribute to his father. These sons, be they filial or rebellious, speak to anxieties about a "loss of innocence" and also allude to the very people that the father's errand has tried to vanish.

CHAPTER 5

Disrupting the Garden

THE INVASION OF THE MACHINE
AND THE VANISHING AMERICAN

The idyll of Huck and Jim is a dream at whose heart lurks a nightmare.
—Leslie Fiedler, *Love and Death in the American Novel*

In an advertisement for a 1953 children's novel, the eponymous protagonist, Danny, is described as being akin to a farm boy, an "unspoiled, naïve" American who, like his adult counterpart, is "a vanishing breed" (Hass BR12). Encouraging adults to identify with this idealized boy, the advertisement continues, "Meeting him—if it happened that you spent your youth in a small town—is like meeting yourself coming around a corner. He is Everyboy as he was before our kids were blasé at 11 and sophisticated at 13. And he is wonderful" (Hass BR12). The celebration of the farm boy's innocence is pitted against the more mature generation of the 1950s. Bemoaning the loss of innocence of the nation's citizens while also suggesting that the younger generation has gained a level of experience and maturity absent in the farm boy, the writer compares Danny to Mark Twain's Tom Sawyer and Huckleberry Finn. This nostalgia for small-town America was predominant in postwar American literature, including children's books like *Danny*, where iconic nineteenth-century pastorals became a reference point for new interpretations of adolescence in the twentieth century. The entrance of the machine into this rural idyll, in particular, served as the setting for playing out the tensions embodied within adolescence, a "period of peril and freedom; an odyssey of psychological self-discovery and growth; and a world apart, with its own values, culture, and psychology" (Mintz 5).

For Leo Marx, author of *The Machine in the Garden* (1964), the loss of the idealized boyhood represented by the nineteenth-century pastoral underscored the tension between the agrarian myth and industrial progress in twentieth-century American culture. What Twain in his lifetime referred to as the "now-departed and hardly-remembered raft-life" of his boyhood days (*Life on the Mississippi* 21), Marx saw as a manifestation of one of the driving conflicts of modern American life. For Twain this threat is represented by the powerful steam engine, whereas for Marx this same threat takes the form of the more sinister and deadly atomic bomb. In drawing a parallel between the experiences of the past and the present, Marx hit on a sensitive element of the national character: a tendency to represent the nation as a white, male youth. This idealized boy was rough, so close to nature that he could practically be hewn from the earth itself—the advertisement for *Danny* notes how the farm boy runs about "barefooted" and has a "native shrewdness"—and he reveled in playing games that involved the outdoors. A more sober account of the farm boy might include the tension between his playful demeanor and the responsibility of manhood, characterized by the intense pressure that plagues Huck as he grapples with the ethics of slavery. The farm boy, much like the frontier that Twain carefully re-creates in *Huckleberry Finn*, becomes a symbol of a vanishing American past, though this past is whitewashed in a manner similar to Aunt Polly's fence.

It is for this reason that many have taken issue with Leo Marx's interpretation of the machine in the garden myth, arguing that the cultural landscape of the United States was much more varied and textured than his scholarship would indicate. In his criticism of the desire to recover a preindustrial past, American literary scholar Walter Benn Michaels argues that tales of the American frontier served to strengthen national identity. In particular, the literary representation of a lone American Indian came to symbolically represent a "vanishing" American past that enabled those who romanticized this figure in their writing to support the "idea of an ethnicity that could be threatened or defended, repudiated or reclaimed" (232). Lora Romero, whose work focuses on nineteenth- and twentieth-century American literature, adds that for these writers, American Indians "represent a *phase* that the human race goes through but which it must inevitably *get over*" (393;

emphasis in original). Citing James Fenimore Cooper's *The Last of the Mohicans* (1826) as an example, Romero demonstrates how the figure of the Vanishing American came to represent a longing for the innocence that was associated with the frontier and eventually, as I have suggested, with small-town America through country boys such as Danny. Set against the shifting ideals associated with adolescence in the twentieth century, which children's literature scholar Sarah Chinn persuasively argues was shaped largely by the attitudes and behaviors of immigrant youth in large American cities, industrialization became a mechanism for providing the freedom once associated with the countryside, though social reformers remained skeptical about the implications of these "freedoms" (gambling, movie houses, and extramarital sex were among the chief concerns) (Chinn 10). At the turn of the twentieth century, Chinn observes, "adolescents were growing up in major cities, rather than on farms or in small towns" (14).

The shifting cultural values surrounding adolescence, and the increasing inclusion of young females in youth studies, meant that the "vanishing" farm boy, and the women and ethnic minorities this adolescent figure erased from national memory, increasingly became a site of ambivalence about innocence after World War II. Indeed, as scholars of bad boy literature (the genre to which Twain's boys' books belong) argue, the emergence of semiautobiographical writing like Twain's was a symptom of a deeper fear about a rapidly changing lifestyle. As Tim Prchal asserts in his 2004 essay on bad boy literature, the bad boy prefigured later redefinitions of American masculinity and could be recognized by his "affinity with nature" (188, 194). Kenneth Kidd has similarly argued in *Making American Boys* (2004) that bad boy literature, which was initiated with Thomas Bailey Aldrich's *The Story of a Bad Boy* (1869), is among one of several strains of "boyology," an amateur study of boyhood that first originated in the nineteenth century and gradually gained momentum with the advent of child psychology in the early twentieth century (1). In these popular nineteenth-century works of boys' fiction, the farm became a favorite backdrop for the bad boy's mischief, anticipating later "preservationist" efforts to save both boy and farm life (Kidd 34). Idealized for its association with nature, the farm seemed to encapsulate what male authors and their adult readers felt was best about boyhood, including the mud, insects, and other elements of nature that provided plenty of space for exercising the wild side of a boy's budding masculinity.

As I convey in this chapter through novels spanning the mid-twentieth and early twenty-first centuries, the disappearance of farm and small-town boys and their replacement with the literary "Everyboy" dramatized the crisis that came with an age of technology, echoing earlier nineteenth-century lamentations about the decline of open territory; this shift also gave rise to an adolescent figure that was much more flexible and stretched beyond the white, middle-class, and male identity categories of earlier variants of this boy figure. Indeed, as my example of Leslie Marmon Silko's *Gardens in the Dunes* (1999) indicates, the farm boy was completely reimagined and replaced by the very people this figure had once excluded from the national narrative. The novel, written primarily from the perspective of a young American Indian girl, revises this narrative through its engagement with the bloody colonial history of the United States. In contrast with previous challenges to the innocence of boyhood in such canonical works as J. D. Salinger's *The Catcher in the Rye* (1951), which I will address presently, the "vanishing American" slowly began to disrupt nineteenth-century notions of masculinity, including the positive, yet damaging, vision of a feminized landscape realized in the image of the garden and the more critical depiction of women as a civilizing force that threatened to erode the "rough" manhood represented by frontiersmen (Meyer 13).[1] By the time of the twenty-first century, the interpretation of the frontier as a garden where men could regain their youth had dramatically shifted in response to a sharp rise in the availability of technology and consumer products. In closing, I demonstrate how popular young adult novelist M. T. Anderson addresses the shifting cultural interpretations of the machine in the garden myth by merging youth and technology in a deeply disturbing dystopian society where consumption has completely destroyed the environment, making a gardenlike retreat from the machines that have fueled the "progress" of this futuristic civilization impossible. In *Feed* (2002), it is an adolescent girl, notably—not a boy—who rebels against the technology causing this destruction.

"I'll Go to Hell": The Fall into Experience

In J. D. Salinger's *The Catcher in the Rye* (1951), the idealized farm boy is replaced with a very different kind of Everyboy from Danny: a rich prep school teenager living in Manhattan who represents the anxieties of his generation. Disenchanted with modern society, Salinger's protagonist, Holden Caulfield, chooses to isolate himself and live as an outcast instead of adhering to social expectations. Holden's consistent description of "phony" people and activities in the high society of New York signals his desire to separate himself from the other privileged members of his class. The son of a wealthy lawyer, Holden is primed to enter the very society he detests, and yet he desperately attempts to escape the cloying and suffocating rules of this society to the point that he suffers from a mental breakdown. His descent into madness displays Salinger's ambivalence about the ability for the traditionally lauded spaces of the American frontier to redeem Americans and return them to a state of innocence. Throughout the narrative of *Catcher*, Salinger repeatedly reinforces this view by demonstrating how Holden can no longer access the agricultural landscapes still prominent in western films of the 1950s, much less regain the innocence represented by the heroes who occupy these landscapes. Desperately attempting to recover his lost innocence, Holden chooses instead to escape into a world of fantasy that revives the nineteenth-century agrarian ideal at a time when war rather than an idyllic communion with nature was central to boyhood (Engelhardt 9).

Salinger's emphasis on rural spaces, and ultimately the frontier, as an inaccessible place for young Holden to escape to demonstrates shifting attitudes toward boyhood and adolescence in the 1950s. In the nineteenth century, when boy books proliferated, social reform in cities aimed to move troubled youth out of the city and into the country in order to convert them into good citizens. Charles Loring Brace, the father of the modern foster care movement, helped initiate the mass migration of young people to these rural homes with the establishment of "orphan trains." These trains, according to historian Marilyn Holt, responded to a desire to remove the urban poor from large cities, but they also reflected a desire to escape the "new world of machines" associated with these urban centers (21). While the orphan train signaled the deeply entrenched fear that youth without direction would wreak havoc on American society, it also placed a strong emphasis on the power of the frontier, and the rural life associated with it, to turn bad boys into good ones. By the end of World War II, the redeeming power of the frontier was more fantasy than reality. Farmers, as I will go on to show, had lost their sons in droves as they left for war or the cities that were previously seen as corrupting to youth, and war continued to plague Americans with the heating up of tension between the United States and the Soviet Union. As the Cold War crisis escalated, Hollywood helped fuel American hatred for Communists by creating historical dramas of American victory, primarily through the popular cowboy and Indian films featuring famous actors such as John Wayne. These films presented celebratory narratives of American victory and "achieved a dominant position on the small screen at home as well" (Engelhardt 34).

The narrative of American victory central to the western had infiltrated American culture first through its popularity on the silver screen and then within the home on television sets. The technology used to distribute these films signaled the progress of American society, yet this same progress was seen as being responsible for the closure of the frontier. In his famous frontier thesis, historian Frederick Jackson Turner argued at the turn of the twentieth century that the unique national character of the United States arose out of an evolutionary process involving the western frontier: "The buffalo trail became the Indian trail, and this became the trader's 'trace'; the trails widened into roads, and the roads into turnpikes, and these in turn were transformed into railroads" (11). Eventually, however, this frontier reached its "natural" limits and could no longer allow American settlers to continue to begin again in a "perennial rebirth" (2). With the closure of the frontier, Holden cannot really set out for the West, like the romantic hero of films from the era, but is instead contained in the artificial landscapes and gardens of Manhattan. Even when he does dream of escaping the city, these visions of rural life draw on popular tropes in American literature, including the cowboy and small-town America. As Holden admits on a date with a neighborhood girl, these dreams are his last-ditch effort to escape the routine lifestyle and expectations of boys in his class, for whom fast cars, corny plays, and other mundane topics become the norm and everyone fits neatly into "little boxes," as Pete Seeger famously declared in the 1963 cover version of Malvina Reynolds's folk song.[2]

The psychological turmoil that Holden experiences can be attributed in part to the rapid mechanization of American culture, especially in relation to work culture. The bosses, time clocks, and machines that made it necessary for workers to adjust to a very regimented schedule were a popular source of anxiety in the 1950s, so much so that the famous child psychologist Erik Erikson declared that the United States was entering a time of "upset identities" (422). This identity crisis gave rise to bad boys like Holden, who celebrated the rugged individualism of early pioneers of the American West and mourned the loss of the freedom associated with the closure of the frontier. In his 1960 study of youth, American writer and social theorist Paul Goodman analyzes the social institutions that gave rise to these bad boys, who began to buck tradition in response to a shift in cultural values that failed to live up to their idealism and in response to demoralizing economic conditions that made it difficult for youth to grow up. In a world where the "system" rules, growing up is not merely difficult, it is actually "absurd." *Growing Up Absurd* (1960), like many of the other works of literary criticism and psychological studies of the day, focused exclusively on the crisis of identity for young men. Goodman, echoing fears about the breakdown of the family structure, describes the dilemma of 1950s male youth as a crisis of values: without a father whose values he can admire and emulate, the young boy is left searching for a role model outside of the family; however, society, like the father, fails the boy and makes it impossible for him to grow up (102). By failing these youth, Goodman believed that a new generation of "beat" and "resigned" men would enter American society (9).

From this brief overview, *Growing Up Absurd* would appear to be a critique of social values and the systems that uphold these values. Certainly, the family was a central part of the system that Goodman sees as contributing to the toxic environment that was preventing American youth from growing into men; however, he also turned to the environment itself and to the economic changes that began to uproot the family by turning this generation's fathers into a set of resigned adults who answered to the "boss" and lived their lives by the clock. Drawing on the agrarian roots of the

nation, Goodman argues that the infiltration into society of machines, which men no longer knew how to fix or use, had upset the
balance between man and nature. In terms of the agrarian ideal
that Jefferson upheld, the bond between the farmer and his land
had been wiped out. The machine now ruled. "Because it [the Jef-
fersonian ideal] has failed to cope with technological changes and
to withstand speculation," continues Goodman, "'farming as a way
of life' has succumbed to cash-cropping dependent on distant mar-
kets, and is ridden with mortgages, tenancy, and hired labor. Yet
it maintains a narrow rural morality and isolationist politics, is
a sucker for the mass culture of Madison Avenue and Hollywood,
and in the new cities . . . is a bulwark against genuine city culture"
(198). Like the resigned fathers in his previous diatribe, the farmers are also "sell outs" who could hardly serve as role models for
disillusioned youth. But Goodman does make some concessions for
the farmers, despite their failure to maintain a stable relationship
to the land—certainly partly a result of increasing technology that
made such manual labor less of a necessity—and sees the farmer
as a last stand, even if a weak one, against the decaying effect of
the city, which has all but rid youth of the golden years of childhood, or so Goodman would have his readers believe.

In *The Catcher in the Rye*, Holden attempts to recover the rapidly vanishing farm life that is viewed as being authentically
American in contrast to the superficial society found in the city.
The natural topography associated with the pastoral, with rural
spaces that include the farm, are a staple of Holden's literary imagination. When Holden first begins to recount his three-day adventure in Manhattan, he recalls some of the books he has recently
read, including Thomas Hardy's *The Return of the Native* (1878),
W. Somerset Maugham's *Of Human Bondage* (1915), and Karen
Blixen's *Out of Africa* (1937). Out of these three books, Holden appears to prefer Hardy's and Blixen's novels, both of which prominently feature agricultural life. In Hardy's *The Return of the Native*, the beautiful and exotic Eustacia Vye attempts to escape the
English countryside and return to the city life that she was accustomed to in her girlhood. In her efforts to achieve her dream, she
becomes romantically involved with a young diamond trader, Clym
Yeobright, who has recently returned from Paris and is currently
trying to begin a new career as a schoolteacher to the rural poor.

Eustacia's dream of living in Paris with her new lover is eventually dashed as she realizes that Clym is set on remaining in the heath, and after a series of dramatic events she ends up drowning herself in a river out of despair. *Out of Africa* appears less dramatic, with its focus on a young Dutch woman who begins a coffee farm in Africa. Although the weather and other events test her resolve, this venture is much more successful and represents a more harmonious relationship with the countryside than Hardy's novel, where the female character despises the remote rural village where she lives. Holden admits that he has "read it [*Out of Africa*] already, but I wanted to read certain parts over again" (22). Based on his interest in the pastoral, we can assume that it is the rural setting that in part attracts Holden to these novels.

Holden's reading choices are integral to an understanding of *Catcher* within the tradition of the machine in the garden myth. Our hero, though tumbling into experience like a typical American Adam, is also preoccupied with the rapidly declining spaces for the American imagination. The yeoman, who was so essential to the agrarian ideal promoted by influential figures like Thomas Jefferson, began losing his charms as the machine encroached on previously untouched lands. In the closing to his chapter on the machine, Leo Marx adds that "the pastoral ideal remained of service long after the machine's appearance in the landscape. It enabled the nation to continue defining its purpose as the pursuit of rural happiness while devoting itself to productivity, wealth, and power. It remained for our serious writers to discover the meaning inherent in this contradiction" (226). The fact that the American pastoral continues to find a place within literary criticism is testament to Marx's assertion of its lasting power. Part of its staying power, according to Lawrence Buell, is due to the unique dynamic between nature and civilization that is at work within the genre, which is much more complex than a simple escape from civilization. Buell argues that the American pastoral "cannot be linked to a single ideological position. Even at its ostensibly most culpable moment—the moment of willful retreat from social and political responsibility—it may actually be more strategized than mystified" (14). Citing classic writers of pastoral like Henry Thoreau alongside more contemporary writers like Leslie Marmon Silko, Buell underlines a different contradiction within pastoral writing from Marx, revealing it as a much more flexible genre in the process that includes women and people of color rather than attempting to "vanish" them. It is perhaps this dynamic, along with its ability to serve as the backdrop for multiple American national myths, including the virgin land and American Adam, that makes the American pastoral such an important genre within the literary landscape (McWilliams 72).

In the context of Salinger's novel, the pastoral genre serves as the mechanism for exploring the cultural changes contributing to his young hero's anxiety, compelling Holden to desperately seek to recover the vanishing frontier. At the beginning of the 1950s, U.S. newspaper headlines were already more devoted to war than to the charm of farming life. With page after page covering new developments in the Cold War, especially the recent events in Korea, it seemed machines and the men who wielded them were of more importance than nature. Yet on the day of *Catcher*'s release in 1951, there was one major headline that turned the nation's attention back west: "Water Lacking amid Flood; Human Dikes Help Stem Tide." The article describes displaced families and wild animals whose lives are disrupted by the unexpected swelling of the Kansas River (Blair 1, 8). If nature could be destructive, though, it was nothing compared to the machines that were now a fundamental part of the power struggle between the United States and the Soviet Union. As one Salinger critic remarks, "apart from [a few] stories . . . all the other articles on the front page bore on the struggle between East and West" (Ohmann 16). Even if the United States' latest power struggle took center stage, the side stories that American literary critics Carol and Richard Ohmann view as the familiar padding to the otherwise "serious" news weren't irrelevant. The flood in Kansas City may not have seemed as immediately relevant to 1950s readers, but it was a reminder of the vast tracts of land that were slowly drifting to the periphery of the cultural imagination, much like the story of the Kansas City flood drifting to the background of the major headlines in the *New York Times*.

Salinger crafts a character who is equally devoted to preserving these pastoral landscapes as he is to preserving innocence. Even the classic quote where Holden dubs himself the "catcher in the rye" is a highly pastoral scene, where Holden envisions himself in a vast wheat field filled with little children that he must catch before the youngsters accidentally fall off a nearby cliff. The setting is crucial here, as it represents an idealized space that is reminiscent of the yeoman who once held an important role in shaping American national ideals. The farm, and the rural life it represented, was a veritable dream of freedom from the drudgery of city life (despite the fact that such work was in fact hard and grueling), but this dream was no longer possible to realize as the stories of farm life became just that—stories. As early as the turn of the twentieth century, it became common to symbolize the disappearance of rural life through depictions of the farm boy, which continued well into the Cold War and beyond. In one 1990 article from the *New York Times*, this approach can be seen as the decline of small-town America is dated back to the 1950s, when "half the people and most of the businesses have left the barren buttes and prairies" of North Dakota (Wilkerson). The author warns readers about the prevalence of this decline, claiming, "nobody knows precisely how many small towns around the country have vanished in recent decades" (Wilkerson).

The 1950s marked a pivotal turning point when boys began to leave farms in a mass exodus, in part due to economic pressures and patriotic duties (the Korean and Vietnam wars would both call more men away from the farms and into the barracks). Holden's interest in rural life, then, is not surprisingly displaced from the American landscape. As mentioned previously, Holden's literary escapes are set in the Scottish Highlands and Kenya, far from Holden's home in Manhattan. However, Holden will turn his attention back home when he formulates an escape plan from the city, a wild scenario where he lives out his days in a log cabin. Holden first reveals his plan to one of his romantic interests, Sally Hayes, at the end of an evening date, when he proposes that the two run off and live in the country in Massachusetts or Vermont: "We could live somewhere with a brook and all and, later on, we could get married or something. I could chop all our own wood in the wintertime and all. Honest to God, we could have a terrific time! Wudduya say? C'mon! Wudduya say? Will you do it with me? Please!" (147). In this passage, Holden hardly mimics the self-reliant American Adam who sets out nobly alone (Lewis 5). Instead, he pleads with his date as he tries to convince her that domestic life outside of the city is better than one in it. His disgust with this life is apparent well before this passage as he whines about "phonies," but just a few pages earlier Holden makes a claim that is more revealing than his previous complaints, when he asserts that unlike the "terrific bores" that he usually hangs out with, he dislikes talking about cars. "I'd rather have a goddam horse. A horse is at least *human*, for God's sake. A horse you can at least—" (145). Holden stops midsentence so that he never reveals what you can do with a horse, but his comment begins to hint at his preference for a nonmechanical form of transportation, one, not coincidentally, that would be readily available to a farmer.

Holden's dream of retreating to a farming community will be dashed when his date declares that it is just too "fan*tas*tic" to carry out (147; emphasis in original), and in many ways such spaces were already radically transformed by the 1950s when the novel is set. Holden, in search of this vanishing space with the power to rejuvenate the experienced, will develop an even more "fantastic" dream as he relocates his ideal abode from the brooks of Massachusetts to the prairies of the Midwest. This time Holden will not make the same mistake and invite a fellow traveler along; instead, he determines to set out on his own in pursuit of the same domestic dream, but one that does not include a female companion who is already socialized to the norms of city life and upper-class society. As he begins to imagine another alternative to city life, Holden relates to his little sister, Phoebe, how life on a ranch in Colorado will provide the quiet atmosphere he desires (183–184). When his sister mocks him and says, "Don't make me laugh. You can't even ride a horse," Holden simply replies, "Who can't? Sure I can. Certainly I can. They can teach you in about two minutes" (184). Holden's reply, while naïve, suggests that he still holds a romantic view of agricultural life.

Holden's claim about the ease of taking part in the agrarian ideal reflects the often poetic descriptions of agricultural labor in the 1950s. In one article in the *New York Times*, "The Hired Man—a Vanishing American" (1950), the farmer's fields where the hired hand works are described as "a living soil blanketed, in its virgin state, by the richest of green grasses" (Davis 16). The entrance of the machine in this ideal space creates a "shift of emphasis from the vital to the non-vital, from men to machines and to the machine-state," and helps explain the anxiety at the root of Holden's iden-

tity crisis (16). Though the *New York Times* article appeared a year
before the release of *Catcher*, the attitude about a lost agricultural
space and the rise of a machine age is reflected in Holden's continued desire to escape to such a place. As his exchange with his sister Phoebe reveals, Holden believes that he can recover the idealized state of country life by moving farther west to live on a ranch,
the home of the American cowboy who was a staple of Hollywood
films of the era. The cowboy, as American writer Tom Engelhardt
explains, was just one of several figures that emerged out of the
battles between Americans and the Native inhabitants of the
western frontier and became a central part of the commercial culture consumed by boys of the era (35). Toy "pop" guns, plastic soldiers, comics, television shows, and other products positioned the
child as consumer and continued to keep alive the triumphalist vision of victory culture in the Cold War (147–148). Holden's focus
on work as a form of manual labor, where daily tasks are either
completely done by hand or else with the help of traditional farm
animals, seeks to recover the masculinity depicted in boy culture:
packaged and distributed to little boys nationwide, these ideals
lost their potency and thrust the adolescent into "a culture of triumphalist despair with money in their pockets" (133).

The idealization of manual labor in *Catcher* underscores prevailing attitudes about the psychological complexity of adolescence
in the mid-twentieth century. In *Childhood and Society* (1950),
Erik Erikson offers case studies of ego development in the United
States, Germany, and Russia, and concludes that the farm boy is
"the descendant of Founding Fathers who themselves were rebel
sons" (399). As Erikson explains this connection, he begins to reassert the familiar narrative of men conquering the frontier and the
clash between nature and civilization that Marx helped popular-
ize in his study of the machine in the garden myth. Erikson outlines how the Founding Fathers helped usher in a new era of manhood through their relationship with the natural landscape, which
due to the fact that it had never been settled before, "permitted an
exploitation of the continent which was crudely masculine, rudely
exuberant, and, but for its women, anarchic" (399). The efforts of
the founders and the inheritor of their mission—the farm boy—
shaped the United States into a new image that departs from the
rural life of England, for these inheritors "have made conquered

earth comfortable and machinery almost pleasant, to the envy of the rest of the world" (399). What Erikson outlines in this passage is a masculine legacy that combines several American national myths but which importantly focuses on the way that farming and industrialization have helped propel the nation to the center of the world stage. In this way, Erikson echoes much of the national rhetoric of the time but importantly identifies the farm boy as the key figure in this narrative of ascendancy.

In light of such complications, Salinger, via his noble hero, Holden, offers a third and final alternative. If the lakes are dry and the fields are failing, then there may still be small pockets of isolated countryside where a man can settle and avoid society. Holden describes this little abode as follows: "I'd build me a little cabin somewhere with the dough I made and live there for the rest of my life. I'd build it right near the woods, but not right *in* them, because I'd want it to be sunny as hell all the time" (219). Salinger critics, curious about the reclusive life led by Holden's creator, speculate that the author's desire for peace and quiet may be reflected in lines such as these (Bloom 12–13). Indeed, just two years after the publication of *Catcher*, Salinger would find a home in an isolated area of Cornish, New Hampshire, and would rarely be in the public eye again—even his publications slowed to a trickle and then completely stopped. Regardless of the veracity of such rumors, Holden's final fantasy of escape ultimately positions the young hero in the far reaches of the West. His desire for seclusion thus begins in the Northeast (where Salinger finally ended up), then farther afield in the Rocky Mountains of Colorado, and at last in an unnamed town that is simply identified as being "somewhere out West" (218). The lack of specificity in Holden's final plan confirms what even he acknowledges—that it is "crazy" and unrealistic—but it speaks to a deeper desire to reclaim the rejuvenating lands mythologized in American tales and even in the national newspapers, where "vanishing Americans" are farmers, hired hands, and young boys living a simpler life in the country.

That Holden considers his final plan as a means for controlling his and his family's exposure to the corrupt world is reflected in a later passage when Holden explains how his cabin will serve as a protective space from the outside world. Not only will he "hide" his future children inside the cabin walls (219), but those who are allowed to enter must follow a prescribed set of rules, which are not surprisingly linked to his obsession with authenticity (no phonies allowed!). His younger sister, Phoebe, and his brother D. B. are the only two family members that Holden will permit to enter this sanctuary, and even D. B. may only come on the condition that he writes "only stories and books" (225). As Holden imagines his reclusive life, he appears to draw on the pastoral literature that he favors, picturing a spectacular image of himself as a romantic hero. He is, for example, "cool as all hell" as he returns home after nearly twenty years in his cabin, and his mother cries and begs for her son to return (225). This fantasy will quickly come to a close, though, when he meets to say a final goodbye to his sister and harshly rejects her plan to join him on his hitchhiking adventure. In a fit of anger, Holden admits, "I'm not going away anywhere. I changed my mind" (228). Holden's decision to stay and his bitterness in admitting this decision reflect his mixed emotions about preserving innocence. Even in the oft-quoted final lines of the story, he admits that "the thing with kids is, if they want to grab for the gold ring, you have to let them do it, and not say anything. If they fall off, they fall off, but it's bad if you say anything to them" (232).

The three rural spaces that dominate Holden's imagination indicate that Salinger's hero is caught up in the debate about man versus machine that, while less talked about than the events of the Cold War, certainly was a felt loss for Americans still captivated by the American West. As Marx suggests, nostalgia for an agrarian past could be found in the writing of famous American authors, most notably in Mark Twain's *Adventures of Huckleberry Finn*. Reflecting a desire to return to an "innocent" American past, these authors used the pastoral to comment on the shifting relationship with the frontier as farm life became less integral to American society. Salinger participates in this tradition of utilizing the adolescent boy to attempt to recover a communion with nature but crafts a hero who is beyond repair, forced to accept the loss of his childhood days and the vision of America that vanished along with it. It is this acceptance of the impossibility of rejuvenation through the landscape that departs from earlier nineteenth-century narratives. While the iconic image of Huck's raft being smashed on the river may seem to foreclose a return to innocence, the famous conclusion where Huck "light[s] out for the Territory" continues to give this young rebel a chance to regain elements of the innocent life he led during his time on the raft with Jim. In ultimately turning away from the previous century's promise of renewal through the American frontier, Salinger underscores the disturbing possibility that the machine in the mid-twentieth century brought to the forefront: that the United States might not always be victorious, and that even the very notion of "victory" could come into question at a time when the boundaries between opposing sides in the power struggle against communism became increasingly blurred.

Recovering the Garden
in an Indigenous Past

Salinger's vision of the "vanishing American" reveals a deep-rooted nostalgia for an imagined past that was predominant in postwar America. As Svetlana Boym argues in *The Future of Nostalgia* (2001), this longing urges the nostalgic to seek out an impossible goal, a past time, and in the process to "turn it [history] into private or collective mythology, to revisit time like space, refusing to surrender to the irreversibility of time that plagues the human condition" (xv). In her third novel, *Gardens in the Dunes* (1999), Laguna Pueblo writer Leslie Marmon Silko explores these themes of nostalgia, revival, trauma, and memory by turning back time in order to reclaim the history buried by the machine in the garden myth. For Silko, this myth isn't about the desire for white male youth to recover their "innocent" boyhood days; instead, it is about the political ramifications of westward expansion and the inevitable industrialization that radically reshaped the land that was once home to numerous American Indian tribes. Returning to the period of the mid-nineteenth century, Silko follows the journey of her child protagonist, Indigo, along with Indigo's adolescent sister, simply known as "Sister Salt." The girls are two of the last surviving members of a fictional tribe called the Sand Lizards. Separated from their family during a military raid of an American Indian ceremony called the Ghost Dance, the girls manage to briefly reunite with their aged grandmother in the ancestral gardens of their tribe before they are separated once again after being captured by the local Indian police. Because of her young age, Indigo is sent away to boarding school in Riverside, California. Escaping from the school in order to find her sister, Indigo is thwarted in her plans to return to the old gardens of her people when she is placed under the guardianship of a well-intentioned but misguided white American couple after being discovered hiding among the lilac bushes in their yard. Although she desires to return to the gardens that for centuries provided her people a safe haven from invaders, Indigo will spend much of the narrative traveling away from this sacred place, across the United States and as far as Corsica, before she will finally realize her dream of returning home.

Indigo's transnational travel experience contrasts with Holden's journey through the streets of New York City, which prompts him to long for the city of his childhood. Indeed, despite her more traumatic past, Indigo is revitalized by the pain of nostalgia and is able to successfully reconstruct her home, whereas Salinger's hero completely falls apart and ends up in a sanatorium, with his ability to successfully reintegrate into society being ambiguous at best. The wildly different conclusions for this pair may, in part, be due to their relationship to the gardens that they seek. For Holden, these gardens are easily transplanted, first in the Northeast and eventually in an unnamed remote town out west. For Indigo, however, there is only ever one garden, and that is the one where she grew up with her mother, Grandma Fleet, and Sister Salt. In the words of one reviewer, *Gardens* is very much a "revitalization story" (Willard 141), what Silko describes as an attempt to recover a different way of seeing the world, one that is not dependent on division or a sense of ownership (Arnold 11). Through the character of Indigo, Silko envisions a young female heroine who has the ability to cultivate the soil under extreme conditions, rejecting romantic accounts of the vanishing American Indian and the farm boy who would go on to replace this literary figure.

The story of Indigo's relationship to her ancestral land draws on the old association with women and gardens. Yet Silko carefully constructs these gardens in order to acknowledge the history of colonization on a global scale, picking up on the political tone of her previous novel, *Almanac of the Dead* (1991). In the opening passage, readers are presented with an idyllic scene of "datura

blossoms round and white as moons" and the white sand of the
desert wet with the "heavenly" scent of a fresh rain (13). This rev-
erie will be broken as the narrator turns to the thoughts of the el-
der and more responsible sibling, Sister Salt, who recalls the chaos
and shouting of her grandmother during a police raid. "Run! Run
get your little sister! You girls go back to the old gardens!" (13).
The gardens, it is later revealed, are a safe haven for the sisters
and their family, a secret location once used by the girls' tribe before the U.S. government wiped out most of the tribal members
through war, disease, and relocation policies. In the present, these
ancient gardens are much like the Sand Lizard tribe, ravaged by
time and unfortunate circumstances, but the girls will soon begin
to nurture the desert sand and bring forth buds of new life. With
the help of Grandma Fleet, the little family is able to produce a
good harvest filled with beans, squash, peaches, sunflowers, and
"brilliant red amaranth," all intended for the practical purpose of
eating (50–51). This period of peace and harmony will be disrupted
when the family is visited by misfortune once more with the passing of Grandma Fleet, who dies under the shade of the little peach
trees in the revitalized gardens.

The time in the old gardens is thus framed as a lesson in colonial history as the girls alternate between experiences of life and
death. Each lesson they learn from their grandmother during her
last days is intended to help them survive, and they carefully guard
the young plants they grow to ensure they will not die of starvation or be eaten by insects. This mode of engagement with the garden is in sharp contrast with that of the white women whom Indigo will later encounter after her escape from Indian boarding
school. Upon discovering a giant glass house (Indigo does not yet
know this is a greenhouse), the child is amazed to find the room
filled with beautiful, exotic plants. The plants, orchids once prized
by the owner's deceased mother, are now tended by a new tenant, a
New England intellectual named Hattie. Hattie's understanding of
plants is naïve at times, as she does not sense what Indigo clearly
sees as an excessive and impractical, albeit beautiful, use of the
gardens. Upon her arrival, for example, Indigo wonders, "Where
did they get all the water? The land here was sandy desert nearly
as dry as home—the panic grass and amaranth grew just as they
did at home" (84). Indigo's observation underscores the difficulty of

growing plants in the California desert, and her wonder creates a greater sense of the excess of such a gardening endeavor. This feeling is heightened as Indigo walks deeper into the gardens and observes more flowering plants inside a large glass greenhouse, with "cascading spikes of white wisteria" (84). As she enters the glass house, she will ask an important question that distinguishes the old gardens from the European-style gardens she will encounter from this point on: "Is there anything to eat?" (104).

As Silko describes in a 1998 interview, gardens are "the most political thing of all," precisely because of their connection to land and food (Arnold 3). Indigo's innocent question about food, and her surprise at the size and grandeur of the gardens, begin to mark the difference between those who have access to this land and food and those who do not. In contrast to their struggling gardens in the dunes, the luscious garden of red and white flowering plants, and the orange and lemon groves that encircle them, indicate a clear disregard for practical needs like eating—even the citrus fruit is not eaten. This disregard, or what Silko describes as "conspicuous consumption" (Arnold 20), is grossly exaggerated through another female figure, Hattie's sister-in-law, Susan. When Hattie and her husband, Edward, travel with Indigo back to New England in preparation for a European trip, the family is required to attend the "Masque of the Blue Garden," an elaborate party that Susan puts on annually. In preparation for the ball, Susan spares no expense, completely relandscaping the gardens. In one of her most excessive displays of wealth, she has workers drag two giant beech trees through the main streets of town. As the giant trees slowly make their way through the small streets, Indigo is shocked and observes how "wrapped in canvas and big chains on the flat wagon was a great tree lying helpless, its leaves shocked limp, followed by its companion; the stain of damp earth like dark blood seeped through the canvas" (183). The trees in this passage take on a human persona and even cry out with "low creaks and groans" (183). The passage parallels earlier scenes where Indigo and Sister Salt are similarly towed in a wagon, tied up by their captors to prevent them from escaping.

Indigo's reactions to these gardens of excess encourage readers to see the politics behind gardening practices. The gardens that populate this narrative, as one American literary scholar ob-

serves, "function as images of historical paradigms, of cultural systems; they symbolize values of beauty and concepts of thinking,
they represent social hierarchies" (Köhler 239). Terre Ryan, a creative writer and American literary scholar, develops this idea in
her 2007 reading of *Gardens*, in which she identifies how male
and female gardening practices differ—women might use the garden to gain power in a world where women rarely had the ability
to make decisions outside of the home (125). Ryan concludes that
there is a fundamental split between cultural views of gardens
represented through Silko's American Indian and Euro-American
characters. For the latter, gardening is simply about gaining power
and control, whereas the former see land in terms of practical (i.e.,
food) and spiritual purposes (126). This connection is underscored
in the previously mentioned scene where Grandma Fleet dies under the peach trees in the old gardens. Not only are these gardens
connected to Sand Lizard tribal history, but they also become the
resting place of the matriarch in Indigo's family, ensuring that the
girls will view the gardens as more than just a source of food.

The divide between American Indian and Euro-American gardening practices is further revealed through the men in the novel,
namely Hattie's husband, Edward, and her father, Mr. Abbott. It is
through these characters that Silko includes the most overt examples of colonialism, such as when Edward witnesses the burning of
one of the last natural sanctuaries of wild orchids in the Amazon.
The orchids, as he will later learn, were destroyed by his investor,
who wanted to have a monopoly on the orchid trade to ensure they
received the highest price for their product. This scheming presents an ugly side to gardening, as it is no longer about the creation of beauty but rather the manipulation of the market for economic gain. Mr. Abbott also tries to cultivate the land, but not in
the way that Edward and the other women do. Rather than focusing on ornamental flowers, he chooses to farm the land in the way
that is more consistent with American Indian values of gardening
for practical purposes. Mr. Abbott's garden, in fact, is compared to
other radical nineteenth-century agricultural experiments such as
Brook Farm, founded by George and Sophia Ripley in 1841, which
emphasized communal living. Abbott's farm is a social experiment
that "aim[s] to teach the poor to grow food to supplement their
diets" (155). Yet Silko will place the goodwill of Mr. Abbott into

question when Indigo is lost and then captured by a neighbor, who
sends the girl to a local reservation after failing to believe that she
is staying at the Abbott household. When Indigo arrives, she will
learn that the local tribe can no longer farm due to lack of proper
land, and have instead turned to the sea as the "last, great, boun-
tiful farm" (169). The irony of Abbott's farm, intended to help the
poor immigrant population, is apparent in this discussion between
Indigo and a Matinnecock Indian woman, since he fails to help the
very people who are suffering due to land loss at the expense of
white farmers. Even Hattie, as she frantically searches for Indigo
after she wanders from her parents' house, remarks in disbelief, "I
didn't know there are Indians nearby!" (170).

If gardens are reflective of cultural and political ideology, then
they also reveal more than what is reaped there. That is, gardens
become a site for narrating experience as much as they are a place
for viewing beautiful flowers or harvesting vegetables and other
edible food. In her 2009 essay on *Gardens*, African American literary scholar Stephanie Li argues that "cultural narratives are man-
ifest in nature" (29). Li provides the example of humming bees,
which once soothed Indigo as a child when she played in the old
gardens with Grandma Fleet (29). The sound of the bees grounds
Indigo and connects her to her personal and cultural identity, enabling her to maintain this identity even when she is at risk of losing it after being adopted by Hattie and Edward. As Li contends,
it is for this reason that the "natural world acts as a key source of
stories that are of particular importance to Indigo during her pro-
longed separation from her family" (24). It is through these storytelling practices, moreover, that gardens become sites of resistance, though this resistance takes different forms depending on
the storyteller. For Indigo, who carefully nurtures the gardens that
she grows, going so far as to treat the squash in the old gardens
like "fat babies" (54), the gardens become both a way to preserve
her culture and to embrace new identities, as is evidenced in the
closing scene where she successfully cultivates a rare mix of glad-
iolus in the resource-strained soil of the Indian reservation.

The gardens that feature prominently in Silko's narrative are
contrasted with another important image in American literature:
the machine. Indeed, from the very beginning of the narrative,
readers are confronted with alternating images of the machine and

the garden, supporting Leo Marx's belief in the enduring power of this image in the American literary imagination. One striking image of the transformative power of the machine appears when Indigo's mind returns to her previous home in the town of Needles, which she recalls as a time when her family "learned to talk English while selling baskets to tourists at the train station" (14). The memories of the tourists, much like those of the ravaged gardens, are bitter. In one particularly vivid story, Indigo recalls how her grandmother fought to keep her when a tourist tried to take her away. Using the only English she knew at the time, she repeatedly screamed "No!" to which "the white woman flinched, her face frozen with fear" (19). Confrontations such as this one continue as Indigo finds herself traveling by train, first to the Riverside boarding school, and then to New England with Hattie and Edward. On the first ride, Indigo observes how the Indian children "were cowering or sobbing, crowded four to a seat" and how the older children bully the younger ones, following the matron's order obediently due to their assimilation into white culture after years of boarding school (67). The uninitiated are labeled "wild," and those who refuse to accept the rules die quietly due to sadness (67). On her second trip, Indigo immediately notices the difference in the traveling style, a far cry from the crowded seats of her previous train trip. But when she is caught trying to jump from the train as it passes through her old hometown of Needles, the language shifts back to the more violent images of colonization in previous passages: "Clackety-clack! Clackety-clack! You left home, now you'll never get back. Clackety-clack! Never get back, never get back, get back, get back, the rails sang; even when Indigo put her fingers in her ears she heard the song. She cried until the tears made a wet spot on the pillow. Hattie sat on the edge of her berth and patted Indigo's back. . . . Hattie meant well, but she did not understand" (121). The rhythmic sound of the rails is turned into the teasing taunts of a bully, reminding Indigo of the challenges of returning home. As she first tries to make her escape, a tall man literally bars her path, and, though gentle, Hattie proceeds to put her hand on Indigo's shoulder, indicating that the girl should stay put (121).

The interactions between white and Native people in the above example identify the machine, much like the garden, as a deeply political image. The railroad, in particular, was both an image of

progress and a means for perpetuating common stereotypes about
Native people. In her 1996 essay on the Santa Fe Railway, Shelby
Tisdale, a cultural anthropologist and museum curator, reveals
how railroad companies took advantage of tourists' desire to see
the local populations and would advertise traditional artisanal
crafts among Native tribes (439). Through their advertisements,
the Santa Fe Railway company was able to boost tourism and gen-
erate a new economy whereby Native people could earn a living by
selling small handicrafts, yet the impact of such tourism has been
heavily critiqued. While Tisdale concludes that "the railroad has
played an indirect role in maintaining this [Native] cultural identity by providing a mechanism for marketing it" (457), the descriptions of tourists in *Gardens* clearly cast white Americans as selfish consumers with little to no regard for the very people they are
so eager to see. Rather than treating American Indians as human
beings, the tourists feel free to take anything that might please
them, including little Indigo. This lack of empathy is expanded in
other touristic activities, such as photography. When Indigo's sister returns to Needles with her baby, she is given money to pose
for a picture and is terrified that the camera lens will "steal his
[the baby's] energy" (399). The eye of the camera becomes a means
for preserving an image of Native people that those from the East
Coast of the United States readily paid money to access, underscoring the way that railroads supported tourist activities that reinforced stereotypes about Native people, in this case the Indian
woman with her "papoose," and failed to increase tourists' understanding of these populations (Tisdale 452).

   This view of the negative impact of railroad expansion is in line
with other historical documentation about the role that trains
played within the lives of marginalized groups in the United
States. In the case of American Indians, many tribes were granted
special railroad passes that enabled them to ride the rails free of
charge, but this benefit did not come without its limitations and
risks. Wovoka, a famous Paiute prophet who appears in the opening of *Gardens*, was a real historical figure who avidly traveled the
massive train system out west. In documentation of his travels,
the deplorable conditions of the railroad for American Indians is
revealed, including arbitrary decisions to void passes and unsafe

riding conditions (Ruuska 588–589). Travelers like Wovoka could expect to be asked to ride on the platform of cars, in an effort to keep Natives away from first- and second-class passengers. As a point of comparison, even Chinese passengers were given a boxcar to ride in (Erkkila 54). At a time when the Chinese were treated worse than marginalized European groups such as the Irish or Italians, it is telling that they were given preferential treatment over American Indian passengers. Such decisions were based on a belief that "their [American Indian] identity . . . was fixed, incapable of transitioning to that of fully assimilated American citizen," reflecting race prejudice that often positioned Native people well below other groups of potential Americans, notably western Europeans, who were seen as more adaptable to American culture (Erkkila 56).

Other images of progress that might fall under the larger category of the machine also appear in the narrative, most notably in the final chapters that revolve around the building of a large dam intended to bring freshwater to the new California towns cropping up in this desert country. Though initially the dam is presented as a source of wealth for all, including freed slaves, American Indians, and even a Mexican gypsy, this money is shown to be tainted as it brings all misfortune. As two of her leading characters, Big Candy and Sister Salt, are left penniless after a Mexican gypsy cleverly discovers the site of their hidden safe and robs them of their acquired wealth, Silko makes it clear that any benefits which might come from the dam project are short lived. She further reinforces this point through the different reactions of her characters: Big Candy desperately chases after the gypsy in an effort to recover the stolen cash and nearly dies, whereas Sister Salt, though disappointed about the loss, is more critical of money and its effects on human beings, bitterly crying: "Money! You couldn't drink it or eat it, but people went crazy over it" (398). The dam is further identified as a destructive force when it begins to flood the land in one of the reservation sites, aptly named "Road's End." Sister Salt, Indigo, and their friends describe the dam as "the government's plan to drown all the Indians, and they all laughed and laughed until tears filled their eyes. The only good land left to them now was about to be taken away by the backwater of the dam" (433).

The image of rising water spilling over and flooding Native land is not a new one, and in this way Silko participates in a long tradition of associating machines, especially those that unnaturally harness nature like the dam, with the destruction of Native land. The same technique, used as the basis for the narrative action in *Solar Storms*, also prompts the growth and development of the adolescent protagonist, Angel Wing. Here, however, Indigo, a child figure, is more passive and does not fight the dam builders. Ironically, Silko even positions her older character, Sister Salt, as a worker at one of the construction sites for the dam so that she initially supports, albeit in a minor way, the dam project. Yet Indigo, much like Angel's baby sister, is able to bring unity to her family in a situation of crisis through her apparent innocence and ability to cross between cultures. In the closing scene, this is vividly represented through the child's garden, a rare combination of the traditional beans and squash plants that once inhabited the gardens in the dunes and the beautiful ornamental plants she collected during her trip to Europe. Importantly, Indigo has solved her previous problem with landscape gardening, remarking that the colorful gladioli "weren't only beautiful; they were tasty!" (476).

Indigo's eagerness to develop a hybrid garden, and her movement between white culture and Indian culture, have led many to declare that the novel is an example of "global" literature.[3] Even Silko herself has proclaimed that the novel was inspired by a lecture circuit in Europe, where she found that she identified with some of the same issues that haunted a group of German women (Arnold 4). Published at the end of the 1990s, the novel anticipates many of the concerns about identity that would emerge in the wake of September 11, 2001, including the formation of "flexible" or "fluid" notions of identity not dependent on nationality. Although in many cases the border-crossing and migration patterns that have led to such new constructions of identity are linked to an emerging group of youth in the twenty-first century, Silko associates the same debate about hybridity with her young protagonist. In doing so, she infuses the garden image from the machine in the garden myth with new meaning, using trains and other machines to illustrate not only the damaging nature of colonization but also the empowering possibilities for those who survive such atrocities.

Reemerging from Ash:
Death of the Garden in M. T. Anderson's *Feed*

In the wake of the September 11 terrorist attacks, the myths revived by Cold War scholars became relevant once again. Rhetoric
calling for the strengthening of the "homeland" fueled U.S. nationalism as then-President George W. Bush declared a "War on Terror" that extended to the controversial invasion of Iraq in 2003. As
the Iraq War grew increasingly unpopular in the early 2000s, dystopian young adult (YA) fiction began to flourish, perhaps due to
the tendency for youth to serve as a "measure of the nation's resil-
iency and health in moments of crisis" (Schwebel, "Reading 9/11"
198). In M. T. Anderson's popular YA novel *Feed* (2002), technology
functions as an aid to consumer culture, serving to implant young
minds with subliminal messages about the latest fashion trends.
The "feed," as Anderson refers to it, is a device that is implanted in
children at a young age, developing along with their bodies so that
it begins to work seamlessly with other natural organs and neural
systems. Although the feed makes it possible for those who have
it to chat and find information instantly, it still leaves many feeling empty, which in turn leads the feed to prompt its users to buy
material objects to fill this emotional void. Much like Salinger's
iconic teenager, Holden Caulfield, Anderson's male protagonist, Titus, bemoans the loneliness that he often feels, "even when there
were other people around me" (5). His words reflect a common sentiment that technology, though making it possible to instantly connect with others, is in fact creating a greater chasm between human beings and leaving youth in particular woefully incapable of
handling social situations.

This sentiment reflects some of the more recent concerns in the
YA novel, which has seen a rise in dystopian fiction since the 1990s
(Bradford et al. 108). As Clare Bradford et al. explain in their 2008
study on contemporary children's literature, authors of dystopian
novels "have foregrounded the propensity of communities founded
on common identities, beliefs, and projects to exclude and punish
those outside of them" (107). This view is supported by best sellers
such as Suzanne Collins's *The Hunger Games* (2008) and James
Dashner's *The Maze Runner* (2009), both of which feature adoles-

cents in dangerous worlds where they must fight just for the right
to survive, often with many casualties along the way. But as Bradford et al. suggest, such fictions have the power to transform the
worlds that they speak of and the adolescent reader along with
it. Drawing on the theories of popular utopian studies scholars,
Bradford and her fellow writers argue that "utopian and dystopian tropes carry out important social, cultural, and political work
by challenging and reformulating ideas about power and identity,
community, the body, spatio-temporal change, and ecology" (2).
Bradford has argued elsewhere that Anderson's novel participates
in this tradition of "transformative utopianism" by enabling its
readers to gain "critical distance" from the problems that Anderson identifies and thereby gives them the ability to critique these
issues from their new vantage point ("'Everything Must Go!'" 129).

A closer look at the novel reveals that Anderson structures his
narrative around familiar binaries, including innocence/experi-
ence, machine/human, and male/female. Through his main characters—the aforementioned Titus, who is fully enmeshed in the
consumer culture the feed is created to cultivate and support, and
Violet, a teenage girl who is determined to resist the feed and all
that it represents—Anderson begins to develop a romantic image
of nature. In an early scene following the attack of a hacker, who
breaks into a club on the moon and temporarily renders Titus's
and Violet's feeds dysfunctional, the young couple walk down the
halls of the hospital and discover an enclosed garden that has been
exposed to the elements of the moon. As Titus observes the eerie
picture created by this neglected garden, he notes how "a long time
ago the glass ceiling over the terrarium had cracked, and so everything was dead, and there was moon dust all over everything
out there. Everything was gray" (62). In spite of this gloomy image, Anderson uses it as the backdrop for the budding love of Titus and Violet, foreshadowing the inevitable demise of the couple.
In the closing lines of the chapter, Titus thinks, "She was staring
at me, and I was staring at her, and I moved toward her, and we
kissed. The vines beat against each other out in the gray, dead garden, they were all writhing against the spine of the Milky Way on
its edge, and for the first time, I felt her spine, too, each knuckle of
it, with my fingers, while the air leaked and the plants whacked

each other near the silent stars" (63). These final words from Titus
are in part meant to illustrate what Violet has noticed already—
that Titus is skilled at using metaphor despite growing up with
the feed. The garden, with its ashy, ghostlike foliage, is a primor-
dial space where language and love can thrive. Indeed, the section
that involves the hospital is aptly named "Eden" and is a nod toward Anderson's position regarding technology and its negative effects on the human race.

The link between youth and technology, and its contrast with a
garden-state, is one that is familiar to readers of Anderson's work.
In his later novel, *The Astonishing Life of Octavian Nothing, Vol.
1* (2006), Anderson begins with a similar scene, where the protagonist is raised in a "gaunt house with a garden" and recounts the
"floating lights in the apple-trees" among the garden orchard (3).
The idyllic image of the garden is quickly contradicted when the
narrator, Octavian, reveals that this same garden is surrounded
by a high stone wall intended to keep him and his mother from escaping (3). As children's literature scholar Anastasia Ulanowicz
notes, the novel "begins to deconstruct a cherished American creation myth, suggesting that American national mythology, like any
national mythology, is contingent upon the exclusion of the Other
as well as the exploitation of those who remain within its carefully
contained boundaries" (278). Ulanowicz's assertion is supported
by Sara Schwebel's more recent 2014 article about post-9/11 fiction. In her essay, Schwebel contends that Anderson's recent young
adult novels, namely *Feed* and *Octavian Nothing*, work together to
urge adolescent readers to think critically about the national mythology they present ("Reading 9/11" 197–198). In this case, the
garden imagery, which suggests a prelapsarian state and supports
the myth of American exceptionalism, is dashed by the harsh realities that enter this supposedly innocent space.

But these garden-states are also contrasted with images of a
machine or machinelike body. In the closing chapters of *Octavian
Nothing*, young Octavian is forced to wear a metal mask, his voice
choked and silenced by the bitter metal bit in his mouth. Similarly,
Titus falls into an almost catatonic state as he and his friends begin to experience the malfunctions that Titus witnessed through
the decline of his previous girlfriend, Violet. The machinery may

not be visible from the outside, as in the case of Octavian, but Anderson goes to great pains to discuss how these machines push the young people who use them into a fallen state:

> Everything was not always going well, because for most people, our hair fell out and we were bald, and we had less and less skin. Then later there was this thing that hit hipsters. People were just stopping in their tracks frozen. At first, people thought it was another virus, and they were looking for groups like the Coalition of Pity, but it turned out that it was something called Nostalgia Feedback. People had been getting nostalgia for fashions that were closer and closer to their own time, until finally people became nostalgic for the moment they were actually living in, and the feedback completely froze them. It happened to Calista and Loga. We were real worried about them for a day or so. We knew they'd be all right, but still, you know. Marty was like, "Holy fuckin' shit, this is so Nike fucked." (278)

As Titus reveals, the malfunctions have literally short-circuited the minds of their users, trapping them in a perpetual present. The degeneration of bodies, which Titus begins with, is just one among many concerns in an era where technology rules. The final line, "this is so Nike fucked," further enforces the message of the danger of technology, specifically corporate-run operations of surveillance. The insertion of "Nike" even at such a grave moment marks the complete control of corporations, who have effectively brainwashed youth through constant advertising (called "bannering" in the novel) and by taking over the education of youth and replacing it with School™. The fact that the boys are only worried "for a day or so" also points to the short-term thinking of youth, who are now so wrapped up in the here and now that they cannot look beyond to the future and the possible consequences of their actions.

The fusion of youth and technology in a bionic body is not a new image in science fiction. As children's literature scholar Victoria Flanagan argues in *Technology and Identity in Young Adult Fiction* (2014), "Young adult narratives that are set in technofuturistic worlds are typically concerned with exploring how technologically modified bodies might extend or challenge normative definitions of what it means to be a human being" (16). In her reading of Anderson's *Feed*, Flanagan explores the way that his and other contemporary dystopian YA novels create futuristic surveillance societies as a way of presenting a fractured subject with powerful agentic potential. That is, the adolescents who populate these worlds are able to skillfully navigate between multiple selves as a way of subverting the system and upsetting it in powerful ways (128). Flanagan concludes that *Feed* fails to offer a positive outlook on the potential of a posthuman subject (here I follow Flanagan and define "posthuman" as living in a world ruled by technology and/or being a physical product of that technology through the aid of medical science [14]), arguing that the novel sends the message that "resistance is completely futile" in the surveillance culture in which these characters exist (135). However, as Sara Schwebel points out, *Feed* does call on its readers to exert a power that its characters fail to uphold ("Reading 9/11" 198). I agree with Schwebel and would add that Anderson is hopeful his adolescent readers will adopt the more "adult" or experienced view of the author himself and learn how to use technology in a savvy way that avoids the pitfalls of corporatization. Clare Bradford makes a similar argument when she acknowledges the way that Anderson effectively uses technology to advertise his work and to cultivate his media persona with his fans. She observes how "the author implied by *Feed* and constructed through Anderson's website occupies a critical distance from mainstream society, positioning young readers to see him as an exceptional adult, one who does not conform to mainstream norms" ("'Everything Must Go!'" 135). In short, while Anderson may be critical of technology within the pages of *Feed*, his media persona suggests that technology can be used in a powerful way to make changes, so long as this self does not totally subsume the user's identity in the real world.

Anderson prefigures this kind of agency within *Feed* through the creation of Titus's love interest, Violet. Violet, who, importantly, was given a choice to get the feed, is eager to participate in activities that she views as "normal," including dancing, partying, and shopping. However, she also can't help but expose herself as an outsider during these games as she remains deeply critical of the system the feed has created. In one particular outburst, Violet erupts and screams at one of Titus's friends, calling the girl a "monster" since she chose to get plastic surgery to imitate the sores that everyone is getting all over their bodies (202). In her mind, the choice to intentionally mutilate one's body is evidence of the decline of civilization, and she screams in fury that this act is proof that everyone is completely controlled by the feed. Of course, she is in part right, as Anderson makes clear through the actions of the characters. Just with a suggestion from the feed, characters will purchase items or change their looks, and in the earlier garden scene everyone is so depressed by the absence of the feed that they watch in awe as one friend, who was not touched by the hacker, narrates a show she is watching on the feed. Yet Anderson also quickly moves from Violet's outburst to her complete breakdown. Already feeling the effects of her feed's malfunction, Violet no longer has the strength to resist the pressures of the feed and appears incredibly fragile. As Titus notes, "she had broken somehow, and she was broken, and, oh fuck, she was sagging and I grabbed her to help her, and she was shaking, and her eyes were all white and rolling around, and she couldn't talk anymore" (202). Violet's silencing due to the malfunction of the feed is similar to the metal bit placed in Octavian's mouth. Both characters are literally choked into silence, though in Octavian's case it is important to note that the metal mask was given to him by force rather than choice.

In presenting the most rebellious character in such a fragile state of decline, Anderson questions the ability of youth to successfully contradict powerful social forces. In earlier chapters, Violet embraces the typical role of rebel that is often ascribed to adolescents. When discussing the effects of the feed, Violet asserts, "I'm not going to let them catalog me. I'm going to become invisible" (98). Violet follows through and successfully confuses the system used to categorize her shopping preferences by asking for random things like a searchlight (which she then asks to have installed on her stomach) and other odds and ends. She refers to these acts as "resisting" and urges Titus to resist along with her. Yet Titus, more skeptical than Violet, only sees resisting as a kind of game and quickly resumes his normal purchasing habits when he returns home. This choice is shown to be better in the long run after Violet learns that her decision to resist has in fact closed off any possibility of receiving funding to have her feed fixed. As she listens to the final decision from FeedTech, the company who owns the feed technology, she is told that she is not a *"reliable investment"* and that *"we might be able to create a consumer portrait of you that would interest our investment team"* (247; emphasis in original). As Feed-Tech's report indicates, if Violet wants to survive, she must give up on resisting the feed's suggestions to buy products and become an ideal consumer. In short, her only choices are to give into the system or to face certain death (the ultimate silencing force). In this way, Violet fails to live up to other popular heroines of dystopian YA novels, such as the immensely popular Katniss Everdeen and Beatrice/Tris Prior, who manage to outwit the systems of surveillance in their respective worlds.

Although she is ultimately unsuccessful in her attempts to resist, Anderson's choice to use a female character to act as the mouthpiece of rebellion is in keeping with recent trends in YA fiction, and Violet is an important counter to the traditional subject of humanism, who tends to be white and male (Flanagan 36). On several occasions, Anderson reveals that Violet is more aware of the political and social issues of her times, which may in part be due to her education outside of the corporate system and the late installation of her feed. She often questions Titus about his apathy toward the world around him, such as in the opening scene where she is flabbergasted that he believes the moon, along with the rest of the world, is uninteresting (37). Violet will later encourage Titus to consider the implications of his apathy, such as when she points out that being able to visit the moon is a luxury that many cannot afford:

> "Do you know how much it costs to fly someone to the moon?"
> I guessed. "A lot?"
> "Yeah. Yeah, a lot. He [her father] wanted to come, but it would have been, like, a month of his salary. He saved up for a year to send me. Then I went, and that stuff happened." (103)

Violet's confession reveals why a world where consumption rules might be so difficult for her to navigate. With little financial power, she must find other ways to connect and "feed" her interest in the world around her. While she tries to share these interests with Titus, she doesn't manage to change him much until she is near death, at which point Titus desperately gives her the information she found important when she was healthy. As he stares at her immobile body, Titus tells story after story about the political events happening around the world. As he admits, these stories are "broken," but they represent a conscious act on his part to detach himself from the feed (296). But even as he "trie[s] not to listen to the noise on the feed," Titus is pulled back into the narrative storytelling that he is accustomed to from his youth, switching from the broken tales of news around the world to a cliché story of love that could be a trailer for a Hollywood film (296–298).

Violet's death scene is imperative as it recalls the long-standing relationship between women and gardens that many authors, including Leslie Marmon Silko, draw on in order to assert a sense of female subjectivity. While Violet appears broken and defeated in much of the novel, her voice compels Titus, an extremely unlikable character due to his apathy and even coldness toward others, to reach out and at least try to connect with the world around him. In this moment, then, Anderson plays with the idea of connection that is inspired by the technological invention of the feed. To connect, one must silence the voices of the feed and begin to think more critically about the people and events that are happening in the world. To connect, one must also be willing to tell stories rather than just listen to them. To create rather than consume. In short, Anderson is encouraging his readers through his characters to return to the metaphorical garden-state that he alludes to in the earlier moon scene, where Violet and Titus first begin to form a relationship. Anderson's emphasis on the destructive power of technology underscores the lasting power of the machine in the garden myth, demonstrating its ability to adapt to the different political and cultural circumstances across the decades that span the Cold War, even well into the twenty-first century when Cold War rhetoric was revived in order to support the United States' "War on Terror." Anderson's image of the decaying bodies of youth provides a shocking conclusion to some of the issues that first arose in the 1950s, when anxiety about delinquent immigrant children revived a belief in the power of rural life to redeem American society and return it to a state of innocence. In what follows, I will conclude by looking at how frontier myths continue to pervade American culture in the twenty-first century, focusing on how the adolescent might offer a vision of radical futurity in a moment when national boundaries are becoming increasingly fluid.

The Price of Maturity for the Future of American Studies

But I tell you the New Frontier is here, whether we seek it or not.
—**John F. Kennedy, "The New Frontier"**

For a movement so critical of the culture around it, American Studies recapitulates America in revealing ways. . . . [B]oth have articulated visions of a new and better order; and the insecurity of identifying with an *ought* rather than an *is* has compelled each to continue asking, "Who are we?" and "Where are we heading?"
—**Gene Wise, "'Paradigm Dramas' in American Studies"**

On July 20, 2019, articles commemorating the fiftieth anniversary of the *Apollo 11* landing on the moon began debating the benefits of reopening what John F. Kennedy called the "New Frontier" in his 1960 speech accepting his presidential nomination. Kennedy, who was assassinated only a few years after that speech, would never see the results of the "space race" between the United States and the Soviet Union. But as a child growing up in central Florida, not far from the Kennedy Space Center on Cape Canaveral, I remember all too well the familiar boom from the air pressure changes caused by a returning space shuttle, the power of the rockets roaring even from miles away during a launch, the famous lines to a countdown: ten, nine, eight . . . blast off! When NASA officially redirected its energies in 2011, terminating the space shuttle program, I also remember the sadness about the finality of that decision, especially for my parents' generation who had witnessed the first successful moon landing in 1969. Although I hadn't seen the space program from its start, I have to admit that the idea of never seeing another shuttle streak across the sky seemed strange to me as well. After all, the idea of discovering new life through space exploration had been embedded in my mind at an early age through film and television shows about aliens and planets beyond our solar system.

While at the time it seemed clear that space exploration was off the table, at least for humans, the anniversary of *Apollo 11* rekindled interest in putting men on the moon. The New Frontier was back. As the phrase first coined by John F. Kennedy suggests, space exploration represented more than a chance to advance science and our knowledge of the world around us; for Americans, it also reopened the frontier that had previously been the site of westward expansion. In a 2019 article from the *New York Times*, the possibility of returning to the moon is eagerly embraced. Mapping the Cold War politics surrounding space exploration, the article describes the shuttle program as an American destiny rather than a choice and concludes that "yes, some of us still want to play with spaceships." Quoting Konstantin E. Tsiolkovsky, a Russian rocket scientist, this destiny is viewed as one that will lead to renewed growth: "The Earth is the cradle of humanity, but one cannot remain in the cradle forever." In comparing space exploration to the process of growing up, the *New York Times* revives the historical connection between national identity and youth. Once again, youth becomes a way to imagine the United States' future and to bolster support for projects meant to increase national progress.

The renewed interest in space exploration demonstrates the longevity of national myths about the frontier, where space becomes another place for Americans to expand their presence and colonize. The promise of once again flying into space draws on the original promises of new land and opportunity associated with the frontier and attempts to imagine what a future beyond national borders might look like. What happens if Americans settled on the moon? Or even further out on planets orbiting in our solar system? Such a suggestion of life beyond earth makes even the dystopian future of M. T. Anderson's young adult novel *Feed*, where trips to the moon are part of the tourist industry, seem like a real possibility. But it also raises important questions about the future of the nation, ones that are bound up in the core questions about the relationship between U.S. national identity and youth that I have addressed in this book. In *Growing Up with America*, I have demonstrated how the figure of the adolescent can help revitalize old paradigms by shifting our attention to early engagements with difference at a time when a narrative of wholeness was desirable. At this pivotal historical moment, when space exploration is seen as a way to launch Americans out of the cradle, the adolescent can once again serve as a symbol of radical futurity for the United States. To answer, as American theorist and cultural historian Gene Wise asked in his pivotal 1979 essay on the methods of American studies, "Who are we?" and "Where are we heading?"

Wise's essay, published nearly twenty years after Kennedy's famous "New Frontiers" speech, claimed that one of the key features of the field of American studies is its intricate connection to the nation and questions of identity. For Wise, the answers to these questions were unclear as the United States was about to move into the Reagan era, a period when Cold War sentiment remained strong, accompanied by a renewed zeal for U.S. militarism. Twenty years later, however, a growing trend emerged to reexamine the history of American studies and consider possible futures for both the field and its object of study, the United States. In moving beyond the national narratives that were the subject of the myth and symbol school, new generations of scholars, especially those who took part in the cultural turn of American studies in the 1970s, have begun to map ways for moving beyond the geographical borders of the United States. These studies consider the effects of globalization and the closure of the period known as the "American Century" on U.S. national identity, trying to offer new ways to conceive of the nation in a time of blurred borders and boundaries. Titles that announce this agenda include *Locating American Studies* (1999), *American Studies in a Moment of Danger* (2001), *The Futures of American Studies* (2002), *Hemispheric American Studies* (2008), *Globalizing American Studies* (2010), and *Re-framing the Transnational Turn in American Studies* (2011). If in debates among the first generation of scholars the focus was on how to move "beyond innocence," in this new debate about the state of the field, composed of second- and third-generation scholars, the task has now shifted from breaking with the United States' past to imagining its future. While to a certain extent first-generation scholars were thinking of the nation's future, the emphasis remained on the importance of breaking with an "innocent past." In the present moment, there is agreement among scholars that this past was never innocent to begin with and that the very concept of a nation itself is at stake.

In this scholarship on the future of the field, the need to move beyond the framework of the nation is repeatedly emphasized, with calls to radically reconfigure approaches to American studies. Those taking part in this conversation have asked, in various ways, how the field might relocate itself in order to see from new perspectives (Edwards and Gaonkar 17). While youth might offer such a perspective, there is an overwhelming silence on the topic of youth that repeats an alarming pattern within the field that first emerged in the beyond innocence debate that I covered earlier in chapter 1. In the past five years alone, not a single article on youth, even accounting for different terminology such as "teenager" and "adolescent," has appeared in *American Quarterly*. Youth has always held a contentious role in the field from its very origins, viewed as a threat to the hard-won maturity gained through the elevation of American literature to a respectable status, but the continued absence of youth from current discussions within American studies foreclose the very futures scholars are seeking at this critical moment. In closing, I want to consider the price of maturity for the future of American studies, and how the role of the figure of the adolescent at this pivotal moment in the field might help advance scholarship on national identity.

At a time when the global is disrupting traditional notions of the nation, the adolescent can help scholars of American studies, as well as others invested in thinking about childhood and youth, to reframe the current conversation about futurity. Not yet a full citizen but with the power to engage in global politics, the adolescent, as a figure of rebellion, serves to break down boundaries dividing nations and engages with the power dynamics at play within the field. As the burgeoning work in childhood and youth studies indicates, adolescents are bound up in the power structures that define national identity, both on a local and international level. In our present moment, globalization has shifted the ways that youth participate as citizens in a global economy (Ventura 238) so that young people are now intricately linked to changes occurring at both the national and global levels in the twenty-first century (Maira and Soep xv). Within the United States alone, youth protests across the country have shown a new level of activism historically attributed to the 1960s. In well-executed movements addressing topics ranging from gun violence, climate change, and immigration, youth are demonstrating their desire to participate as active citizen subjects. However, this participation extends beyond the domestic sphere. The impact of globalization, in particular, is shifting the way youth view themselves and how their acts of rebellion might serve as a symbol of the state of the nation. Youth as active *global* citizen subjects, with the ability to think beyond the traditional category of national identity, respond to growing concerns about the ability of the term "American" to continue to accurately describe those with national ties to the United States.

Despite the significance of the relationship between youth and national identity in our present moment, American studies scholars continue to have an uncomfortable relationship with youth and in this sense follow in the footsteps of the first generation of scholars who participated in the beyond innocence debate of the 1950s. The field's desire for maturity (or, better yet, to *remain* mature) continues to limit the engagement with the figure of the adolescent as an object of study, a point that becomes evident with a closer look at some of the scholarly accounts of the future of the field from the twenty-first century. These authors often make a nod toward the radical potential of youth, only to abandon this thread of their argument in favor of other methodological possibilities. In Janice Radway's frequently cited 1998 American Studies Association presidential address, "What's in a Name?," the potential for youth to shape the field is quite literally a footnote in her larger argument.[1] Relating how one of her questions about renaming the association was inspired by a conference presentation at Duke University where the "youth" of students in subaltern studies enabled them to ask new questions of the field (75), Radway views youth as bound up in the futurity of the field.[2] In her example, the "innocence" of youth in fact becomes an advantage because these young scholars do not have predetermined answers to the questions they are asking. George Lipsitz, another prominent second-generation scholar of American studies, similarly views youth in terms of their active potential to enact change. Using the example of the Tielman Brothers, an Indonesian popular rock band in the Netherlands, Lipsitz notes in his recent historical study of the field, *American Studies in a Moment of Danger* (2001), how even in the 1950s youth "found an opportunity to insert themselves into the national spotlight through commercial culture" and that the group's eventual international success and blend of different national music traditions "helped redefine the 'nation' and its boundaries" (310–311).[3]

In response to calls for new paradigms that can cope with the shifting position of the United States in a global landscape, Donald Pease and Robyn Wiegman, who alongside Radway and Lipsitz might be associated with a more mature second generation of scholars in American studies, bring together several voices from both senior and emerging scholars in their edited collection *The Futures of American Studies* (2002).[4] In order to begin to chart how to handle the stretching boundaries of the field and break once and for all with the exceptionalist thinking that has overshadowed American studies since its founding as an academic field of study in the 1950s, the duo attempt to provide an overview of several different critical orientations for a more global American studies. Launching their exploration of the "futures" of the field through a return to Gene Wise's influential essay "'Paradigm Dramas' in American Studies: A Cultural and Institutional History of the Movement" (1979), the editors make the by now familiar turn to the past in order to anticipate the future. Describing Wise's essay as a "founding gesture," Pease and Wiegman suggest that through his argument Wise "gave monumental status to an origin retrospectively invoked, thereby giving the past authority over the contours of the present in a management strategy that seemed to contextualize, if not override, the present threat of rupture and incoherence" (2). The anxiety that the pair identify as shaping Wise's exploration and review of the state of the field in the 1970s, which they claim prevented several possible futures, can in fact help us understand the current state of the field, which I have begun to locate in the preoccupation with futurity at the turn of the new millennium. Viewed as a moment when the American Century would finally come to a close, the year 2000 marked a moment of rupture within the field similar to that of the 1960s, when radical social movements transformed American studies to the point that leaders such as Gene Wise could no longer recognize it.

The implications of this earlier rupture can be found in the anxiety about futurity in the present moment. In Pease and Wieg-

man's vision of a new American studies, the need to reconceptualize the nation as a place with fluid rather than fixed borders
is attributed to the rapid globalization of the 1990s. Anthropologist Arjun Appadurai, famous for his identification of the "scapes"
of globalization in *Modernity at Large* (1996), argued during the
previous decade that we "need to think beyond the nation" ("Patriotism and Our Futures" 411), and Mary Louise Pratt, who is
an expert in Latin American studies, similarly suggests in a 1991
article that we ought to consider "*contact zones*" as sites of exchange where "cultures meet, clash, and grapple with each other"
(34; emphasis in original). With the nation no longer serving to define the "imaginary communities" that bind people together, questions about the state of American studies and its primary object
of study, the United States, remain central to efforts to imagine
a global future. As of yet, however, it seems that the field has not
found a consistent method for approaching American studies without "America." As Robyn Wiegman suggests, the "prevailing relation between historical time and national entity has begun to fracture, confounding our earlier assurance that time and place could
define, without question, the legitimacy of our objects of studies"
("Futures" 5). Donald Pease has elsewhere underscored the impact
of the movement away from traditional notions of the nation for
the field, identifying the "transnational turn" as "the most significant reimagining of the field of American studies since its inception" ("Introduction: Re-mapping" 1).

If acknowledging that the global relationships of the United
States and their impact on its citizens was one radical step toward
a new future for the field, the next might be expanding the markers of identity studied in order to reconceive U.S. national identity itself. Youth, as I have begun to suggest, provides one possibility for doing so. One recent example from youth movements of the
twenty-first century includes the expanding protests against gun
violence. In Florida, a group of high school students from Parkland
helped initiate the March for Our Lives rally, part of their Never
Again campaign for gun control, which quickly gained national attention. The protests became one of many school "walkouts" for
different causes, the most recent of which has been the global protests against climate change. Young people participating in these
campaigns are choosing to leave school to make their voices heard

by national politicians and to enact change, but their efforts expand beyond the national sphere and take part in a larger international youth movement. In the case of the recent protests against
climate change, launched by Swedish teenager Greta Thunberg
in 2018, protests began across the pond in Europe before making their way to the United States. In one report from Kawika Pegram, a student protester in Hawaii, the teenager's admiration for
the leaders of March for Our Lives led him to information about
the climate change protests (Anzilotti). Youth like Pegram use social media to stay informed about domestic issues, but as his example demonstrates they can and often are led to international
movements for social change. These movements intersect with one
another, leading young people from one campaign to the next, and
are part of a global network of youth activism that is redefining
adolescent rebellion and how young people imagine themselves as
citizens of a nation.

What I find interesting about these examples of American
youth activism is not so much how young people become politically engaged but how this engagement gives them different ways
to participate as citizen subjects. In the coverage of these youth
movements, many teenagers are denouncing traditional narratives about the dependency of youth and utilizing media to connect with others unrelated to them by nationality. Their sense of
an identity is grounded in their youth and their belief in the social
causes they support, a way of bonding that Arjun Appadurai first
suggested in his 1990s work on globalization (420). This way of relating through activism is reflected in contemporary American literature as well, including two recent novels by award-winning authors Thanhha Lai and Linda Sue Park. In Lai's case, her National
Book Award winner, *Inside Out and Back Again* (2011), employs
the figure of the refugee to reflect on national guilt from international conflicts stemming from the Cold War crisis. Her young protagonist, Kim Hà, flees from South Vietnam after the fall of Saigon
and must forge relationships with other young people to survive
the racism of rural Georgia in the American South. In contrast,
Park's more journalistic novel, *A Long Walk to Water* (2010), anticipates youth interest in the topic of climate change and focuses
on a South Sudanese refugee who goes on to begin a campaign
for building water wells in his home country as an adult. Both

books aim to address young readers as members of a world community and to direct them toward new participatory modes of citizenship—in Park's case, young readers are encouraged to fund-
raise for Water for South Sudan, a charity started by Salva Dut
whose story inspired the novel.

These examples from both real and fictional youth do not provide easy solutions to the questions about U.S. national identity
in the twenty-first century. Those who seek to define adolescents,
and even younger children, as exemplars of global citizenship
must grapple with the history of imperialism undergirding this
concept, which has eerie echoes in the national myths that dominated in the Cold War. In a 2007 article in the *Wall Street Journal*, young people are described as "inconvenient youths," a play on
words that alludes to former vice president Al Gore's 2006 documentary film on climate change. Youth here are depicted as pesky
children who chide their parents to pay more attention to the effects of climate change; they are environmental activists on a mission to turn attention to the present moment rather than the future ahead. The belittling of youth, attempting to silence rather
than empower them, appears in the trailer for another documentary film with the same title. In Slater Jewell-Kemker's 2012 film
about her journey as a teenager to help protect the environment,
she narrates images of her younger self on the screen, explaining
how she and her friends were "paraded" onstage at the 2008 Environment G8 Summit in Kobe, Japan (*"An Inconvenient Youth"*).
Jewell-Kemker's observation about her employment as a tool for
greedy politicians resonates with criticism of today's youth movements as well, when adults cast suspicion on the ability of teenagers to understand complex political issues.

In the past, children did participate in similar events as the
Environmental G8 Summit in order to support the United States'
Cold War agenda. Historical newspaper articles show young white,
middle-class girls like Jewell-Kemker distributing clothing, toys,
and other items for relief efforts to war-torn countries that included Korea and Hungary ("Gifts for Korea" 12), along with hand-
made scrapbooks espousing ideal American values. But youth
were not simply pawns for politicians; they were actively seeking
ways to counter this authority despite their limitations as citizen
subjects, including not yet having the right to vote. In her study

of Arthurian cinema, Susan Aronstein, a scholar of medieval literature and popular culture, remarks how in the 1960s youth were
already revolting against the "new Frontier" and the "tyranny of
conformity" created by those in power by the time of John F. Kennedy's death in 1963 (82). Young people continue this fight today,
as the waves of new protests for different social causes ranging
from gun violence to climate change demonstrate. In the Lako-
ta-led One Mind Youth Movement, a 2016 editorial shows children
running across prairie fields in a protest meant to raise awareness
about the destruction that completion of the Dakota Access Pipeline would cause. The teenagers leading this movement, or "water warriors" as they call themselves, participate in a much longer
struggle for sovereign rights for Native tribes, but their message
about the destruction of land is clear: protecting the land is nonne-
gotiable, and it is time for adults to listen to those who will inherit
the problems of today's generation (Gebreyes).

The entanglement of youth and national identity in the twenty-
first century underscores the continued importance of thinking
about the figure of the adolescent. As scholars seek to find new
ways of constructing identity that extend beyond the nation, the
adolescent provides a way both to revitalize old paradigms, drawing attention to the fractured identities of the twentieth century
and the global politics that shaped Americans' views of themselves, and to offer new methodological approaches to current issues. Here I have advocated for a childhood studies approach,
which has begun gaining traction in the field of American studies since I first began writing this book in 2012. In the past five
years alone, a number of articles on childhood in *American Quarterly* have appeared, placing young people at the center of the field
for the first time since its inception. These publications include
essays by Marah Gubar, Sara Schwebel, Jennifer Helgren, Susie Woo, Laura Briggs, and Kiara Vigil, among others.[5] At least in
part, it seems, the anxiety about innocence and the immaturity
that a focus on youth was once seen as representing is starting to
dissipate. This shift, which unfortunately fails to extend to older
youth, seems timely given the political changes happening within
the United States in the twenty-first century, and it's a trend that I
hope will gain increasing momentum. With the United States setting its sights on new, far-off horizons, we may once again be living

in a time where the myths originating in the frontier shape constructions of national identity. If that turns out to be the case, the boom and the roar may not just be sounds from space shuttles; it will be from the young people themselves who oppose the resurrection of the United States' imperial legacy.

NOTES

Introduction. The Specter of Youth in the Cold War

The epigraph is from *Playing in the Dark*, by Toni Morrison. Copyright © 1992. Used by permission of the author.

1. See, for example, essays in an ongoing debate about the role of the child in academic scholarship among scholars in children's literature and childhood studies. These include Marah Gubar's "Risky Business: Talking about Children in Children's Literature Criticism" (2013), Kenneth Kidd's "Children's Culture, Children's Studies, and the Ethnographic Imagination" (2002), Mary Galbraith's "Hear My Cry: A Manifesto for an Emancipatory Childhood Studies Approach to Children's Literature" (2001), Gertrud Lenzer's "Children's Studies: Beginnings and Purposes" (2001), Karen Coats's "Keepin' It Plural: Children's Studies in the Academy" (2001), and Richard Flynn's "The Intersection of Children's Literature and Childhood Studies" (1997).

2. I refer here to letter 3 from de Crèvecoeur's *Letters from an American Farmer* (1782).

3. For a full discussion of these scientific developments, see Carolyn Steedman's *Strange Dislocations: Childhood and the Idea of Human Interiority, 1780–1930* (1995).

4. I am indebted to Jane Knowles and Robert Allen Skotheim for this term, which I first encountered in their 1961 review in *American Quarterly*.

Chapter 1. Beyond Innocence

The epigraph is from *The Liberal Tradition in America*, by Louis Hartz. Copyright © 1955 and renewed 1983 by Louis Hartz. Used by permission of Houghton Mifflin Harcourt. All rights reserved.

1. In the Spring 2005 issue of *American Literary History*, Amy Kaplan and George Lipsitz both offer compelling responses to Leo Marx's attacks on contemporary American studies scholarship, an essay that appears in the same issue. In "On Recovering the 'Ur' Theory of American Studies," Marx views the younger generation of American studies scholars as emerging after a period he identifies as the "Great Divide." The "AD," or "After the Divide," scholars are characterized by their interest in a more diverse, multicultural America,

whereas the "BD," or "Before the Divide," scholars were more deeply invested in a homogeneous America (124).

2. In his preface to *Literary Reflections* (1993), Lewis touchingly refers to his time stationed in Italy during the war, where he "happened upon a copy of *Moby-Dick* in an Armed Forces edition and read it right through" (xvi). Lewis's encounter with Melville's masterpiece is presented as on par with a religious conversion, his whole world literally "turned around" by the novel's vision of the clash of the new and old worlds. This clash was experienced by many of Lewis's peers, and it was this defining historical moment that prompted them to search for the basis of a renewed national identity in the literature of the past.

3. Lewis observes that Whitman "begins after that recovery, as a child, seeming self-propagated, and he is always going *forth*" (50; emphasis in original). As he explains in the full passage, Whitman has made the complete transformation to the childlike state that Thoreau idealizes and desires. It is this "recovery" of childhood that Lewis suggests is the key difference between Whitman and his literary predecessor.

4. Smith described this intense period of his life as "a sort of super-graduate seminar" (qtd. in Bridgman).

5. This definition sounds strikingly similar to the one provided by Gillian Avery in her study of American children's literature. In her chapter on boys' books, Avery writes, "Even Peck's Bad Boy, crude and spiteful as he seems to the modern reader, will fight to protect a smaller boy or a schoolgirl. There is no malice in the idealized Bad Boy; it is just that he is born to trouble, and he is resigned to the fact that the cards are stacked against him" (199).

6. Miller's friendship with James B. Conant, a former colleague at Harvard who became the ambassador to Germany in 1953, is one example of the types of connections that gave him personal insight into U.S. foreign policy (Guyatt 148–149).

7. See Vivian Wagner's "Unsettling Oz: Technological Anxieties in the Novels of L. Frank Baum" (2006) for more on this relationship between childhood and technology.

8. Marx makes a similar connection between the child's loss of innocence and the machine in his reading of the Try-Works passage in Melville's *Moby-Dick* (1851). This section of the novel is where the youthful protagonist, Ishmael, observes his shipmates burning whale blubber for its precious oil. As he describes this process in minute detail, he will compare the fires of the try-works to the mad quest of Ahab. This scene is much darker than the earlier chapter "A Squeeze of the Hand," in which Ishmael finds pleasure in using his bare hands to help remove the whale oil and the confusion that often occurs as he slips between grabbing the whale flesh and those of his fellow companions. Marx concludes that for Ishmael, "the distance between these two episodes is the unbridgeable gulf between a childlike self, intoxicated by thoughts of innocent love, and the outer world of ruthless, adult aggressiveness" (305). He will later claim that Ishmael outgrows his "childish pleasure" and enters a sorrowful world of adulthood (309). In these passages, as in his reading of *Huckleberry Finn*, Marx pits childhood against adulthood, innocence against experience, and settles his readings on the difficulty of transcending from one state to another. He is, to put it briefly, brought again to the stage of adolescence.

Chapter 2. American Adam (and Eve)

The epigraph is from *The American Adam*, by R. W. B. Lewis. Copyright © 1955 by the University of Chicago Press. Used by permission of the publisher.

1. Schwebel is the editor of the first critical edition of *Island of the Blue Dolphins* (2016), and she has also helped develop a digital humanities project, the Lone Woman Digital Archives, that brings together hundreds of original documents about the real Nicoleño woman that inspired O'Dell's novel.

2. For more information on the critical reception of O'Dell's *Island of the Blue Dolphins*, see Melissa Kay Thompson's "A Sea of Good Intentions: Native Americans in Books for Children" (2001) and Debbie Reese's "A Critical Look at O'Dell's *Island of the Blue Dolphins*" (2016).

3. See, for example, Susan Naramore Maher's "Encountering Others: The Meeting of Cultures in Scott O'Dell's *Island of the Blue Dolphins* and *Sing Down the Moon*" (1992).

4. Karana's experience in the village is reminiscent of Freud's definition of the uncanny. As Freud explains in "The Uncanny" (1919), the uncanny is both *heimlich* (homely, familiar, etc.) and *unheimlich* (unhomely, strange, etc.) at the same time (132–134). It is this tension between the familiar and unfamiliar that makes it impossible for Karana to continue living in the village.

5. Karana's interaction with the native animals, while sympathetic, does mirror the more violent acts of colonization enacted by the Russian-led Aleut tribe. For instance, Karana clips the wings of a few birds in order to prevent them from flying off. The cave also is a pivotal moment that marks the end of Karana's solitude. It is shortly thereafter that she befriends a female member of the Aleut tribe, Tutok, and then longs for human companionship. Her wish is soon fulfilled as a Spanish ship comes to "rescue" her. Forced to wear a "scratch[y]" dress instead of her native clothes, Karana's future remains uncertain in this final scene (172).

6. See Francine Prose's discussion of Carol Gilligan's study of adolescent girls in, *Making Connections: The Relational Worlds of Adolescent Girls at Emma Willard School* (1990), in her 1990 *New York Times* article, "Confident at 11, Confused at 16."

7. Marie's behavior was the result of severe childhood abuse. Her biological mother, according to Vernon, "burned [her] with cigarettes and hot wires . . . and pushed [her] out of a car . . . in an attempt to lose her" (41).

8. "Adoption is a very big issue for us," Hogan observes. "I had my own troubles with social services and I began to think that it was really important to write the story of what happens to children when they go home and try to search out their families, or when they are taken away from family and brought into another culture" (*Conversations with American Novelists* 198).

9. Hogan scholars Christine Jespersen, Jill Fiore, and Irene Vernon have made similar arguments about Angel's scars.

10. It is worth noting that Ishmael's survival is made possible when a ship named *Rachel* discovers him lost at sea. The ship's name alludes to a story from the Hebrew Bible, where Rachel's son Joseph became a leader of the Israelites.

11. See, for example, Laura Virginia Castor's "Claiming Place in Wor(l)ds: Linda Hogan's *Solar Storms*" (2006), Jill Fiore's "Narrative as Landscape:

A Home Beyond Boundaries in Linda Hogan's *Solar Storms*" (2010), Theresa Smith's "Landscape as Narrative: Traveling the Sacred Geography of the Anishinaabeg" (2010), and Christine Jespersen's "Unmapping Adventure: Sewing Resistance in Linda Hogan's *Solar Storms*" (2010).

12. Hogan describes harsh and torrential rain as "male" while soft, steady rain is "female" (317, 349). Her story, while focused on an unnamed northern tribe, may also be drawing on the cultural traditions of the Navajo, where rain is gendered in this way based on how hard or soft it falls.

13. As Silvia Schultermandl notes, the name Angel chooses for her sister, Aurora, also symbolizes the future since Angel associates the aurora borealis with the spiderwebs in matrilineal creation stories from Native culture (79–80); the name thus embodies the tribe's longing for a new future filled with hope and promise rather than pain and despair.

14. The novel is also filled with biblical imagery. In this particular passage, the red alligator's demise brings to mind the slaughter of the innocents in Egypt at the order of King Herod. The gator's squeal can be related to the cry of the infant in this mass episode of infanticide.

Chapter 3. From Virgin Land to Virgin Girl

The epigraph is from *Lay of the Land: Metaphor as Experience and History in American Life and Letters*, by Annette Kolodny. Copyright © 1975 by the University of North Carolina Press. Used by permission of the publisher. www.uncpress.org.

1. Kolodny notes that the land was often described as a woman by white male explorers, and more specifically as a mother: this mother-land cared for her children and provided for their needs. To disturb the balance between mother and child by attempting to collect more power constituted nothing short of incest.

2. The remarks of these literary critics are cited in a television interview with Nabokov hosted by Pierre Berton. The 1958 episode of *Close Up* also features a guest appearance by Lionel Trilling.

3. For more about the historical allusions in *Lolita*, see Susan Mizruchi's "*Lolita* in History" (2003).

4. While I doubt Fiedler would have anticipated this use of his argument, Gillian Avery, in the first comprehensive history of U.S. children's literature, adopts Fiedler's definition of the good bad boy as a way of explaining the bad boy movement in literature, which began with the publication of Thomas Bailey Aldrich's *The Story of a Bad Boy* (1869). Cases such as Avery's serve as interesting moments of crossover, where American studies scholarship actually helps legitimate the field of children's literature. It is only now that American studies scholars are starting to really band together and consider what children's literature might be able to do for them.

5. Her actions, while clearly intended to suggest Lolita is like a prostitute, also pervert the middle-class invention of the allowance.

6. I say Nabokov here rather than Humbert because Humbert never makes this connection, which is evident because he does associate another character,

Jean Farlow, with American Indians. Upon first meeting Jean, Humbert comments, "she was handsome in a carved-Indian sort of way, with a burnt sienna complexion" (104).

7. Clare Bradford critiques Nodelman's application of postcolonial theory to children's literature (*Unsettling Narratives* 7). Most importantly, she argues that Nodelman ignores how race affects children's experience of the world around them. Nodelman, as so many scholars before him, therefore begins from the assumption that all children enjoy the privileges of white, middle-class living. The fact that many children have in fact lived under colonial rule distinguishes their experience from those who have never experienced such conditions. In the case of Lolita, her condition as sexual chattel places her in a power relationship that parallels that of colonizer and colonized more strongly than the child in Nodelman's essay. The racialization of her body also hints at her otherness and challenges the white privilege that a girl of her age and status would normally enjoy.

8. In the seventh stanza of Wordsworth's poem, the narrator describes the child-at-play: "Behold the Child among his new-born blisses, / A six years' Darling of a pygmy size! / See, where 'mid work of his own hands he lies, / Fretted by sallies of his mother's kisses, / With light upon him from his father's eyes!" (lines 86–90).

9. Eugenides has also confirmed this influence. In an interview with *3am Magazine*, the author states that his "biggest literary influences are the great Russians: Nabokov, Tolstoy, and the great Jewish Americans: Bellow and Roth." He makes a similar claim in interviews with the *Paris Review* and *Bomb* magazine.

10. I am thinking, for example, about the numerous reports about LA gangs and even policies implemented to deport deviant boys of Latino origin. See, for example, Gustavo Adolfo Guerra Vásquez's "Homies Unidos: International Barrio Warriors Waging Peace on Two Fronts" in the edited collection *Youthscapes* (2005) for more on youth gangs and their depiction in the U.S. media.

11. Sissen becomes an early example of the emasculating effect of the feminine space of the Lisbon home. A boy whose name is similar to the derogative word "sissy," Sissen's entry is less threatening than Baldino's because he does not pose a threat to the girls. Baldino, who is a bully and the son of a local mobster, uses the sewer system to spy on those around him, and through these activities he is metaphorically associated with the underground activities of his father. The fact that the Lisbon girls' father, the only male in the household, chooses to invite Sissen instead of a "bad boy" like Baldino is symbolic since Mr. Lisbon is regularly characterized as a weak male figure.

12. I am thinking, in particular, of Cecilia's tendency to wear black underwear under a white wedding dress. From the beginning of the novel, this outfit is described as one that she "always wore" and has a haunting effect given the young girl's age and decision to commit suicide (4). Considering the racial division of the suburb and the larger political issues of the 1990s, Cecilia's wardrobe is no doubt symbolic. The black underwear, only revealed as the young girl rides her bicycle, is akin to the dark underside of white suburbia, a place that African Americans are discouraged from entering.

13. See, for example, the Canadian Broadcasting Corporation's (CBC) December 1992 video report on Nayirah's testimony, entitled "To Sell a War—Gulf War Propaganda."

14. Erdrich's poem first appeared in her collection of poems entitled *Jacklight* (1984).

15. See Baenen, "A Dark Event Inspires Erdrich's New Novel," 23 May 2008.

16. See, for example, Sunaina Maira's *Missing: Youth, Citizenship, and Empire after 9/11* (2009). In addition, the horrific misidentification of Kimberly Lowe, a Creek Indian, as a Muslim American demonstrated the extent to which anyone with darker skin color was subject to racism and hate crimes in the aftermath of the September 11 terrorist attacks. See Natsu Saito's "The Cost of Homeland Security" in *Radical History Review* for more on Lowe's murder.

17. I use the word "testimony" here on purpose, since Evelina is very much witnessing the aftereffects of a town tragedy.

18. Since plagues are traditionally associated with insects and other "creepy-crawlies," according to John Gamber, it is likely that Erdrich intended this image to refer to white settlement of Native lands (143). Certainly, Gamber insists, we can see how "an excessively large, migrating, white mass of life clamping down on the American landscape, overusing the land and starving out the indigenous population bears some slight similarities to Native history over the past few 100 years" (144).

Chapter 4. Extraordinary Boys on an Errand

The first epigraph is from *Errand into the Wilderness*, by Perry Miller (Cambridge, Mass.: The Belknap Press of Harvard University Press), Copyright © 1956 by the President and Fellows of Harvard College. Copyright © renewed 1984 by the President and Fellows of Harvard College. The second epigraph is from *Progressive Historians*, by Richard Hofstadter, copyright © 1968 by Richard Hofstadter. Used by permission of Alfred A. Knopf, an imprint of the Knopf Doubleday Publishing Group, a division of Penguin Random House LLC. All rights reserved.

1. In a commemorative piece in the *Horn Book*, Judith Hartzell writes, "Believing that war books sell best during wartime, Mick tried to send the manuscript from China to his editors at Harper in 1945. It was intercepted at the border by an Air Force censor who returned it, saying 'it would give aid and comfort to the enemy.' This amused Mick greatly: the book came entirely from his imagination" (232).

2. In "Family Romances," Freud describes how the young child, in an asexual phantasy, wishes to have his parents replaced by people of nobler birth (239). The child's desire for this parental exchange stems not from hatred of his parents but love. Freud writes that it is the father, in particular, whom the child venerates through this phantasy, as the child identifies positive attributes he/she formerly identified in the father in the "grander people" that replace him (240).

3. It is important to note that while young Americans might find these mo-

ments in the text to be funny, the colonial implications of the relationship between Tien Pao and the airmen make them less so. Indeed, when teaching this novel in Shanghai, I found that many of my Chinese students were troubled by this scene and a similar one where the airmen try to take a picture of the sleeping Tien Pao with his pet pig.

4. Banks's earlier novel, *The Book of Jamaica* (1980), also involved the movement of the white protagonist (in this case an adult) between U.S. and Jamaican cultures.

5. As Jim O'Loughlin argues, Bone's journey is patterned after Mark Twain's *Adventures of Huckleberry Finn* (1885) (36). An equally important influence, however, is Walt Whitman's "Song of Myself" (1881–82). References to Whitman's masterpiece appear in I-Man's very name and in Bone's determination to discover "I-self."

6. After getting a tattoo of two crossed bones on his forearm, Chappie adopts the nickname "Bone," which is both a reminder of his childhood days—he recalls the skull and crossbones of Captain Hook in *Peter Pan*—as well as his desire to be tough as bone in order to overcome the personal challenges he faces on the streets after running away from his abusive stepfather (80–81).

7. I am using the term "kinship" here in the sense that Judith Butler employs it in *Antigone's Claim: Kinship Between Life and Death* (2000), where she argues that kinship relations are not bound solely by blood. Drawing on recent work in anthropology, Butler asserts that this "radical kinship" is one where consent—the choosing of family—is privileged over relations we are born into and provides family alternatives for those who either do not have blood ties or who have various reasons for wanting to disassociate from these relations (74).

8. One of the scenes that most explicitly references the Cold War intervention in the Caribbean occurs when I-Man explains how the locals reuse old tarps left from the U.S. military invasion of Grenada in order to cover up their illegal ganja crops. According to I-Man, the tarps are "de bes' t'ing 'bout dat invasion so as t' mek de ganja reach him fulfillment undisturbed 'neath de Jamaican sun an' den return to Babylon an' help create de peaceable kingdom dere" (330). In this passage, I-Man recognizes the benefits of the U.S. soldiers' presence, yet his words emphasize the fact that the United States was invading rather than helping the islanders. It is only by mere chance that the rubbish left behind comes to good use.

9. Armbruster-Sandoval is not suggesting that Alexie's intent was to critique former president George W. Bush. Rather, he is suggesting that the theme of fatherhood and forgiveness in *Smoke Signals* connects to larger issues surrounding the United States' past actions toward American Indians. Armbruster-Sandoval frames his discussions with questions raised by his former undergraduate students: "When Thomas asks, 'how do we forgive our fathers,' is he talking about our biological fathers or he is talking about our founding fathers?" (125). It is by way of these questions that Armbruster-Sandoval makes a case for reading *Smoke Signals* in relation to former "fathers'" (i.e., presidents') actions.

10. I refer to *Smoke Signals*, the film version of Alexie's short-story collection *The Lone Ranger and Tonto Fistfight in Heaven* (1993), since it is the sub-

ject of Armbruster-Sandoval's essay. However, it's worth bearing in mind that although there are differences between these two texts, the events discussed in relation to the film also occur in the stories featuring Arnold, Victor, and Thomas.

11. An example is when Joseph Ellis, in *Founding Brothers* (2000), devotes a long chapter to a dinner party hosted by Thomas Jefferson. By structuring his book around ordinary events like eating dinner, Ellis makes this celebrated national leader seem infinitely more human. The act of eating, drinking, and entertaining—activities familiar to us all—make Jefferson's life seem a little less glamorous and a little more ordinary.

12. Readers might also associate the cover image to the Virginia Polytechnic Institute and State University (more commonly known as "Virginia Tech") massacre, which took place a mere eighteen days after *Flight*'s publication and resulted in the deaths of thirty-two students after the shooter, Seung-Hui Cho, a young man studying English at the university, opened fire on campus classrooms on the morning of April 16, 2007. This and other heavily publicized school shootings like Columbine contribute to the potency of the image of the young male as a figure of domestic terror and violence, but in the case of the Virginia Tech shootings the male is significantly cast as "outsider" (Cho, despite growing up in the United States, is referred to as a South Korean immigrant in news reports of the mass shooting).

13. Other instances of burning homes are in Marilynne Robinson's *Housekeeping* (1980) and William Faulkner's "Barn Burning" (1939). Ralph Armbruster-Sandoval also connects the burning of the house to the burning rage inside Native people. He remarks that the "firewater" Arnold drinks is a way of dealing with "centuries of conquest, colonization, genocide" but that it never completely removes the pain which derives from this traumatic past (132).

Chapter 5. Disrupting the Garden

The epigraph is from *Love and Death in the American Novel*, by Leslie Fieldler, originally published in 1960 and reprinted by Dalkey Archive Press in 1998.

1. In "Work, Play, and Power: Masculine Culture on the Automotive Shop Floor, 1930–1960," Stephen Meyer identifies two major types of American masculinity: "rough" and "respectable." As one might imagine, "rough" manhood is associated with outdoor activities as well as fighting, gambling, and swearing, whereas "respectable" masculinity often positions the man indoors in professions considered to be white-collar work, an environment that supposedly restricts men's ability to maintain their natural male instincts (15–16).

2. Malvina Reynolds wrote and composed "Little Boxes" in 1962, but it was the cover version by Seeger that helped the song gain national attention. Reynolds would later produce her own recording of the song in 1967, which was part of her record *Malvina Reynolds Sings the Truth*.

3. See, for example, Angelika Köhler's 2002 essay, "'Our human nature, our human spirit, wants no boundaries': Leslie Marmon Silko's *Gardens in the Dunes* and the Concept of Global Fiction."

Epilogue. The Price of Maturity for
the Future of American Studies

The first epigraph is from John F. Kennedy's inaugural address ("The New Frontier") on July 15, 1960, available from the John F. Kennedy Presidential Library and Museum. The second epigraph is from "'Paradigm Dramas' in American Studies: A Cultural and Institutional History of the Movement," by Gene Wise, *American Quarterly* 31.3 (1976): 293–294. © The American Studies Association. Reprinted with permission of Johns Hopkins University Press.

1. In the edition I cite, Radway's first name is shortened to "Jan," but since her full name is used in other sources and may be more recognizable to those in the field of American studies, I use "Janice" in my references here.

2. The question Radway is referring to here is: "In order to promote work that would further reconceptualize the American as always relationally defined and therefore as intricately dependent upon 'others' that are used both materially and conceptually to mark its boundaries, would it make sense to think about renaming the association as an institution devoted to a different form of knowledge production, to alternative epistemologies, to the investigation of a different object?" (59).

3. Lipsitz also addresses childhood in his argument about the impact of globalization on the field in "'Sent for You Yesterday, Here You Come Today': American Studies Scholarship and the New Social Movements" (1998) but frames his discussion more in relation to the child's vulnerability in the face of global forces. Citing data from the United Nations, Lipsitz comments on the inequality of power and the uneven distribution of wealth around the world. "In Africa, Asia, and Latin America close to 500,000 children die every year from malnutrition or from completely preventable diseases," he announces in a line that could have just as easily appeared in an advertisement for a national charity (204). "The 'Pocahontas' pajamas worn by some of our most affluent children," he later adds, "are made under sweatshop conditions by low-wage women workers in Haiti," to reiterate his main points about the global flows of capital (205). Lipsitz, even if only in passing, identifies here how the child is both a producer and a consumer and the ways in which these children are participants in a global marketplace.

4. This collection bears the same name as the 1998 special issue of *Cultural Critique*, which Wiegman edited, and features Lipsitz's essay "'Sent for You Yesterday, Here You Come Today,'" which appears in a revised form in his later book *American Studies in a Moment of Danger* (2001).

5. The essays referred to above include Marah Gubar's "Entertaining Children of All Ages: Nineteenth-Century Popular Theater as Children's Theater" (2014), Sara Schwebel's "A Children's Book, Nineteenth-Century News, and Multimedia Approaches to American Studies" (2018), Jennifer Helgren's "Native American and White Camp Fire Girls Enact Modern Girlhood, 1910–39" (2014), Susie Woo's "Imagining Kin: Cold War Sentimentalism and the Korean Children's Choir" (2015), Laura Briggs's "Central American Child Migration: Militarization and Tourism" (2016), and Kiara Vigil's "Charles Eastman's 'School of the Woods': Re-creation related to Childhood, Race, Gender, and Nation at Camp Oahe" (2018).

WORKS CITED

Abate, Michelle Ann. *Tomboys: A Literary and Cultural History*. Philadelphia: Temple University Press, 2008. Print.

Adams, Mikaëla. "Savage Foes, Noble Warriors, and Frail Remnants: Florida Seminoles in the White Imagination, 1865–1934." *Florida Historical Quarterly* 87.3 (2009): 404–435. JSTOR. Web. 4 Apr. 2017.

Alexie, Sherman. *Flight: A Novel*. New York: Black Cat–Grove/Atlantic, 2007. Print.

Alger, Horatio. *Tattered Tom, or, The Story of a Street Arab*. Boston: Loring, 1871. Print.

Anderson, M. T. *Feed*. Cambridge, Mass.: Candlewick Press, 2002. Print.

Anzilotti, Eillie. "How Kids Organized the Massive School Walkout Demanding Action on Climate Change." *Fast Company*, 15 Mar. 2019. Web. 18 July 2019. <www.fastcompany.com/90318935/how-kids-organized-the-massive-school-walkout-demanding-action-on-climate-change>.

Appadurai, Arjun. "Patriotism and Its Futures." *Public Culture* 5 (1993): 411–429. Print.

Armbruster-Sandoval, Ralph. "Teaching *Smoke Signals*: Fatherhood, Forgiveness, and 'Freedom.'" *Wicazo Sa Review* 23.1 (2008): 123–146. Project Muse. Web. 8 Feb. 2013.

Arnett, Jeffrey Jensen. "G. Stanley Hall's *Adolescence*: Brilliance and Nonsense." *History of Psychology* 9.3 (2006): 186–197. Print.

Arnold, Ellen. "Listening to the Spirits: An Interview with Leslie Marmon Silko." *Studies in American Indian Literatures* 10.3 (1998): 1–33. JSTOR. Web. 4 Jan. 2017.

Aronstein, Susan. *Hollywood Knights: Arthurian Cinema and the Politics of Nostalgia*. New York: Palgrave Macmillan, 2005. Print.

Avery, Gillian. *Behold the Child: American Children and Their Books, 1621–1922*. Baltimore: Johns Hopkins University Press, 1994. Print.

Baecker, Diann. "Surviving Rescue: A Feminist Reading of Scott O'Dell's *Island of the Blue Dolphins*." *Children's Literature in Education* 38.3 (2007): 195–206. Springer. Web. 5 Mar. 2017.

Baenen, Jeff. "A Dark Event Inspires Erdrich's New Novel." *Bismarck Tribune*, 23 May 2008. Web. 11 Nov. 2019. <https://bismarcktribune.com/news/state

-and-regional/a-dark-event-inspires-erdrich-s-new-novel/article_32f7f1da
-c3f2-518b-ba54-e3915168a33b.html>.

Banks, Russell. *Rule of the Bone*. New York: HarperCollins, 1995. Print.

———. "Russell Banks: The Art of Fiction CLII." *Paris Review* 40.147 (1998):
50–88. Literature Online. Web. 15 Feb. 2013.

Baym, Nina. "Melodramas of Beset Manhood: How Theories of American Fiction Exclude Women Authors." *American Quarterly* 33.2 (1981): 123–139.
Web. 14 May 2019.

Benn Michaels, Walter. "The Vanishing American." *American Literary History*
2.2 (1990): 220–241. JSTOR. Web. 15 Feb. 2017.

Bernstein, Robin. *Racial Innocence: Performing American Childhood from Slavery to Civil Rights*. New York: New York University Press, 2011. Print.

Bhabha, Homi, ed. "Introduction: Narrating the Nation." In *Nation and Narration*. New York: Routledge, 1990. 1–7. Print.

"Bizarre Love's Baby Soft 1975 TV Commercial." YouTube. Web. 2 Feb. 2017.
<www.youtube.com/watch?v=l7IP5SV6GqQ>.

Blair, William. "Water Lacking amid Flood; Human Dikes Help Stem Tide."
New York Times, 16 July 1951. ProQuest Historical Newspapers. 2 Feb.
2017. Web. 1, 8.

Blake, William. *Songs of Innocence and Songs of Experience*. New York:
J. Lane, 1901. n.p. Project Gutenberg. Web. 11 Mar. 2013. <www.gutenberg
.org/dirs/etext99/sinex10h.htm>.

Blixen, Karen. *Out of Africa*. 1937. New York: Penguin, 2011. Print.

Bloom, Harold. *J. D. Salinger's The Catcher in the Rye*. New York: Infobase,
2007. Print.

Boland, Kerry. "'We're All the Same People'?: The (A)Politics of the Body in
Sherman Alexie's *Flight*." *Studies in American Indian Literatures* 27.1
(2015): 70–95. Project Muse. Web. 5 Feb. 2017.

Borstelmann, Thomas. *The Cold War and the Color Line: American Race Relations in the Global Arena*. Cambridge, Mass.: Harvard University Press,
2001. Print.

Bosman, Julie. "Obama Sharply Assails Absent Black Fathers." *New York
Times*, 16 June 2008. Web. 18 Feb. 2014. <www.nytimes.com/2008/06/16/us
/politics/15cnd-obama.html>.

Boyd, Brian. *Vladimir Nabokov: The American Years*. Princeton: Princeton University Press, 1991. Print.

Boym, Svetlana. *The Future of Nostalgia*. New York: Basic Books, 2001. Print.

Bozeman, Theodore Dwight. "The Puritans' 'Errand into the Wilderness' Re-
considered." *New England Quarterly* 59.2 (1986): 231–251. JSTOR. Web. 18
Mar. 2012.

Bradford, Clare. "'Everything Must Go!': Consumerism and Reader Positioning
in M. T. Anderson's *Feed*." *Jeunesse: Young People, Texts, Cultures* 2.2. (2010):
128–137. Project Muse. Web. 22 Feb. 2017.

———. *Unsettling Narratives: Postcolonial Readings of Children's Literature*.
Waterloo, Ont.: Wilfrid Laurier University Press, 2007. Print.

Bradford, Clare, Kerry Mallan, John Stephens, and Robyn McCallum. *New
World Orders in Contemporary Children's Literature: Utopian Transformations*. Basingstoke: Palgrave Macmillan, 2008. Print.

Bridgman, Richard. "In Memoriam: The American Studies of Henry Nash Smith." *American Scholar* 56 (1987): 263. Web. 2 Feb. 2013.

Briggs, Laura. "Central American Child Migration: Militarization and Tourism." *American Quarterly* 68.3 (2016): 573–582. Project Muse. Web. 5 Feb. 2017.

———. *Somebody's Children: The Politics of Transracial and Transnational Adoption*. Durham, N.C.: Duke University Press, 2012. Print.

Buell, Lawrence. "American Pastoral Ideology Reappraised." *American Literary History* 1.1 (1989): 1–29. JSTOR. Web. 4 Mar. 2017.

Burnett, Frances Hodgson. *Giovanni and the Other: Children Who Have Made Stories*. New York: Charles Scribner's Sons, 1892. Print.

Bush, George W. "America's New War: President Bush Talks with Reporters at Pentagon." CNN, 17 Sept. 2001. Web. 3 Feb. 2013. <http://transcripts.cnn.com/TRANSCRIPTS/0109/17/se.09.html>.

Butler, Judith. *Antigone's Claim: Kinship between Life and Death*. New York: Columbia University Press, 2000. Print.

Canadian Broadcasting Corporation. "To Sell a War—Gulf War Propaganda." Directed by Neil Docherty. Dec. 1992. YouTube. Web. 2 Feb. 2017. <www.youtube.com/watch?v=yaR1YBR5g6U>.

Capra, Frank, dir. *The Battle of China*. 1944. Why We Fight series. Synergy Entertainment, 2007. DVD.

Castor, Laura Virginia. "Claiming Place in Wor(l)ds: Linda Hogan's *Solar Storms*." *MELUS* 31.2 (2006): 157–180. JSTOR. Web. 16 Apr. 2014.

Cattelino, Jessica R. "Casino Roots: The Cultural Production of Twentieth-Century Seminole Economic Development." In *Native Pathways: American Indian Culture and Economic Development in the Twentieth Century*. Ed. Brian Hosmer and Colleen O'Neill. Boulder: University Press of Colorado, 2004. 66–90. Print.

Chinn, Sarah. *Inventing Modern Adolescence: The Children of Immigrants in Turn-of-the-Century America*. New Brunswick, N.J.: Rutgers University Press, 2009.

Choy, Catherine Ceniza, and Gregory Paul Choy. "Transformative Terrains: Korean Adoptees and the Social Constructions of an American Childhood." In *The American Child: A Cultural Studies Reader*. Ed. Caroline Levander and Carol Singley. New Brunswick, N.J.: Rutgers University Press, 2003. 262–279. Print.

Clark, Beverly Lyon. *Kiddie Lit: The Cultural Construction of Children's Literature in America*. Baltimore: Johns Hopkins University Press, 2003.

Coats, Karen. "Keepin' It Plural: Children's Studies in the Academy." *Children's Literature Association Quarterly* 26.3 (2001): 140–150. Project Muse. Web. 10 Mar. 2012.

Colapinto, John. "Nabokov's America." *New Yorker*, 30 June 2015. Web. 8 June 2016. <www.newyorker.com/books/page-turner/nabokovs-america>.

Collado-Rodríguez, Francisco. "Back to Myth and Ethical Compromise: García Márquez's Traces on Jeffrey Eugenides's *The Virgin Suicides*." *Atlantis* 27.2 (2005): 27–40. Academic OneFile. Web. 20 Sept. 2012.

Communist Culture in China: Red Chinese Battle Plan. Quality Information Publishers, 1967. DVD.

Connor, Michael, and Joseph White. "Fatherhood in Contemporary Black America: An Invisible Presence." *Black Scholar* 37.2 (2007): 2–8. JSTOR. Web. 10
Apr. 2017.

A Conversation with Meindert DeJong. Calvin Media Foundation, 2008. DVD.

Cooper, Lydia. "Beyond 9/11: Trauma and the Limits of Empathy in Sherman
Alexie's *Flight*." *Studies in American Fiction* 42.1 (2015): 123–144. Project
Muse. Web. 22 Feb. 2017.

Coughlan, Robert. "How We Appear to Others: U.S. 'Envoys-Ordinary,' Widely
Criticized, Still Succeed in Winning Foreign Hearts." *Life*, 23 Dec. 1957.
Web. 5 Apr. 2019. 150–156.

Davis, Kenneth S. "The Hired Man—A Vanishing American: The Machine Age
in Farming Is Transforming a Rugged Individualist into a 'Factory Hand.'"
New York Times, 23 July 1950. 16; 34–35. ProQuest Historical Newspapers.
Web. 26 Nov. 2016.

de Crèvecoeur, J. Hector St. John. *Letters from an American Farmer*. 1782. Intro. and notes by Susan Manning. Oxford: Oxford University Press, 1997.
Print.

DeJong, Meindert. *The House of Sixty Fathers*. Illus. Maurice Sendak. New
York: HarperCollins, 1956. Print.

de la Durantaye, Leland. "Lolita in *Lolita*, or the Garden, the Gate and the Critics." *Nabokov Studies* 10 (2006): 175–197. Project Muse. Web. 4 Sept. 2012.

Delbanco, Andrew. "The Puritan Errand Re-Viewed." *Journal of American Studies* 18.3 (1984): 343–360. JSTOR. Web. 18 Mar. 2012.

DeLuzio, Crista. *Female Adolescence in American Scientific Thought, 1830–
1930*. Baltimore: Johns Hopkins University Press, 2007. Print.

Denning, Michael. *The Cultural Front: The Laboring of American Culture in the
Twentieth Century*. New York: Verso, 1996. Print.

———. "'The Special American Conditions': Marxism and American Studies."
American Quarterly 38.3 (1986): 356–380. Web. JSTOR. 2 Sept. 2018.

"Domestic Abuse on Rise as Economy Sinks." NBC News, 10 Apr. 2009. Web. 20
Mar. 2017. <www.nbcnews.com/id/30156918/ns/health-health_care/t
/domestic-abuse-rise-economy-sinks>.

Duane, Anna Mae. *Suffering Childhood in Early America: Violence, Race, and
the Making of the Child Victim*. Athens: University of Georgia Press, 2010.
Print.

———, ed. Introduction to *The Children's Table: Childhood Studies and the Humanities*. Athens: University of Georgia Press, 2013. 1–14. Print.

Edelman, Lee. *No Future: Queer Theory and the Death Drive*. Durham, N.C.:
Duke University Press, 2004. Print.

Edwards, Brian T., and Dilip Parameshwar Gaonkar, eds. "Introduction: Globalizing American Studies." *Globalizing American Studies*. Chicago: University
of Chicago Press, 2010. 1–44. Print.

Ellis, Joseph. *Founding Brothers: The Revolutionary Generation*. 2000. New
York: Vintage Books–Random House, 2002. Print.

Ellison, Ralph. *Invisible Man*. 1952. New York: Penguin Books, 1965.

Engelhardt, Tom. *The End of Victory Culture: Cold War America and the Disil-
lusioning of a Generation*. 1995. New York: BasicBooks, 2007. Print.

Erdrich, Louise. "Erdrich Bases New Novel on Lynching." Interview by Jeff Baenen. *Los Angeles Times*, 28 June 2008: n.p. Web. 15 Jan. 2014. <http://articles.latimes.com/2008/jun/28/entertainment/et-erdrich28>.

———. *The Plague of Doves: A Novel*. New York: Harper Perennial, 2008. Print.

———. "The Strange People." *Poetry*, n.d. Web. 8 Feb. 2014. <www.poetry foundation.org/poems-and-poets/poems/detail/43082>.

Erikson, Erik. *Childhood and Society*. 1950. New York: W.W. Norton, 1963. Print.

Erkkila, Catherine Boland. "American Railways and the Cultural Landscape of Immigration." *Buildings and Landscapes: Journal of the Vernacular Architecture Forum* 22.1 (2015): 36–62. *Project Muse*. Web. 5 May 2017.

Eugenides, Jeffrey. Interview. *3am Magazine*, 2003. Web. 8 Sept. 2012. <www.3ammagazine.com/litarchives/2003/sep/interview_jeffrey_eugenides.html>.

———. "Jeffrey Eugenides." Interview by Jonathan Safran Foer. *BOMB* 81 (Fall 2002): n.p. Web. 12 Sept. 2012. <http://bombmagazine.org/article/2519/jeffrey-eugenides>.

———. "Jeffrey Eugenides, The Art of Fiction No. 215." *Paris Review* 199 (Winter 2011): n.p. Web. 12 Sept. 2012. <www.theparisreview.org/interviews/6117/the-art-of-fiction-no-215-jeffrey-eugenides>.

———. *The Virgin Suicides*. New York: Warner Books, 1993. Print.

Fiedler, Leslie. *An End to Innocence: Essays on Culture and Politics*. Boston: Beacon Press, 1955. Print.

———. *Love and Death in the American Novel*. 1960. Intro. Charles Harris. Champaign, Ill.: Dalkey Archive Press, 1997. Print.

Fiore, Jill. "Narrative as Landscape: A Home Beyond Boundaries in Linda Hogan's *Solar Storms*." *Studies in American Indian Literatures* 22.4 (2010): 71–79. Project Muse. Web. 19 May 2014.

Fischer, Nina. *Memory Work: The Second Generation*. Basingstoke: Palgrave Macmillan, 2015. Print.

Fisher, Philip, ed. Introduction to *The New American Studies: Essays from Representations*. Berkeley: University of California Press, 1991. vii–xxii. Print.

Flanagan, Victoria. *Technology and Identity in Young Adult Fiction: The Posthuman Subject*. New York: Palgrave Macmillan, 2014. Print.

Flynn, Richard. "The Intersection of Children's Literature and Childhood Studies." *Children's Literature Association Quarterly* 22.3 (1997): 143–145. Project Muse. Web. 18 Apr. 2018.

Forman-Brunell, Miriam, and Leslie Paris, eds. Introduction to *The Girls' History and Culture Reader: The Twentieth Century*. Chicago: University of Illinois Press, 2011. 1–14. Print.

Freud, Sigmund. "Family Romances." 1909. In *The Standard Edition of the Complete Psychological Works of Sigmund Freud, Volume IX (1906–1908): Jensen's "Gradiva" and Other Works*. Trans. James Strachey. London: Vintage, 2001. 235–242. Print.

———. *The Uncanny*. Trans. David McLintock. New York: Penguin Books, 2003. Print.

Fuller, Randall. "Errand into the Wilderness: Perry Miller as American

Scholar." *American Literary History* 18.1 (2006): 102–128. Project Muse. Web. 18 Mar. 2012.

Gaines, Donna. *Teenage Wasteland: Suburbia's Dead End Kids*. 1990. Chicago: University of Chicago Press, 1998.

Galbraith, Mary. "Hear My Cry: A Manifesto for an Emancipatory Childhood Studies Approach to Children's Literature." *The Lion and the Unicorn* 25.2 (2001): 187–205. Project Muse. Web. 20 Apr. 2018.

Gamber, John. "So, a Priest Walks into a Reservation Tragicomedy: Humor in *The Plague of Doves*." In *Louise Erdrich: Tracks, The Last Report on the Miracles at Little No Horse, The Plague of Doves*. Ed. Deborah Madsen. New York: Continuum, 2011. 136–151. Print.

Gamerman, Ellen. "Inconvenient Youths." *Wall Street Journal*, 29 Sept. 2007. Web. 15 July 2019. <www.wsj.com/articles/SB119101716857043113>.

Gavanas, Anna. "Domesticating Masculinity and Masculinizing Domesticity in Contemporary U.S. Fatherhood Politics." *Social Politics: International Studies in Gender, State, and Society* 11.2 (2004): 247–266. Project Muse. Web. 12 Nov. 2011.

Gebreyes, Rahel. "Meet the Young People Who Are Standing Up Against the Dakota Access Pipeline." *HuffPost*. 11 Apr. 2016. Web. 10 Apr. 2019. <www .huffingtonpost.co.uk/entry/dakota-access-pipeline-protesters_us_ 581ca039e4b0aac62483a72c>.

"Gifts for Korea Set: Camp Fire Girls Being Asked to Prepare 'Friendship Boxes.'" *New York Times*. 15 Apr. 1954. ProQuest Historical Newspapers. Web. 2 Feb. 2017. 12.

Giles, Paul. *Virtual Americas: Transnational Fictions and the Transatlantic Imaginary*. Durham, N.C.: Duke University Press, 2002. Print.

Goodman, Paul. *Growing up Absurd: Problems of Youth in the Organized Society*. 1960. New York: New York Review Books, 1972. Print.

Graham, Sarah. "Unfair Ground: Girlhood and Theme Parks in Contemporary Fiction." *Journal of American Studies* 47.3 (2013): 589–604. Print.

Griswold, Jerry. *Fatherhood in America: A History*. New York: BasicBooks– HarperCollins, 1993. Print.

Gubar, Marah. "Entertaining Children of All Ages: Nineteenth-Century Popular Theater as Children's Theater." *American Quarterly* 66.1 (2014): 1–34. Project Muse. Web. 15 Apr. 2018.

———. "Risky Business: Talking about Children in Children's Literature Criticism." *Children's Literature Association Quarterly* 38.4 (2013): 450–457. Literature Online. Web. 10 Feb. 2019.

Guerra Vásquez, Gustavo Adolfo. "Homies Unidos: International Barrio Warriors Waging Peace on Two Fronts." In *Youthscapes: The Popular, the National, the Global*. Ed. Sunaina Maira and Elisabeth Soep. Philadelphia: University of Pennsylvania Press, 2005. 103–118. Print.

Guyatt, Nicholas. "'An Instrument of National Policy': Perry Miller and the Cold War." *Journal of American Studies* 36.1 (2002): 107–149. JSTOR. Web. 18 Mar. 2012.

Hall, G. Stanley. *Adolescence: Its Psychology and Its Relations to Physiology, An-*

thropology, Sociology, Sex, Crime, Religion and Education. Vol 2. New York: D. Appleton, 1904. Print.

———. "The Awkward Age." *Appleton's Magazine*. July 1908: 149–156. Hathi-Trust. Web. 15 Nov. 2018.

"Hans Christian Andersen Awards." International Board on Books for Young People, 22 Apr. 2013. Web. 2 Feb. 2013. <www.ibby.org/index.php?id=273>.

Hardy, Thomas. *The Return of the Native*. 1878. Seattle: Amazon Digital Services, 2012. Kindle.

Hartz, Louis. "The Coming of Age of America." *American Political Science Review* 51.2 (1957): 474–483. JSTOR. Web. 5 Apr. 2015.

———. *The Liberal Tradition in America: An Interpretation of American Political Thought Since the Revolution*. 1955. Intro. Tom Wicker. Orlando: Harcourt, 1991. Print.

Hartzell, Judith. "Happy Centennial, Meindert DeJong!" *Horn Book*. Mar.–Apr. 2006: 227–233. *Academic Search Premier*. Web. 7 Jan. 2013.

Hass, Victor P. "Scooping the Town: Danny." *New York Times*, 6 Sept. 1953. ProQuest Historical Newspapers. Web. 26 Nov. 2016. BR12.

Hassan, Ihab. "The Idea of Adolescence in American Fiction." *American Quarterly* 10.3 (1958): 312–324. JSTOR. Web. 18 Mar. 2012.

Helgren, Jennifer. "Native American and White Camp Fire Girls Enact Modern Girlhood, 1910–39." *American Quarterly* 66.2 (2014): 333–360. Project Muse. Web. 20 Apr. 2018.

Herbold, Sarah. "'(I have camouflaged everything, my love)': Lolita and the Woman Reader." *Nabokov Studies* 5 (1998/1999): 71–98. Project Muse. Web. 4 Sept. 2012.

Hines, Maude. "Playing with Children: What the 'Child' is Doing in American Studies." *American Quarterly* 61.1 (2009): 151–161. Project Muse. Web. 14 Mar. 2012.

"Hitchiti-Mikasuki Creation Story." *Indigenous Peoples' Literature*. Compiled by Glenn Welker, 24 Nov. 2013. Web. 11 Feb. 2013. <www.indigenouspeople.net/hitchiti.htm>.

Hodgson, Godfrey. *The Myth of American Exceptionalism*. New Haven: Yale University Press, 2009. Print.

Hofstadter, Richard. *The Progressive Historians*. New York: Knopf, 1968. Print.

Hogan, Linda. "Linda Hogan." In *Conversations with American Novelists: The Best Interviews from the Missouri Review and the American Audio Prose Library*. Ed. Kay Bonetti et al. Columbia: University of Missouri Press, 1997. 184–200. Print.

———. *Solar Storms*. New York: Simon & Schuster, 1995. Print.

———. *The Woman Who Watches Over the World: A Native Memoir*. New York: W.W. Norton, 2001. Print.

Holt, Marilyn Irvin. *The Orphan Trains: Placing Out in America*. Lincoln: University of Nebraska Press, 1992. Print.

Hubler, Angela. "Female Adolescence and Its Discontents." In *Growing Up Postmodern: Neoliberalism and the War on the Young*. Ed. Ronald Strickland. Lanham, Mass.: Rowman and Littlefield, 2002. 169–180. Print.

Ibarrola-Armendariz, Aitor, and Estibaliz Vivanco. "Undone and Renewed by Time: History as Burden and/or Opportunity in Sherman Alexie's 'Flight.'" *Atlantis* 35.2 (2013): 27–45. JSTOR. Web. 23 May 2017.

Immerman, Richard, and Petra Goedde, eds. Introduction to *Oxford Handbook of the Cold War*. Oxford: Oxford University Press, 2013. 1–14. Print.

"Indian Child Welfare Act of 1978." National Indian Child Welfare Association, n.d. Web. 10 Nov. 2019. <www.nicwa.org/families-service-providers>.

Iriye, Akira. "Historicizing the Cold War." In *Oxford Handbook of the Cold War*. Ed. Richard Immerman and Petra Goedde. Oxford: Oxford University Press, 2013. 15–31. Print.

Jacobs, Ronald. *Race, Media, and the Crisis of Civil Society: From Watts to Rodney King*. New York: Cambridge University Press, 2000. Print.

Jacobs, Sue-Ellen, Wesley Thomas, and Sabine Lang, eds. Introduction to *Two-Spirit People: Native American Gender Identity, Sexuality, and Spirituality*. Urbana: University of Illinois Press, 1997. 1–18. Print.

Jaggi, Maya. "All Rage and Heart." *The Guardian*. 3 May 2008. Web. 12 Apr. 2017. <www.theguardian.com/books/2008/may/03/featuresreviews .guardianreview13>.

James, Henry. *Daisy Miller*. 1879. New York: Dover, 1995. Print.

———. *The Portrait of a Lady*. 1881. Ware, Hertfordshire: Wordsworth Editions, 1999. Print.

Jenkins, Lee. "Studies in Classic American Literature and American Studies." *D. H. Lawrence Review* 37.2 (2012): 44–59. EBSCO. Web. 9 June 2016.

Jespersen, Christine. "Unmapping Adventure: Sewing Resistance in Linda Hogan's *Solar Storms*." *Western American Literature* 45.3 (2010): 274–300. Project Muse. Web. 21 Oct. 2013.

Jewell-Kemker, Slater. "*An Inconvenient Youth* Documentary Preview." Vimeo. Uploaded by Slater Jewell-Kemker, 2012. Web. 18 July 2019. <https://vimeo .com/36197312>.

Johnson, Robyn. "A World without Fathers: Patriarchy, Colonialism, and the Male Creator in Northwest Tribal Narratives." *American Indian Quarterly* 38.3 (2014): 342–373. JSTOR. Web. 20 Feb. 2017.

Johnston, Elizabeth. "'Deadly Snares': Female Rivalry, Gender Ideology, and Eighteenth-Century Women Writers." *Studies in the Literary Imagination* 47.2 (2014): 1–21. Project Muse. Web. 10 May 2017.

Kaplan, Amy. *The Anarchy of Empire in the Making of U.S. Culture*. Cambridge, Mass.: Harvard University Press, 2002. Print.

———. "A Call for a Truce." *American Literary History* 17.1 (2005): 118–134. JSTOR. Web. 20 June 2016.

———. "'Left Alone with America': The Absence of Empire in the Study of American Culture." In *Cultures of United States Imperialism*. Ed. Amy Kaplan and Donald Pease. Durham, N.C.: Duke University Press, 1993. 3–21. Print.

Kennedy, John F. "The New Frontier: Acceptance of Democratic Nomination for President." John F. Kennedy Presidential Library and Museum, 15 July 1960. Web. 10 June 2019. <www.jfklibrary.org/learn/about-jfk/historic -speeches/acceptance-of-democratic-nomination-for-president>.

Kidd, Kenneth. "Children's Culture, Children's Studies, and the Ethnographic

Imagination." *Children's Literature Association Quarterly* 27.3 (2002): 146–155. Project Muse. Web. 15 Apr. 2018.

———. *Making American Boys: Boyology and the Feral Tale*. Minneapolis: University of Minnesota Press, 2004. Print.

Kincaid, James. *Erotic Innocence: The Culture of Child Molesting*. Durham, N.C.: Duke University Press, 1998. Print.

Kirby, Lisa. "Interrogating Suburbia in *The Virgin Suicides.*" *Academic Exchange Quarterly* 11.1 (2007): 51–55. Academic OneFile. Web. 6 Sept. 2012.

Klein, Christina. "Family Ties and Political Obligation: The Discourse of Adoption and the Cold War Commitment to Asia." In *Cold War Constructions: The Political Culture of United States Imperialism, 1945–1966*. Ed. Christian Appy. Amherst: University of Massachusetts Press, 2000. 35–66. Print.

Knowles, Jane, and Robert Allen Skotheim. "'Innocence' and 'Beyond Innocence' in Recent American Scholarship." *American Quarterly* 13.1 (1961): 93–99. JSTOR. Web. 12 Mar. 2012.

Koerper, Henry. "More on Arthur Sanger's Skullduggeries." *Pacific Coast Archaeological Society Quarterly* 52.2 (2016): 17–42. Print.

Köhler, Angelika. "'Our human nature, our human spirit, wants no boundaries': Leslie Marmon Silko's *Garden in the Dunes* and the Concept of Global Fiction." *American Studies* 47.2 (2002): 237–244. JSTOR. Web. 22 Jan. 2017.

Kolodny, Annette. *The Lay of the Land*. Chapel Hill: University of North Carolina Press, 1975. Print.

Kuklick, Bruce. "Myth and Symbol in American Studies." 1972. In *Locating American Studies: The Evolution of a Discipline*. Ed. Lucy Maddox. Baltimore: Johns Hopkins University Press, 1999. 71–90. Print.

Kunce, Catherine. "Feasting on Famine in Linda Hogan's *Solar Storms.*" *Studies in American Indian Literatures* 21.2 (2009): 50–70. Project Muse. Web. 21 Oct. 2013.

Ladino, Jennifer. "'Sovereignty of the Self': Interspecies Ethics in Sherman Alexie's *Face.*" *Studies in American Indian Literatures* 25.4 (2013): 28–47. Project Muse. Web. 12 Apr. 2017.

Lai, Thanhha. *Inside Out and Back Again*. New York: HarperCollins, 2011. Print.

Latham, Don. "'Manly-Hearted Women': Gender Variants in Louise Erdrich's Birchbark House Books." *Children's Literature* 40 (2012): 131–150. Project Muse. Web. 15 Jan. 2014.

Lavezzo, Kathy, and Harilaos Stecopoulos. "Leslie Fiedler's Medieval America." *American Literary History* 22.4 (2010): 867–887. Project Muse. Web. 15 Feb. 2017.

Lawrence, D. H. *Studies in Classic American Literature*. 1923. Cambridge: Cambridge University Press, 2003. Print.

Lenzer, Gertrud. "Children's Studies: Beginnings and Purposes." *The Lion and the Unicorn* 25.2 (2001): 181–186. Project Muse. Web. 15 Apr. 2018.

Lesko, Nancy. *Act Your Age! A Cultural Construction of Adolescence*. New York: Routledge Falmer, 2001. Print.

Levander, Caroline, and Carol Singley, eds. Introduction to *The American Child: A Cultural Studies Reader*. New Brunswick, N.J.: Rutgers University Press, 2003. 3–12. Print.

Levine, Robert. "'My Ultraviolet Darling': The Loss of Lolita's Childhood." *Modern Fiction Studies* 25.3 (1979): 471–479. Periodicals Archive Online. Web. 4 Sept. 2012.

Lewis, R. W. B. *The American Adam: Innocence, Tragedy, and Tradition in the Nineteenth Century*. 1955. Chicago: University of Chicago Press, 1959. Print.

———. *Literary Reflections: A Shoring of Images, 1960–1993*. Boston: Northeastern University Press, 1993. Print.

Li, Stephanie. "Domestic Resistance: Gardening, Mothering, and Storytelling in Leslie Marmon Silko's *Gardens in the Dunes*." *Studies in American Indian Literatures* 21.1 (2009): 18–37. Project Muse. Web. 22 Mar. 2017.

Limerick, Patricia Nelson. *The Legacy of Conquest: The Unbroken Past of the American West*. New York: W.W. Norton, 1987. Print.

Lipsitz, George. *American Studies in a Moment of Danger*. Minneapolis: University of Minnesota Press, 2001. Print.

———. "Our America." American Literary History 17.1 (2005): 118–134. JSTOR. Web. 20 June 2016.

———. "'Sent for You Yesterday, Here You Come Today': American Studies Scholarship and the New Social Movements." *Cultural Critique* 40 (1998): 203–225. Project Muse. Web. 15 June 2019.

Lowry, Lois. Introduction to *Island of the Blue Dolphins*, by Scott O'Dell. New York: Houghton Mifflin Harcourt, 2010. v–xi. Print.

Luce, Henry. "The American Century." *Life*, 17 Feb. 1941: 61–65. Print.

Lutkehaus, Nancy. *Margaret Mead: The Making of an American Icon*. Princeton, N.J.: Princeton University Press, 2008. Print.

Maher, Susan Naramore. "Encountering Others: The Meeting of Cultures in Scott O'Dell's *Island of the Blue Dolphins* and *Sing Down the Moon*." *Children's Literature in Education* 23.4 (1992): 215–227. ERIC. Web. 20 Mar. 2017.

Maira, Sunaina. *Missing: Youth, Citizenship, and Empire after 9/11*. Durham, N.C.: Duke University Press, 2009. Print.

Maira, Sunaina, and Elisabeth Soep, eds. Introduction to *Youthscapes: The Popular, the National, the Global*. Philadelphia: University of Pennsylvania Press, 2005. xv–xxxv. Print.

Marcovitz, Hal. *Scott O'Dell*. New York: Infobase, 2008. Print.

Marx, Leo. *The Machine in the Garden*. 1964. New York: Oxford University Press, 2000. Print.

———. "On Recovering the 'Ur' Theory of American Studies." *American Literary History* 17.1 (2005): 118–134. JSTOR. Web. 20 June 2016.

May, Henry. *The End of American Innocence: A Study of the First Years of Our Own Time, 1912–1917*. 1959. Foreword by David Hollinger. New York: Columbia University Press, 1992. Print.

McAlexander, Patricia Jewell. "The Creation of the American Eve: The Cultural Dialogue on the Nature and Role of Women in Late Eighteenth-Century America." *Early American Literature* 9.3 (1975): 252–266. JSTOR. Web. 5 May 2019.

McQuade, Mike. "Is It Time to Play with Spaceships Again?" *New York Times*. 15 July 2019. Web. 22 July 2019. <www.nytimes.com/2019/07/15/science/apollo-moon-space.html>.

McWilliams, John. "The Rationale for 'The American Romance.'" *boundary 2* 17.1 (1990): 71–82. JSTOR. Web. 12 Mar. 2017.

Mead, Margaret. *Coming of Age in Samoa: A Psychological Study of Primitive Youth for Western Civilization*. New York: William Morrow, 1928. Print.

———. *Male and Female: The Classic Study of the Sexes*. 1949. New York: Harper Perennial, 2001. Print.

Medovoi, Leerom. *Rebels: Youth and the Cold War Origins of Identity*. Durham, N.C.: Duke University Press, 2005. Print.

Meyer, Steven. "Work, Play, and Power: Masculine Culture on the Automotive Shop Floor, 1930–1960." In *Boys and Their Toys? Masculinity, Technology, and Class in America*. Ed. Roger Horowitz. New York: Routledge, 2001. 13–32. Print.

Mickenberg, Julia. "American Studies and Childhood Studies: Lessons from Consumer Culture." *American Quarterly* 58.4 (2006): 1217–1227. Project Muse. Web. 14 Mar. 2012.

Miller, Perry. *Errand into the Wilderness*. Cambridge, Mass.: Belknap Press of Harvard University Press, 1956. Print.

Mintz, Steven. *Huck's Raft: A History of American Childhood*. Cambridge, Mass.: Harvard University Press, 2004. Print.

Mizruchi, Susan. "*Lolita* in History." *American Literature* 75.3 (2003): 629–652. Project Muse. Web. 20 Oct. 2011.

Moon, Set-Byul. "Mapping the Terrain of New Black Fatherhood in Contemporary African American Literature." *Trans-Humanities Journal* 10.1 (2017): 53–80. Project Muse. Web. 22 Apr. 2017.

Morrison, Toni. *Playing in the Dark: Whiteness and the Literary Imagination*. Cambridge, Mass.: Harvard University Press, 1992. Print.

Nabokov, Vladimir. Interview by Pierre Berton. *Close Up*. CBC. New York, 19 Nov. 1958. Television.

———. *Lolita*. 1955. New York: Vintage Books–Random House, 1997. Print.

———. *Speak, Memory: An Autobiography Revisited*. 1998. Introduction by Brian Boyd. New York: Knopf, 1999. Print.

Nelson, Claudia. "Introduction: Fictions about Fatherhood." *Children's Literature Association Quarterly* 18.3 (1993): 98–99. Project Muse. Web. 12 Jan. 2013.

Niebuhr, Reinhold. *The Irony of American History*. Chicago: University of Chicago Press, 1952. Print.

Noble, David. *Death of a Nation: American Culture and the End of Exceptionalism*. Minneapolis: University of Minnesota Press, 2002. Print.

Nodelman, Perry. "The Other: Orientalism, Colonialism, and Children's Literature." *Children's Literature Association Quarterly* 17.1 (1992): 29–35. Project Muse. Web. 30 Oct. 2012.

O'Brien, Sharon. Commentary for R. Gordon Kelly's "Literature and the Historian." In *Locating American Studies: The Evolution of a Discipline*. Ed. Lucy Maddox. Baltimore: Johns Hopkins University Press, 1999. 110–113. Print.

O'Dell, Scott. *Island of the Blue Dolphins*. 1960. Introduction by Lois Lowry. New York: Houghton Mifflin Harcourt, 2010. Print.

Ohmann, Carol, and Richard Ohmann. "Reviewers, Critics, and 'The Catcher in the Rye.'" *Critical Inquiry* 3.1 (1976): 15–37. JSTOR. Web. 22 Mar. 2017.

O'Loughlin, Jim. "The Whiteness of Bone: Russell Banks' *Rule of the Bone* and the Contradictory Legacy of *Huckleberry Finn*." *Modern Language Studies* 32.1 (2002): 31–42. JSTOR. Web. 5 Feb. 2013.

Park, Linda Sue. *A Long Walk to Water*. 2010. London: Oneworld, 2018. Print.

Pease, Donald. "Introduction: Re-Mapping the Transnational Turn." In *Re-Framing the Transnational Turn in American Studies*. Ed. Winfried Fluck, Donald Pease, and John Carlos Rowe. Hanover, N.H.: Dartmouth College Press, 2011. 1–46. Print.

———. *The New American Exceptionalism*. Minneapolis: University of Minnesota Press, 2009. Print.

Pease, Donald, and Robyn Wiegman, eds. "Futures." In *The Futures of American Studies*. Durham, N.C.: Duke University Press, 2002. 1–42. Print.

Pember, Mary Annette. "Mary Annette Pember: A Young Boy's Journey to Standing Rock." Indianz.com. Ho-Chunk Inc. 23 Sept. 2016. Web. 20 July 2019. <www.indianz.com/News/2016/09/23/mary-annette-pember -a-young-boys-journey.asp>.

Perry, Armon, Dana Harmon, and Mikia Bright. "A Package Deal? African American Men's Perspectives on the Intersection of Marriage and Fatherhood." *Women, Gender, and Families of Color* 1.2 (2013): 124–142. Project Muse. Web. 15 Mar. 2017.

Person, Leland, Jr. "The American Eve: Miscegenation and a Feminist Frontier Fiction." *American Quarterly* 37.5 (1985): 668–685. JSTOR. Web. 10 May 2019.

Pilgrim, David. "Racial Stereotypes." In *Encyclopedia of American Race Riots*. Ed. Walter Rucker and James Nathaniel Upton. Westport: Greenwood Press, 2007. 2:528–531. Print.

Podruchny, Carolyn. "Werewolves and Windigos: Narratives of Cannibal Monsters in French-Canadian Voyageur Oral Tradition." *Ethnohistory* 51.4 (2004): 677–700. Project Muse. Web. 10 June 2016.

Pratt, Mary Louise. "Arts of the Contact Zone." *Profession* (1991): 33–40. JSTOR. Web. 10 May 2019.

Prchal, Tim. "The Bad Boys and the New Man: The Role of Tom Sawyer and Similar Characters in the Reconstruction of Masculinity." *American Literary Realism* 36.3 (2004): 187–205. JSTOR. Web. 15 Feb. 2017.

Proehl, Kristen. "Politicizing Youth: Childhood Studies on Social Change." *American Quarterly* 64.1 (2012): 171–180. Project Muse. Web. 20 Oct. 2013.

Prose, Francine. "Confident at 11, Confused at 16." *New York Times*, 7 Jan. 1990. Web. 20 Apr. 2019. <www.nytimes.com/1990/01/07/magazine /confident-at-11-confused-at-16.html>.

Prucha, Francis Paul. *The Great Father: The United States Government and the American Indians*. Lincoln: University of Nebraska Press, 1984. Print.

Radway, Jan. "What's in a Name?" In *The Futures of American Studies*. Ed. Donald Pease and Robyn Wiegman. Durham, N.C.: Duke University Press, 2002. 45–75. Print.

Rainwater, Catherine. "Intertextual Twins and Their Relations: Linda Hogan's *Mean Spirit* and *Solar Storms*." *Modern Fiction Studies* 45.1 (1999): 93–113. Project Muse. Web. 21 Apr. 2012.

Ransaw, Theodore. "The Good Father: African American Fathers Who Positively

Influence the Educational Outcomes of Their Children." *Spectrum: A Journal on Black Men* 2.2 (2014): 1–25. Project Muse. 24 Jan. 2017.

Raphael, Ray. *Founding Myths: Stories That Hide Our Patriotic Past*. New York: New Press, 2004. Print.

Reese, Debbie. "A Critical Look at O'Dell's *Island of the Blue Dolphins*." *American Indians in Children's Literature*. 16 June 2016. Web. 10 Apr. 2019. <https://americanindiansinchildrensliterature.blogspot.com/2016/06/a-critical-look-at-odells-island-of.html>.

Richardson, Joe. "Florida Black Codes." *Florida Historical Quarterly* 47.4 (1969): 365–379. JSTOR. Web. 15 Feb. 2017.

Ringel, Paul. *Commercializing Childhood: Children's Magazines, Urban Gentility, and the Ideal of the American Child, 1823–1918*. Amherst: University of Massachusetts Press, 2015. Print.

Romero, Lora. "Vanishing Americans: Gender, Empire, and New Historicism." *American Literature* 63.3 (1991): 385–404. JSTOR. Web. 30 Jan. 2017.

Rosaldo, Renato. "Imperialist Nostalgia." *Representations* 26 (1989): 107–122. JSTOR. Web. 3 Mar. 2019.

Russell, David. *United States Author Series: Scott O'Dell*. New York: Twayne, 1999. Print.

Russell, Karen. "Karen Russell: Interview." Interview by Patrick Ryan. *Granta* 11 (Nov. 2011): n.p. Web. 15 May 2019.

———. *Swamplandia! A Novel*. New York: Vintage–Random House, 2011. Print.

Ruuska, Alex. "Ghost Dancing and the Iron Horse: Surviving through Tradition and Technology." *Technology and Culture* 52.3 (2011): 574–597. Project Muse. Web. 5 May 2017.

Ryan, Terre. "The Nineteenth-Century Garden: Imperialism, Subsistence, and Subversion in Leslie Marmon Silko's *Gardens in the Dunes*." *Studies in American Indian Literatures* 19.3 (2007): 115–132. Project Muse. Web. 22 Mar. 2017.

Said, Edward. *Orientalism*. 1978. New York: Random House, 1994. Print.

Saito, Natsu Taylor. "The Cost of Homeland Security." *Radical History Review* 93 (2005): 53–76. Academic Search Premier. Web. 15 Feb. 2014.

Salaita, Steven. "Concocting Terrorism off the Reservation: Liberal Orientalism in Sherman Alexie's Post-9/11 Fiction." *Studies in American Indian Literatures* 22.2 (2010): 22–41. Project Muse. Web. 6 Apr. 2013.

Salinger, J. D. *The Catcher in the Rye*. New York: Little, Brown, 1951. Print.

Sánchez-Eppler, Karen. *Dependent States: The Child's Part in Nineteenth-Century American Culture*. Chicago: University of Chicago Press, 2005. Print.

Schaub, Thomas. *American Fiction in the Cold War*. Madison: University of Wisconsin Press, 1991. Print.

Schultermandl, Silvia. "Fighting for the Mother/Land: An Ecofeminist Reading of Linda Hogan's *Solar Storms*." *Studies in American Indian Literatures* 17.3 (2005): 67–84. Project Muse. Web. 21 Oct. 2013.

Schwebel, Sara. "A Children's Book, Nineteenth-Century News, and Multimedia Approaches to American Studies." *American Quarterly* 70.3 (2018): 715–719. Project Muse. Web. 18 Apr. 2018.

——. *Child-Sized History: Fictions of the Past in U.S. Classrooms*. Nashville: Vanderbilt University Press, 2011. Print.

——. "Reading 9/11 from the American Revolution to U.S. Annexation of the Moon: M. T. Anderson's *Feed* and *Octavian Nothing*." *Children's Literature* 42 (2014): 197–223. Project Muse. Web. 2 Mar. 2017.

——, ed. *Island of the Blue Dolphins: The Complete Reader's Edition*. Oakland: University of California Press, 2016. Print.

Scott, James F. "Beat Literature and the American Teen Cult." *American Quarterly* 14.2 (1962): 150–160. JSTOR. Web. 18 Mar. 2012.

Sell, Ted. "Tiny Skeleton Recalls 1835 Island Saga: Bones Believed Those of Mystery Hermit's Child." *Los Angeles Times*, 5 July 1954: 1–2. Lone Woman and Last Indians Digital Archive, University of South Carolina. Web. <http://calliope.cse.sc.edu/lonewoman/home/Sell1954>.

Shostak, Debra. "'A story we could live with': Narrative Voice, the Reader, and Jeffrey Eugenides's *The Virgin Suicides*." *Modern Fiction Studies* 55.4 (2009): 808–832. Project Muse. Web. 12 Sept. 2012.

Sielke, Sabine. "The Politics of the Strong Trope: Rape and the Feminist Debate in the United States." *American Studies* 49.3 (2004): 367–384. JSTOR. Web. 8 May 2017.

Silko, Leslie Marmon. *Gardens in the Dunes: A Novel*. New York: Simon & Schuster, 1999. Print.

Singley, Carol. *Adopting America: Childhood, Kinship, and National Identity in Literature*. New York: Oxford University Press, 2011. Print.

Smith, Henry Nash. *Virgin Land: The American West as Symbol and Myth*. 1950. Cambridge, Mass.: Harvard University Press, 1970. Print.

Smith, Theresa. "Landscape as Narrative: Traveling the Sacred Geography of the Anishinaabeg." *Studies in American Indian Literatures* 22.4 (2010): 61–71. JSTOR. Web. 10 Apr. 2011.

Smoke Signals. Dir. Chris Eyre. Miramax Films, 1999. DVD.

Steedman, Caroline. *Strange Dislocations: Childhood and the Idea of Human Interiority, 1780–1930*. Cambridge, Mass.: Harvard University Press, 1995. Print.

Stegner, Page. *Escape in Aesthetics: The Art of Vladimir Nabokov*. New York: Dial Press, 1966. Print.

Steinle, Pamela Hunt. *In Cold Fear: The Catcher in the Rye Censorship Controversies and Postwar American Character*. Columbus: Ohio State University Press, 2000. Print.

Stockton, Kathryn Bond. *The Queer Child, or Growing Sideways in the Twentieth Century*. Durham, N.C.: Duke University Press, 2009. Print.

Strother, Ruth. *Margaret Mead: Cultural Anthropologist*. Edina, Minn.: ABDO, 2009. Print.

Tarr, Anita. "Fool's Gold: Scott O'Dell's Formulaic Vision of the Golden West." *Children's Literature Association Quarterly* 17.1 (1992): 19–24. Project Muse. Web. 21 Apr. 2012.

——. "An Unintentional System of Gaps: A Phenomenological Reading of Scott O'Dell's *Island of the Blue Dolphins*." *Children's Literature in Education* 28.2 (1997): 61–71. ERIC. Web. 5 Mar. 2017.

Thomas, Evan. "Founders Chic: Live from Philadelphia." *Newsweek*, 8 July

2001: n.p. Web. 14 June 2019. <www.newsweek.com/founders-chic-live-philadelphia-154791>.

Thomas, M. Wynn, and John Turner. "'Whitman, the great poet, has meant so much to me': Lawrence's *Studies in Classic American Literature, 1919–1923.*" *Walt Whitman Quarterly Review* 21.2 (2003): 41–64. Print.

Thompson, Melissa Kay. "A Sea of Good Intentions: Native Americans in Books for Children." *Lion and the Unicorn* 25.3 (2001): 353–374. Project Muse. Web. 21 Apr. 2012.

Tisdale, Shelby. "Railroads, Tourism, and Native Americans in the Greater Southwest." *Journal of the Southwest* 38.4 (1996): 433–462. JSTOR. Web. 5 Apr. 2017.

Trilling, Lionel. *The Liberal Imagination.* 1950. Introduction by Louis Menand. New York: New York Review Books, 2008. Print.

Trites, Roberta. *Disturbing the Universe: Power and Repression in Adolescent Literature.* Iowa City: University of Iowa Press, 2000. Print.

True, Jacqui. *The Political Economy of Violence against Women.* Oxford: Oxford University Press, 2012. Print.

Tucker, Nancy Bernkopf. *Taiwan, Hong Kong, and the United States, 1945–1992.* New York: Twayne, 1994. Print.

Turner, Frederick Jackson. *The Frontier in American History.* 1920. New York: Henry Holt, 1921. Digital.

Twain, Mark. *Adventures of Huckleberry Finn.* 1885. New York: Dover, 1994. Print.

———. *Life on the Mississippi.* 1883. Sydney: ReadHowYouWant, 2008. Print.

Tyler May, Elaine. "'The Radical Roots of American Studies': Presidential Address to the American Studies Association, November 9, 1995." *American Quarterly* 48.2 (1996): 179–200. JSTOR. Web. 20 Mar. 2016.

Ulanowicz, Anastasia. "American Adam, American Cain: *Johnny Tremain, Octavian Nothing*, and the Fantasy of American Exceptionalism." *Lion and the Unicorn* 35.3 (2011): 267–295. Project Muse. Web. 2 Oct. 2016.

Valentino, Gina. "'It All Does Come to Nothing in the End': Nationalism and Gender in Louise Erdrich's *The Plague of Doves.*" In *Louise Erdrich: Tracks, The Last Report on the Miracles at Little No Horse, The Plague of Doves.* Ed. Deborah Madsen. New York: Continuum, 2011. 121–135. Print.

Ventura, Abbie. "Post-Fordist Nation: The Economics of Childhood and the New Global Citizenship." In *The Nation in Children's Literature: Nations of Childhood.* Ed. Christopher (Kit) Kelen and Björn Sundmark. New York: Routledge, 2013. 235–245. Print.

Vernon, Irene. "'We Were Those Who Walked out of Bullets and Hunger': Representation of Trauma and Healing in *Solar Storms.*" *American Indian Quarterly* 36.1 (2012): 34–49. Project Muse. Web. 21 Oct. 2013.

Vigil, Kiara. "Charles Eastman's 'School of the Woods': Re-creation related to Childhood, Race, Gender, and Nation at Camp Oahe." *American Quarterly* 70.1 (2018): 25–53. Project Muse. Web. 5 Apr. 2018.

Von Eschen, Penny. "Who's the Real Ambassador? Exploding Cold War Racial Ideology." In *Cold War Constructions: The Political Culture of United States Imperialism, 1945–1966.* Ed. Christian Appy. Amherst: University of Massachusetts Press, 2000. 110–131. Print.

Wagner, Vivian. "Unsettling Oz: Technological Anxieties in the Novels of L. Frank Baum." *Lion and the Unicorn* 30.1 (2006): 25–53. Project Muse. Web. 4 July 2018.

Waldstreicher, David. "Keeping It in the Family: Post-DNA" Rev. of *Founding Brothers*, by Joseph Ellis. *Reviews in American History* 29.2 (2001): 198–204. JSTOR. Web. 8 Feb. 2013.

Wapshott, Nicholas. *Ronald Reagan and Margaret Thatcher: A Political Marriage*. New York: Sentinel, 2007. Print.

Weikle-Mills, Courtney. *Imaginary Citizens: Child Readers and the Limits of American Independence, 1640–1868*. Baltimore: Johns Hopkins University Press, 2013. Print.

Weisman, Brent. "Nativism, Resistance, and Ethnogenesis of the Florida Seminole Indian Identity." *Historical Archaeology* 41.4 (2007): 198–212. JSTOR. Web. 20 Apr. 2017.

Welter, Barbara. "The Cult of True Womanhood: 1820–1860." In *Locating American Studies: The Evolution of a Discipline*. Ed. Lucy Maddox. Baltimore: Johns Hopkins University Press, 1999. 43–70. Print.

Wesselhoft, Conrad. "'Blue Dolphins' Author Tells Why He Writes for Children." *New York Times*. 15 Apr. 1984. Web. 3 Mar. 2017. <www.nytimes.com/1984 /04/15/nyregion/blue-dolphins-author-tells-why-he-writes-for-children .html>.

Whitman, Walt. "Song of Myself." In *Leaves of Grass and Other Writings*. 1855. Ed. Michael Moon. New York: W.W. Norton, 2002. 26–77. Print.

Wiegman, Robyn. "Introduction: The Futures of American Studies." *Cultural Critique* 40 (1998): 5–9. JSTOR. Web. 10 Apr. 2019.

Wilkerson, Isabel. "With Rural Towns Vanishing, States Choose Which to Save." *New York Times*, 3 Jan. 1990. Web. 20 Nov. 2016. <www.nytimes.com/1990 /01/03/us/with-rural-towns-vanishing-states-choose-which-to-save.html>.

Willard, William. Rev. of *Gardens in the Dunes*, by Leslie Marmon Silko. *Wicazo Sa Review* 15.2 (2000): 139–141. Project Muse. Web. 5 Apr. 2017.

Wise, Gene. "'Paradigm Dramas' in American Studies: A Cultural and Institutional History of the Movement." 1979. In *Locating American Studies: The Evolution of a Discipline*. Ed. Lucy Maddox. Baltimore: Johns Hopkins University Press, 1999. 71–90. Print.

Woo, Susie. "Imagining Kin: Cold War Sentimentalism and the Korean Children's Choir." *American Quarterly* 67.1 (2015): 25–53. Project Muse. Web. 22 Mar. 2018.

Wood, Gordon. *Revolutionary Characters: What Made the Founders Different*. New York: Penguin Books, 2006. Print.

Wordsworth, William. "Ode: Intimations of Immortality from Recollections of Early Childhood." *Bartleby*, n.d. Web. 4 Sept. 2012. <www.bartleby.com /101/536.html>.

INDEX

CPSIA information can be obtained
at www.ICGtesting.com
Printed in the USA
LVHW041917200820
663743LV00002B/251

9 780820 357812